DESCARTES AND THE ENLIGHTENMENT

Descartes and the Enlightenment begins with an examination of the role played by the concepts freedom, mastery, and progress in Descartes' writing. Peter Schouls argues that these concepts express a vital and fundamental feature of Descartes' thought, and his careful and detailed examination of the conjunction and use of these concepts in Descartes' writings shows that they play the same role in Descartes' works as they do in writing typical of the eighteenth-century Enlightenment.

In order to avoid facile and vague generalizations about the eighteenth century, Schouls limits himself to discussion of a single part of the spectrum of acknowledged Enlightenment reflection, namely, the French *philosophes*. While the relationship between Descartes and Enlightenment thinkers is often characterized as one of animosity and rejection, Schouls shows that this is true only on a superficial examination. The main feature of the relationship is one of profound affinity—an affinity which is shown in the eighteenth century's assimilation of central elements from Descartes' writing. Schouls' study shows that the *philosophes* are, and acknowledge themselves to be, Descartes' progeny.

Peter A. Schouls is a member of the Department of Philosophy, University of Alberta.

McGill-Queen's Studies in the History of Ideas

DESCARTES AND THE ENLIGHTENMENT

Peter A. Schouls

McGill-Queen's University Press
Kingston and Montreal

© McGill-Queen's University Press 1989
First published in Canada in 1989 by
McGill-Queen's University Press
ISBN 0-7735-1014-1
Legal deposit first quarter 1989
Bibliothèque nationale du Québec

Printed in Canada on acid-free paper

Published in the United Kingdom in 1989
by Edinburgh University Press
ISBN 0-8522-4562-9

This book has been published with the help of a grant from the
Canadian Federation for the Humanities using funds provided by
the Social Sciences and Humanities Research Council of Canada.

Canadian Cataloguing in Publication Data
Schouls, Peter, 1937–
Descartes and the Enlightenment

(McGill-Queen's studies in the history of ideas)
Includes index.
Bibliography: p.
ISBN 0-7735-1014-1

1. Descartes, René, 1596–1650—Influence.
2. Enlightenment. 3. Philosophy, French—18th
century. 4. France—Intellectual life—18th century.
I. Title. II. Series.

B1875.S38 1989   194   c88-090451-8

To Jeanette

Contents

Acknowledgments

For the academic year of 1981–82 the Social Sciences and Humanities Research Council of Canada awarded me a Time Release Stipend; for 1983–84 the University of Alberta allowed me a Study Leave. The penultimate draft of this book was completed during the first of these periods; during the second it was given its present form. I am deeply grateful to both the Council and the University for their generous support of my work.

I am indebted to many of my students, particularly to the students who took my graduate seminars, and to graduate students Kevin O'Brien (for proofreading and many pertinent comments along the way) and Donna Dorsey (for compiling the index). Many colleagues, especially Cameron MacKenzie and Frederick Van De Pitte, made valuable suggestions at various stages.

My greatest indebtedness is to my friends and colleagues Richard Bosley, Hendrik Hart, and John King-Farlow. During 1982–83 each of these read the complete first draft and made numerous very helpful suggestions for improvement.

Three forthcoming articles draw upon parts of this book. These are: "Descartes and the Idea of Progress," *History of Philosophy Quarterly* 4, no. 4 (1987): 423-33; "Descartes: la primauté du libre vouloir sur la raison," *Dialogue* 25, no. 2 (1986): 211-21; and "Descartes as Revolutionary," *Philosophia Reformata* 52, no. 1 (1987): 4-23. I thank the editors of these journals for permission to use this material.

Throughout my life and work there is the joy of my wife's presence. To her I dedicate this book.

DESCARTES AND THE ENLIGHTENMENT

Introduction

THIS STUDY is about *freedom, mastery,* and *progress,* primarily as these concepts function in Descartes' works. This triad represents the core of Enlightenment thought. My discussion of these concepts is intended to reveal Descartes' relationship to the Enlightenment.

Enlightenment thought was preoccupied with human freedom. It was preoccupied with freedom from prejudice and from political and social oppression, with freedom from drudgery, pain, and anxiety. It was equally interested in mastery, and hence in the power which scientific knowledge was supposed to give to humanity, for it was believed that scientific knowledge would allow each person to become master of his destiny. This preoccupation with such mastery expressed the Enlightenment's concern for freedom in a positive sense: it insisted on freedom from all sorts of oppression in order that each person would be able to achieve the freedom which consists in mastery of his destiny. Finally, the Enlightenment was deeply concerned with progress. It believed that through the development of scientific knowledge man would be able to give an ever more concrete expression to the ideal of being free from prejudice, from arbitrary dominion by others, from drudgery, pain, and anxiety. It held that progress in science would allow ever greater realization of the ideal of being master of one's destiny both in this life and (if there were one) in the life to come. The ideal expressed through this triad of concepts may well be called that of autonomy.

This ideal of autonomy reveals the mainstream of Enlightenment thought. For many, the assertion that the ideal of the Enlightenment is that of autonomy and that this ideal finds its clear expression through concepts like those of freedom, mastery, and progress, will hardly need a defence. Support for it is quite readily available in well-known general accounts of eighteenth-century thought, as well as in important discussions of particular thinkers of the Enlightenment. Such accounts and discussions one finds, for example, in the authoritative works of Crane Brinton, Alexandre Koyré, Aram Vartanian, Isaiah Berlin, Peter Gay, and Ira Wade. I shall draw upon these and others at appropriate places. If they do not present their story in precisely the terms which I use, they do so in closely related terms.

Although the triad of concepts introduced above reveals the mainstream of Enlightenment thought, discussion of this triad should not be confined to the Enlightenment. Descartes had already articulated the Enlightenment's ideal, and these concepts occupy as central a position in his thought as in that of the eighteenth century. When Descartes published his major works during the fourth and fifth decades of the seventeenth century, he gave clear expression to an ideal which is still often, if not generally, said to have been born more than half a century later. The truth of the matter is that the eighteenth century's Enlightenment thinkers did little more than widely disseminate an inherited ideal. Many received their inheritance directly from Descartes; some received it from Descartes by way of John Locke. In either case they were often unwilling to acknowledge their debt.[1] Contemporary writers have also too often ascribed an exaggerated originality to eighteenth-century thought.[2] This persistence has hindered our understanding both of Descartes' position, and of the Enlightenment's. In this study I shall explore important aspects of the Enlightenment through a discussion of the works of Descartes.

I want to examine the role played by the concepts of freedom, mastery, and progress in Descartes' writings. Since these concepts are often said to belong peculiarly to the Enlightenment, such an examination calls for repeated reference to the eighteenth century in order to show that the concepts through which the ideal of autonomy

1. For some of the main reasons for this reticence, see the excellent account in Vartanian's *Diderot and Descartes*, pp. 34, 40, 308-09.

2. Not all writers have ascribed such a self-made character to the Enlightenment. Wade (in *The Intellectual Origins of the French Enlightenment*) characterizes the spirit of Cartesianism as identical with that of the Enlightenment (cf. p. 241 and pp. 656-57). And Brumfitt (in *The French Enlightenment*) rightly concludes that because of its "questioning spirit" the Enlightenment "may not unfairly be placed under his [Descartes,] banner" (p. 33). Even important differences among the *philosophes*, he argues, are often the result of emphasis on one aspect of Descartes' position and disregard of another (p. 32).

finds expression in Descartes' thought are in fact those which also occupy a central position in Enlightenment thought. The more contentious claim is, of course, that these concepts function centrally in Descartes' works. My study therefore especially calls for careful and detailed examination of the conjunction and uses of these three concepts in Descartes' works in order to show that they play the same role there as they do in writings typical of the eighteenth century.

A study such as this presents several dangers. One must be especially on guard against facile generalizations about either Descartes or later thinkers. This danger is greatest with respect to Descartes. There exist no studies which provide detailed support for the thesis that a triad of concepts like freedom, mastery, and progress does in fact play a fundamental role in his thought. Instead, relating Descartes' position to that of the eighteenth century has often been a matter of vague generalities. After three decades, Vartanian's indictment still holds: "Only too often, in attempting to state the relationship of Descartes to the Enlightenment *in toto*, the former's doctrine has unavoidably been quintessentialized to an almost deceptive generality."[3] Vartanian's solution has been to take a specific aspect of Descartes' position, his naturalism, and to compare it with the naturalistic thought of a particular member of the Enlightenment, Diderot. The result, *Diderot and Descartes, A Study of Scientific Naturalism in the Enlightenment*, is an excellent work, devoid of superficiality. It is still one of the very few studies which successfully relates Descarte to the eighteenth century.[4]

My own intention is to deal with a more general aspect of Descartes' stance than that which Vartanian discussed. In dealing with freedom,

3. Vartanian, *Diderot and Descartes*; p. 3.

4. Although, in this paragraph I have had in mind books written in English, with respect to literature in French the situation is not much different. There are, of course, excellent studies of Descartes in French. Among these are Gouhier's two books: *Essais sur Descartes* and *La Pensée Métaphysique de Descartes*. Neither of these contain a discussion of free will. In Gilson's older (but still very valuable) *Discours de la Méthode* there is an account of free will, but it is strictly confined to a discussion of thinking, and of error. In three of Roger Lefèvre's works on Descartes, free will receives considerable attention, namely, in *L'Humanisme de Descartes*, *La Pensée Existentielle de Descartes*, and *La Métaphysique de Descartes*. In all of these, the discussion remains restricted to Descartes' position alone. The most extended account of Cartesian freedom in French is Gabaude's *Liberté et Raison, La liberté cartésienne et sa réfraction chez Spinoza et chez Leibniz*. In none of these three volumes does Enlightenment thought enter the picture. And with respect to all of these authors there is no discussion of "free will" in its relations to concepts like "mastery" and "progress."

mastery, and progress I take myself to be examining the very foundations of Descartes' total position. It is my thesis that this triad of
concepts expresses a vital, quite fundamental feature of Descartes'
thought; and it is my foremost aim to prevent this thesis from becoming a "deceptive generality." I intend to meet Vartanian's objection by providing a carefully detailed and documented discussion of
Descartes' writings.

Because there exist many good accounts of the Enlightenment which
provide ample justification for dealing with it in terms of my proposed
triad, the danger of superficiality through over-generalization is slight.
Nevertheless, I shall further guard against vague generalitites by lim-
iting my attention as much as possible to a single part of the spectrum
of acknowledged Enlightenment reflection, eighteenth-century French
thinkers. Among these, I shall restrict myself to the *philosophes*, particularly to men such as d'Alembert, Condillac, and especially, Con-
dorcet.⁵ There is no need to establish that the concepts of freedom,
mastery, and progress do in fact characterize their stance. Neither
need it be established that, in this respect, they are true representatives
of Enlightenment thought.⁶ Both popular and scholarly works support these contentions.

5. The *Sketch for a Historical Picture of the Progress of the Human Mind* (written during
1793-94) is of particular relevance. In it, Condorcet explicitly discusses the importance
of Descartes for the Enlightenment. And he does so as a true representative of the
Enlightenment. As Prior put it: "*Condorcet . . . le dernier des philosophes . . . n'a pas conçu
de système absolutement originale, mais il rassemble toutes les thèories de ses prédecesseurs. Nous
retrouvons chez lui les idées de Voltaire, de Rousseau, de Turgot d'Helvétius, de Condillac, peu
à peu façonnés en un tout harmonieux dont la dernière expression est L'ESGUISSE, sorte de
résumé philosophique du XVIIIe siècle.*" (These sentences are from the opening paragraph
of Prior's introduction to his edition of the *Esquisse d'un Tableau Historique des Progrès
de l'Esprit Humain.* See also Voegelin, who characterized the *Sketch* as possessing a place
"which may be compared to that of a gospel of the Johannine type in the Christian
evangelical literature" because it is "an authorative summary of the creed of the community" (*From Enlightenment to Revolution,* p. 125); and Robinson, *Significant Contributions
to the History of Psychology* p. xxvi: "Condorcet . . . spoke for all the *philosophes* in his
Sketch . . . ". That in the *Sketch* Condorcet spoke for others, that in it he did not present
an absolutely new position, makes it of particular value for my purposes. It should,
however, not be forgotten that Condorcet spoke also for himself and that (although
influenced particularly by Turgot) the material presented and the manner of presentation warrent an evaluation like that of Stuart Hamphire, who called the *Sketch* "one
of the few really great monuments of liberal thought." (See Hampshire's Introduction
to Barraclough's translation of the *Esquisse,* published as *Sketch for a Historical Picture
of the Progress of the Human Mind,* p. ix.)

6. It has long been recognized that the *philosophes* are genuinely representative of
the Enlightenment. As the various essays in a recent book demonstrate, wherever it

Crane Brinton proposes that "Three key clusters of ideas form our model of the world view of the Enlightenment: Reason, Nature, Progress." His explication of this "model"—a model which he intends to characterize Enlightenment thought wherever it was found—shows an affinity with my own proposal, for instance when Brinton writes about it as expressing "an optimistic, this-worldly belief in the power of human beings, brought up rationally from infancy on as nature meant them to be, to achieve steady and unlimited progress toward material comfort and spiritual happiness . . . ."[7] Persons "brought up rationally from infancy on as nature meant them to be" are persons free from prejudice and compelled only by reason—a compulsion to which they freely submit for the sake of achievement of mastery through progress in "material comfort and spiritual happiness." That, as Brinton adds, this model "must be qualified and amended in many ways" almost goes without saying and applies both to his and my own proposal, but I am confident that it is correct and helpful to use a model like this. Because such a model is neither new nor controversial there is no burden of proof on this score. Hence without becoming superficial I can afford to say relatively little about the eighteenth century in this study of Enlightenment concepts. However, a case still needs to be made for Descartes' connection to the Enlightenment. Of the eight chapters which follow, only three chapters (the shorter ones: chapters three, six, and eight) deal specifically with the eighteenth century. It is only in these three chapters that I explicitly relate Descartes to the eighteenth-century Enlightenment.

The case I want to make in the other five chapters is that, in their conjunction, the terms freedom, mastery, and progress are so typical of Descartes' position that it, too, is characterized by the ideal which these concepts express. They are, therefore, not distinctly or solely eighteenth-century concepts: they are also characteristic of a thinker of the seventeenth century.

A corollary of my argument is that we should see Descartes as a progenitor of the Enlightenment. Indeed, we should recognize him as more than that: in crucial respects he is himself a full-grown Enlightenment thinker. D'Alembert, Condillac, and Condorcet may be taken as Descartes' progeny, a progeny that strikingly bears their

---

occurred, Enlightenment reflection shared a common core of ideas, chief among which were those related to freedom, mastery and progress. See Porter and Teich, eds. *The Enlightenment in National Context.* (New York, 1982).

7. Brinton, "Enlightenment," 2:519-25, 521.

ancestor's stamp in likeness of spirit and accomplishments. From the middle of the seventeenth century on there is a continuity of outlook, an identity of posture which affords the proper soil both for Kant's definition of "enlightenment" as man's freeing himself from his self-incurred tutelage, and for the French Revolution's *ni Dieu ni Maître*. However, certainly as far as Descartes is concerned, many will take these statements as anything but incontrovertible.

It is well known that many of the acknowledged leaders of the Enlightenment wrote harsh words about Descartes. Many explicitly, sometimes vehemently, rejected his "rationalism." But they did not reject what Descartes meant by and expected from "reason." They trusted reason and accepted as correct Descartes' description of its mode of operation. Most shared Descartes' high expectation that through the use of reason the sciences would develop to the stage where their application would produce the fruits of health, freedom, and happiness. When they rejected "rationalism" they set aside certain doctrines which Descartes claimed to have reached through rational thought, but which they rejected as dogmas of an insufficiently critical mind or as products of an "impatient imagination."[8] Because of their acceptance of a rational faculty which they took to function in ways described by Descartes (and also because of their acceptance of certain fundamental Lockean notions), it is correct to characterize eighteenth-century thought as Koyré did: a "mixture of Cartesian rationalism and sensualist, nominalist empiricism".[9] When they rejected "rationalism" they set aside neither Descartes' notion of reason nor his firm trust in this reason's promises. Instead, like d'Alembert, they distanced themselves from the position that reason can, or needs to, explain everything. Like d'Alembert, most therefore rejected Descartes' psycho-physical parallelism because it rested on the dogma that thought cannot belong to extension. They rejected the program of deducing the nature of physical objects from what were taken to be purely mental givens. They rejected the identification of matter and extension.[10] When in his *Encyclopedia* entry called "Taste" d'Alembert reflects on "the use and abuse of philosophy," he criticises a philosopher

8. The phrase "impatient imagination" is Condorcet's. *Cf. Sketch*, p. 132. My quotations from the *Sketch* are from Barraclough's translation of the *Esquisse*.

9. Koyré, "Condorcet," p. 131.

10. See Grimsley's *Jean D'Alembert*, pp. 226, 242, 248, 256.

like Descartes for bad taste. Philosophy goes beyond the bounds of good taste when, as metaphysics, it refuses to place "strict limits on the mania for explaining everything," when it disregards "the wise timidity of modern physics."[11]

But not all metaphysics was considered in bad taste. D'Alembert would agree with Condillac:

We must distinguish two sorts of metaphysics. The one, vain and ambitious, wants to search into every mystery. . . . The other more reserved, proportions her researches to the weakness of the human understanding; and not concerning herself about what is above her sphere, but eager to know whatever is within her reach, she wisely keeps within the bounds prescribed by nature. The first makes all nature a kind of magic incantation . . .; the second . . . is as simple as truth itself. The former is the source of innumerable errors, as it fills the mind with vague and indeterminate notions, and with words that have no meaning: the latter . . . helps the understanding to avoid falling into mistakes, to reason exactly, and to frame clear ideas.[12]

The dismissal of the first type constituted the rejection of Descartes' metaphysics, while the admission of the second was the acceptance of Cartesian methodology and epistemology. When eighteenth-century philosophers spoke approvingly of metaphysics, they usually referred to methodology and epistemology. Many of them, though not all, believed they then referred only or primarily to Lockean doctrines. In effect, their adoption of Locke's "metaphysics" makes them rationalists if by "rationalist" we refer to a person who accepts as correct Descartes' view of the workings and role of reason.[13] Locke,

11. See Hoyt and Cassirer, *Encyclopedia Selections*, pp. 362-63.

12. Condillac, *An Essay on the Origin of Human Knowledge*, pp. 2-3. In the opening pages of his *Jean-Jacques Rousseau*, Grimsley draws attention to the fact that some of the *philosophes* explicitly juxtaposed Cartesian metaphysics and Cartesian methodology, rejecting the former and adopting the latter.

13. When the *philosophes* accepted Descartes' view of the workings and role of reason, they would often add that reason by itself cannot do all Descartes thought it could do because, they said, reason needs the co-operation of the senses if *useful* knowledge is to be won. Many, among them d'Alembert and de la Mettrie, believed Descartes to be ignorant about the need for experimentation. This misinterpretation of Descartes has persisted to this day. For an account of the important role which Descartes assigns to experimentation, see my *The Imposition of Method*, chapter 3, part 4. For d'Alembert's misinterpretation of Descartes on this point, see Grimsley's *Jean D'Alembert*, p. 228 and

for one, accepted and expounded this view.[14] The *philosophes*' adoption
of this aspect of Locke made them, sometimes quite unwittingly, accept
Descartes. Through Locke, Cartesian methodology and epistemology
returned to their native soil. Through Locke, Cartesian reductionism
and foundationalism came to be generally accepted by the *philosophes*.
D'Alembert and other *philosophes* were thus right to regard themselves
as "the spiritual heirs of Descartes,"[15] but for many of them the real
foundation of their inheritance was obscured, because their rejection
of Descartes' metaphysics prevented them from seeing their acceptance of Descartes' methodology and epistemology. As many have
pointed out, the *philosophes* acquired their Descartes at a most impres-
sionable age, at school.[16] Consequently as one writer has put it, "no
genuinely philosophical production of the century—save Hume's—
would be free of heavy indebtedness to Descartes."[17]

When the *philosophes* saw themselves as Descartes' spiritual heirs
they often did so for somewhat superficial reasons. But I shall argue
that these reasons had a common source, namely, a shared methodology, a common view of the workings of reason. To use Peter Gay's
rather vague formulation, it was the "intellectual style of Descartes"
which retained its power in the eighteenth century.[18]

The *philosophes* felt a kinship with Descartes based on their perception of his "revolutionary" position. They firmly embraced Descartes'
rejection of the "schools," of whatever smacked of medieval dogma.
They rejoiced in his break with the past, in his introduction of what
they, too, recognized as the healthy, modern, critical mind. In his

---

p. 271. In *Man a Machine*, de la Mettrie writes that Descartes was ignorant of "the value
of experiment and observation, and the danger of cutting loose from them."

14. See Schouls, *The Imposition of Method*, chapters 6, 7, 8. In his review of this book
Stewart supports the position that in the *Essay concerning Human Understanding* Locke
adopted and expounded Descartes' methodology. He also supports the position that
Locke applied this methodology in his works in education—the works through which
his influence on the *philosophes* was perhaps the greatest. Stewart writes: "That Locke
meant the methodology of the *Essay* to carry through to every subject of knowledge is
not particularly problematic: the message is clear enough in his own 'discourse on
method,' the educational tract 'Of the Conduct of the Understanding' . . . ", p. 122.

15. This is Lough's phrase, from his *The Encyclopédie*, p. 143.

16. See, for example, Gay, *The Enlightenment, 2: The Science of Freedom*, p. 146; Grimsley, *Jean D'Alembert*, p. 269; and Vartanian, *La Mettrie's L'HOMME MACHINE*, p. 2.

17. Robinson, *Significant Contributions to the History of Psychology*, pp. xxiii–xxiv.

18. Gay, *The Enlightenment, 2: The Science of Freedom*, p. 146.

Discours préliminaire to the *Encyclopédie*, d'Alembert firmly connected Descartes, criticism, revolution, and modernity:

Descartes at least had the courage to show good thinkers how to shake off the yoke of scholasticism, opinion, and authority—in a word, of prejudice and barbarism; and by this revolt, the fruits of which we are gathering today, he rendered philosophy a service, more difficult perhaps and more essential than all those which it owes to his illustrious successors. He can be regarded as the leader of a conspiracy, the one who had the courage to rise up first against a despotic and arbitrary power.[19]

When Condorcet described the *philosophes* as "a class of men" who devoted "themselves to the tracking down of prejudices in the hiding places where the priests, the schools, the governments and all long-established institutions had gathered and protected them," who "made it their life-work to destroy popular errors," he fittingly described Descartes as well as the *philosophes*.[20]

For Descartes and the *philosophes* a prejudice was any belief which was not authorized by reason. Freedom from what reason had not authorized, and freedom from the consequences of action based on such unauthorized beliefs, was of prime importance to them all. If Brinton is right in endorsing the restriction of the term "Enlightenment" to the eighteenth century, because it was during that period that "the characteristic ideas and attitudes of rationalism had spread from a small group of advanced thinkers to a relatively large educated public," he is at least in part wrong when he claims that it was "The English"—"Locke, Newton, and the early deists like Toland and Tindal"—who "have some claim to being the originators, the adventurers in ideas which the French did no more than develop and spread."[21] "The French" were indeed less innovative than they are often believed to be. But behind "the English," especially behind the *philosophes'* re-

19. This frequently quoted statement from the *Encyclopédie, Discours préliminaire*, p. xxvi, may be found in Gay, *The Enlightenment 2: The Science of Freedom*, p. 149; as well as in Grimsley, *Jean D'Alembert*, p. 269.

20. Condorcet, *Sketch*, p. 136.

21. Brinton, "Enlightenment," p. 519, 523. Elsewhere, Brinton presents what is perhaps a different picture when he calls Descartes "one of the men who prepared for the Enlightenment." See *The Shaping of Modern Thought*, p. 94. But there also Brinton does not fully appreciate the thoroughly revolutionary character of Descartes' thought and Descartes remains, at best, one among a number of more or less important progenitors.

vered Locke, there stood Descartes. And so, in the end, it was a
Frenchman who supplied the original ideas.

In this study I shall deal with Descartes as one who unmistakably
articulated the Enlightenment's central ideas. I shall deal with those
aspects of his position which came to be widely accepted throughout
the Enlightenment—accepted sometimes with an acknowledgment of
their source, but often without this. These aspects will be seen to be
peripheral neither to the Cartesian position nor to most of eighteenth-
century thought. One might say that the spreading of the Enlightenment amounted to the growing acceptance of an integral part of
Descartes' position, the Cartesian concepts of freedom, mastery, and
progress.

To say that the Enlightenment became pervasive once there was a
widespread emphasis on certain parts of Descartes' position is, of
course, not meant to imply that Descartes' was the only important
seventeenth-century influence on the eighteenth century. Next to him
there are, at least, Bacon, Leibniz, Newton, and Locke. Some place
Locke and Newton among the Enlightenment's great progenitors.
Others, more correctly, include them as members of the Enlightenment itself—as does S.C. Brown when he answers his question "Who
belongs to the Enlightenment and who does not?" with "Everyone
would include Diderot, d'Alembert and Voltaire. Everyone will allow
honorary and retrospective membership to Locke and Newton."[22] The
connection between Locke or Newton and the *philosophes* is scarcely
in doubt, but there remains a case for the connection to be made
between Descartes and the *philosophes*—a better case than that for Bacon
or Leibniz, neither of whose thought permeated that of the *philosophes*.
Condorcet summed up the *philosophes'* attitude towards them when
he accused them both of sterility: Bacon's "methods for discovering
truth . . . in no way influenced the course of science" and Leibniz's
"system" "retarded the progress of philosophy."[23] Of neither Bacon
nor Leibniz can it be said that they were the originators of the modern
attitude disseminated by those of whom I take the *philosophes* to be
representative, of the ideal which was expressed through the concepts
freedom, mastery, and progress. My study is intended to demonstrate
that this can be said very clearly of Descartes.

22. Brown ed., *Philosophers of the Enlightenment*, p. vii.
23. These statements are from the *Sketch*, pp. 121, 135.

I

Escape from Bondage

AMONG THE CONCEPTS of freedom, mastery, and progress, that of freedom is the most fundamental to Descartes' works. For mastery presupposes freedom from prejudice and oppression and consists in having the liberty to shape one's own destiny. Progress, in turn, is measured in terms of the extent to which mastery has been achieved. Hence throughout most of this study the discussion of freedom will be central. Because of the interrelatedness of the three concepts, mastery and progress will of course enter the scene; but they will not occupy centre stage until the fifth chapter.

To establish the fundamental nature of Descartes' concept of freedom, I shall consider some general features of his position in chapter 1, and go into more detail in chapter 2. In presenting Descartes as a revolutionary, I shall focus on those acts of freedom which he believes can deliver us from the confinement imposed by our physical and cultural contexts.

In this chapter I shall argue first that Descartes' position may be called that of a revolutionary because his method dictates that if we are to obtain knowledge we must begin by rejecting all beliefs and opinions which we have absorbed from the contexts in which we live. Secondly, I want to make it clear why Descartes holds that his revolutionary procedure, although it involves a radical form of epistemic individualism, does not lead him into relativism. It is important to see how strongly Descartes means his position to oppose relativism, for this allows us to understand (in a later chapter) how the freedom of revolutionary activity can become firmly linked with an absolutism dictated by reason.

I shall go on to deal with both the bondage and the liberation of reason. Because reason is misdirected by what Descartes considers pernicious habits, it is like someone caught in what he regards as a vast web of prejudice. He believes that the impediments can be destroyed in a revolt which calls for the exercise both of freedom and of methodic doubt. How in spite of talk of bondage there can at the same time and without contradiction be mention of the exercise of freedom is a problem which I take up in a discussion that begins the second chapter.

I. REVOLUTION, RELATIVISM, AND TRUTH

Descartes saw the need for what he called a "reformation" of the sciences. Not that he expected himself fully to bring about such a "reformation," but he did expect to make a beginning. For he believed that he had available to him the necessary instrument: his "method of rightly conducting reason." In this section I will, therefore, begin with an exploration of Descartes' use of his method in the rejection of all beliefs which we have absorbed from the contexts in which we live. In other words, I want to begin with a preliminary exploration of what I shall call Descartes' "revolutionary procedure."

First, *Descartes as revolutionary*. Although he speaks of the necessity of bringing about a reformation in the sciences, it seems to me that Descartes should instead be seen as bringing about a revolution. He should not be considered as a revolutionary in some narrow sense of that word; for, as we shall see, he intended to bring about a totally new outlook in all areas of life. The term "reformation" does not cover so radical an activity. Although reformation does away with the old and replaces it with what is new, it is an activity which takes place within an accepted framework within which certain key aspects are considered inviolate by the reformer. Reformation may therefore exist in improving the old by removing imperfections or faults or errors. By contrast, revolution may be taken as radical substitution of everything within a certain framework and of that framework itself. If the term "reformation" is restricted to the activity of amending and the term "revolution" to that of radical substitution, then Descartes' "reformation" ought to be seen as a revolution and Descartes himself should be characterized as a revolutionary rather than as a reformer. He had no sympathy with a reformation which set out merely to amend. Indeed, the only instrument which he considered adequate for the task of bringing about a "reformation" in the sciences precluded mere amendment. This instrument, the method of the *Rules for the Direction of the Mind* and of the *Discourse on the Method of Rightly Conducting the Reason*, called for radical substitution. If revolution consists in two parts, the first being to do away with the old and the second to present the new, then Descartes was sometimes modest with respect to his achievements in the second area but never with respect to his accomplishments in the first.[1]

In the *Discourse*, where he often speaks of the need for *réformer le cors des sciences* (e.g. HR1, 89; AT6, 13),[2] Descartes makes it quite clear that he considers himself to have been entirely successful in carrying out one of his major self-imposed tasks. That task was not limited to removing much of what was old in the realm of science; instead, it was the total rejection of all his own beliefs and opinions, and this of course included total rejection of whatever he had up to then taken to be science. He writes that "as regards all the opinions which up to this time I had embraced, I thought I could not do better than endeavour once for all to sweep them completely away . . . " (ibid.). Well before the end of the *Discourse* he is confident that he has been successful in this endeavour. Old opinions are to be swept "completely away, so that they might later on be replaced, either by others which were better, or by the same, when I had made them conform to the uniformity of a rational scheme" (ibid.). Thus what is new may appear similar to, even identical with the old.

This ostensible re-incorporation of the old may give Descartes' revolution the appearance of being less radical than it in fact is meant to be. However, that is appearance only. For it is crucial that nothing old be retained unless it "conforms to the uniformity of a rational scheme." As he puts it later in the *Discourse*, with respect to doctrines

1. To characterize Descartes' stance as that of the revolutionary because he insists on radical newness, is to use the word "revolutionary" as it has been from the eighteenth century until today. For contemporary insistence on radical novelty as essential to revolution, see, e.g., Arendt, *On Revolution*, p. 40; Brinton, *Anatomy of Revolution*, the opening pages as well as p. 227ff.; Elliot, "Revolution and Continuity in Early Modern Europe," pp. 35-56, p. 40 and 43; Finlayson, *Historians, Puritanism, and the English Revolution*, p. 32–33; and Freidrich, *Revolution*, p. 4. That radical newness was also a defining characteristic of "revolution" for the eighteenth century will become clear as the argument develops.

2. Wherever possible the quotations from Descartes' writings are from Haldance and Ross, *The Philosophical Works of Descartes*, vols. I and II (Cambridge, 1911) abbreviated as HR1 and HR2. The second reference in each case is to the Adam and Tannery *OEuvres de Descartes* (Paris, 1965–75), abbreviated as AT.

and discoveries to be presented in the *Dioptrics* and the *Meteors*, "And I do not even boast of being the first discoverer of any of them, but only state that I have adopted them, not because they have been held by others . . . but only because Reason has persuaded me of their truth" (HR1, 129; AT6, 77). But before one can be persuaded by reason, the old, regardless of whether it is to reappear as the new, is to be swept completely away. The old, as such, can never truly and legitimately find a place in the new.

Descartes did not believe that any of the old would in fact find a place in the new. This is clear from what he says about the *Principles of Philosophy*. In the final paragraph of the "Author's Letter" which serves as preface to the French edition of the *Principles*, he states that what he is about to present is genuinely new rather than the old, partly or even largely, transformed. Its newness is a consequence of the fact that the principles upon which it is founded are themselves new, a "difference which is observable between these principles and those of all other men" (HR1, 215; AT9–2, 20). This stress on newness comes to the fore in all of Descartes' works.

Take, for example, *The Passions of the Soul*, the last work which he prepared for publication. In its first article he speaks of "the defective nature of the sciences," and therefore seems to sound the typically-thorough reformer's note when he says "There is nothing in which the defective nature of the sciences which we have received from the ancients appears more clearly than in what they have written on the passions . . . " However, that the internal correction of defects holds no appeal becomes clear from the continuation of this sentence: "that which the ancients have taught regarding them is both so slight, and for the most part so far from credible, that I am unable to entertain any hope of approximating to the truth excepting by shunning the paths which they have followed." Thus a strategy naturally presents itself. It is the strategy of the person who denies the existence of links with the past rather than that of the one who holds that there is continuity. It is the procedure of the revolutionary rather than that of the reformer: "I shall be here obliged to write just as though I were treating of a matter which no one had ever touched on before me" (HR1, 331; AT11, 327-28).

Of course, speaking of *The Passions*' contents as new was not an idle boast, for there existed no precedent of a consistent attempt at an explanation of mental and physiological phenomena entirely by means of simple mechanical processes. What was presented as new looked new and was in fact different from what had gone before. But its newness in appearance should not obscure the important point that whether or not it looked new, it would, in Descartes' view, be new simply because it could have been presented only after the old had been completely swept away. And this stress on newness is not dictated by the particular subject-matter of *The Passions*. It pertains to the entire realm of knowledge, whatever its subject-matter. As Descartes writes in *The Search after Truth*, with respect to "upsetting all the knowledge . . . hitherto acquired": "I do not wish to be placed amongst the number of these insignificant artesans, who apply themselves only to the restoration of old works, because they feel themselves incapable of achieving new" (HR1, 313: AT10, 509).

If we take seriously the metaphor from the *Discourse* that no systematic knowledge can be attained unless one first takes all one's opinions and "sweeps them completely away," then whatever takes their place can arise only in this newly created void and that which arises in a void cannot fail to be new. Although as we shall see it cannot be *creatio ex nihilo* it is certainly meant to be *creatio de novo*.

Sometimes Descartes speaks as if the *hubris* or, perhaps, the cultural solipsism which seems implicit in these statements is meant to be taken as quite innocent because it is entirely idiosyncratic. In the *Discourse*, for example, we read that "My design has never extended beyond trying to reform my own opinion and to build on a foundation which is entirely my own" (HR1, 90; AT6, 15). In the sentence immediately following he even seems to warn against taking his action as an example. But these warnings are meant for only two groups of people. They hold, in the first place, for those who are "precipitate in judgement." Such persons simply cannot follow Descartes' example even if they would, for they do not have "sufficient patience to arrange their thoughts in proper order" and therefore can not reach valid new results. Not paying attention to "order" is attempting to gain truth unmethodically, and the outcome of that exercise can only be opinion and uncertainty rather than knowledge and certainty. This result is shared by the second group: those who believe "that they are less capable of distinguishing truth from falsehood than some others from whom instruction might be obtained." Such people "are right in contenting themselves with following the opinions of these others rather than in searching better ones for themselves." These warnings amount to saying that attempts at "reformation" are for neither the foolish nor the timid. That leaves the wise and the courageous. And as Descartes well knew, men are more apt to classify themselves as wise and courageous than as foolish or timid. Thus for anyone not satisfied with mere opinion and uncertainty, the complete sweeping away of all beliefs is a necessary condition for obtaining knowledge and certainty.

Even apart from these warnings to the precipitous and timid, Descartes has to say that his design does not extend beyond trying to reform his own opinion and to build on a foundation which is entirely his own. He must say this because his method forces it upon him: everyone has to do it for himself and can only do it for himself. No one, therefore, can build upon anything which we might call a "primary given," on something given through the senses or tradition, by education or by contemporary thought.[3] None of these can provide a solid foundation on which to build a system of knowledge. As he writes in the first of the *Principles*, "in order to examine into the truth it is necessary once in one's life to doubt of all things." Modest though Descartes' "reformation" may seem in some of his comments, very little probing is needed to show it up for what it is, namely a complete and universal revolution. Its intended completeness and universality are dictated by Descartes' method, the instrument whose use he considered necessary for the attainment of truth. For it is this method which requires of whoever searches for truth "to strip oneself of all opinions and beliefs formerly received" (HR1, 90; AT6, 15).

It may seem an exaggeration to speak of the intended universality of Descartes' revolution if the basic principle of the revolution's manifesto merely forbids the acceptance of a primary given as a foundation on which to build science. It will seem less of an exaggeration once we remember that, for Descartes, no action can be called truly human

---

3. I shall use the phrase "primary givens" at several points in this study: it refers to whatever one is initially given in one's experience. The word "experience" I use is the broadest sense in which Descartes would have used it. In that sense, "experience" confronts us with items through perception, through the understanding, through memory and through imagination. I call these "primary givens" before we question their status, before we ask, for example, whether perception gives us accurate knowledge of our surroundings or whether the understanding provides us with correct accounts of whatever can be an object of thought. These questions about status will turn out to be metaphysical questions. Even once these metaphysical questions have been settled, Descartes' criteria of knowledge demand that there still be methodological operations which must be executed on "primary givens" before anything derived from such "givens" can be accepted as an item of knowledge. These metaphysical, epistemological, and methodological issues, and their relevance to "revolution," are a subject of discussion in the remainder of this chapter, and will also surface in the next.

unless it can be called rational; that it cannot be called rational unless it is dictated by knowledge; and that there is no knowledge apart from science. Hence when it is said that no primary given may be accepted as a foundation on which to build science, what does this imply? It implies that no primary given may be accepted as a basis on which to order any part of life, if that part of life is to qualify as truly human. Hence my earlier statement that Descartes intended to bring about a totally new outlook in all areas of life.

The completeness and universality of Descartes' revolution are dictated by his method. This relationship betwen revolution and methodology will be a topic for further discussion. But I should first turn to consider the fact that this revolution's intended universality is also closely related to Descartes' epistemology. This introduces the second topic of this section, namely, that contrary to what some might expect from one who advocates universal and thoroughgoing revolution, Descartes is nevertheless *a thorough opponent of relativism*.

For a set of connected statements to qualify as a (part of a) system of knowledge it must have a "solid foundation"; and this foundation must consist of items which are known not in terms of something else but in terms of themselves. The point of connection of this aspect of Descartes' epistemology with his insistence on sweeping former opinions "completely away" is perhaps clear enough from the outset: the items known in terms of themselves are by definition known in a void, that is, they are known out of context of other items. To make this connection quite clear let us look at intuition, the power through which we are said to "grasp" these foundational items of knowledge, and at clarity and distinctness, the criteria which these items of knowledge are said to meet.

It is in the *Rules for the Direction of the Mind* that Descartes introduces "intuition." As a definition he gives:

By intuition I understand, not the fluctuating testimony of the senses, nor the misleading judgment that proceeds from the blundering constructions of imagination, but the conception which an unclouded and attentive mind gives us so readily and distinctly that we are wholly freed from doubt about that which we understand. (HR1, 7; AT10, 368)

The mind is said to consist of the understanding (comprising both "intuition" and "deduction"), imagination, sense, and memory. Memory is never taken to be a source of knowledge for it can only present that which it has first received from the understanding, imagination, or sense. But it is clear that Descartes also rules out both the senses and the imagination as sources of knowledge, or at least knowledge which may be called "foundational." His purposeful juxtaposition of "fluctuating," "misleading," and "blundering" with "unclouded," "attentive," and "wholly freed from doubt" points to his belief that if we are to gain foundational knowledge we must depend upon the understanding alone. What Descartes wants to dispute is that any "givens" ought to be accepted. For Descartes himself it is beyond dispute that, for example, whatever we sense, or whatever we learn from others, cannot be accepted as a "given." What is thus "given" may be accepted as a point of departure for analysis but, because it lacks clarity and distinctness, must be rejected as a suitable starting point for synthesis.

It must be rejected as a suitable starting point for synthesis, for the construction of systematic knowledge, because what we sense or what we learn from others is always complex. What is complex is not originally clear and distinct, and therefore cannot be grasped in an intuition, which means that it cannot be known. Whatever is sensed or learned can therefore only function legitimately as a point of departure for analysis, for in analysis we attempt to break up the given complex item into ultimate items which are simple, clear, and distinct. It is only from these items that we can commence our synthesis. They are the first that can be intuited. If we cannot break up a given complex item, it is to be rejected, for by definition it will remain opaque to the understanding. And if it can be broken up, that also constitutes its rejection, because even if the same complexity as is given in the original results from the synthesis which is to follow analysis, the item which results is different from the original given. It is now no longer *given* to the mind but is *put together* by the mind itself. In either case, because of the role of intuition, Descartes' epistemology demands the rejection of any complex givens as knowledge. And because whatever is given by means of the senses, or by means of the senses and the imagination combined, is always complex, it is initially to be rejected as knowledge. We come to the same conclusion if, rather than focus on intuition, we say more about the criteria of clarity and distinctness.

The criteria of clarity and distinctness jointly apply to an item if it is legitimately called an item of knowledge. It is not difficult to show that these criteria dictate the contextlessness of items of knowledge grasped as the foundational items of science. Descartes calls "clear" that which "is present and apparent to an attentive mind"; and "the distinct" "is that which is so precise and different from all other objects that it contains within itself nothing but what is clear" (*Principles* HR1, 237; AT8, 22). Therefore to be capable of judging anything properly it is not sufficient just to be fully aware of all of that "thing." That much is compliance with the first criterion, clarity, only. And such compliance may leave the "thing" intricately enmeshed with many other "things," themselves not necessarily clearly in mind. "Clarity" only demands of that on which we pronounce judgement that it be before the mind fully. But that is not sufficient "to be capable of judging of it properly. For the knowledge upon which a certain and incontrovertible judgment can be formed, should not alone be clear but also distinct" (ibid.). And "distinctness" demands that we have before the mind nothing but what pertains to having that item fully before the mind.[4]

Thus these criteria dictate that we cannot initally accept anything as knowledge which is not utterly simple in the sense of not synthetically derived. Even if we are confronted with a complex item which is clear and distinct to others, it cannot be so to us. For, as complex, it is a compound of other items all of which we must ourselves intuit as clear and distinct. Only then can the relations which hold between and among such items be intuited; only then can a complex item be clear and distinct. These criteria therefore demand that at the foundation of science there be utterly simple items, that is, items known apart from any other items. These criteria dictate that at the foundation of science there be items known *per se* rather than *per aliud*.

If they can be known at all, items to be known *per se* can only be known clearly and distinctly. Anything known *per aliud* can be known only if that from which it is derived is also before the mind clearly and distinctly (or at the least is remembered as having been so before the mind). Thus anything known *per aliud* ultimately can be known only if it can be seen as following from the relevant foundation or first principles, i.e. from what is known *per se*. Therefore that which

4. Although I do not accept as viable Descartes' (or any others') doctrines of absolute simplicity and absolute clarity and distinctness, this is not the place to argue against them. In any case, there are sufficiently well-known reasons against doctrines like these (not the least Wittgenstein's in *Philosophical Investigations* I, 46–47, 88f) to have made them archaic notions to most contemporary philosophers.

the senses give us cannot, as given, be known immediately by the understanding. For what is thus given is concrete, enmeshed in its context.

The implications for us at this point are clear. For Descartes, "nature" can be understood only once it has been fitted into the "rational scheme" of mechanics, medicine, or morals. These rational schemes themselves cannot be developed prior to the advancement of the "rational schemes" called metaphysics and physics. Metaphysics and physics, in turn, rest on the prior intuited knowledge of certain concepts and principles known *per se*. And therefore "nature" cannot be known immediately. Neither can we know immediately that which our education or cultural environment places before us. Neither Euclid's *Elements* nor Aristotle's *Ethics*, neither Aquinas's *Summa Theologica* nor Galileo's *Two New Sciences* show that they derive their conclusions from indubitable principles known *per se*. None of them even went so far as to attempt to state these principles. But even had they stated them, and even had they derived their conclusions from them by uninterrupted chains of arguments, I cannot begin at the end, with conclusions. If I am to understand I mush start where they began to understand, at the level of items known *per se*. But such items are not "given."

Descartes' epistemology, therefore, dictates that, whether it is my physical or my cultural context which I attempt to understand, if I am to understand I must understand for myself, radically so. Using words from the opening paragraph of the first Meditation, someone else's "firm and permanent structure in the sciences" is of little use to me for I will not be able to understand it unless I myself "commence to build anew from the foundation." And no foundation is ever given. The foundation is always to be established. Whoever wants to understand will first have to establish his own foundation. Moreover, no foundation can be established apart from obeying the precepts of the method which Descartes proposes. Thus, when he writes that "my design has never extended beyond trying to reform my own opinion and to build on a foundation which is entirely my own," Descartes speaks for himself and, he believes, for whoever seeks to understand. The need for universal revolution is dictated by a methodology which goes hand-in-hand with the criteria of clarity and distinctness, with a doctrine of radical epistemic individualism.

Such a radical form of epistemic individualism at once raises questions about relativism. If each can only "reform" his own opinion, if each must build on a foundation which is entirely his own, how can there be talk of science if (as Descartes does) by science we refer to a system of objective universal truth? How, for that matter, can Descartes without contradiction hold that he speaks for himself and for whoever seeks to understand when he says that one can only "reform" one's own opinion and must build from a foundation entirely one's own? The answer to these questions introduces one of Descartes' fundamental assumptions, and assumption which (as we shall see later) he shares with all major figures of the Enlightenment. It is that each person's reason is like every other person's reason, and that therefore a correct description of the workings of one person's reason holds for all. This fundamental assumption will recur throughout my study. It might be an innocuous assumption if Descartes did not take the workings of reason to be those articulated in his methodology.

Descartes assumes that truth is objective, absolute, and attainable only in one particular way. Because of this assumption he concludes that a description of the way in which a *particular* (set of) truth(s) has been attained is a description of the way reason functions *whenever* it is successful in its pursuit of truth. But once written down, that description may be read by others. And, says Descartes, if these others have also been successful in their pursuit of truth and have become conscious of their reason's operation in this pursuit, then they will find their reason's mode of operation reflected in the statement they read. That statement, being a picture of reason's procedure, is to that extent reason's self-portrait. The fact that others find themselves in this picture indicates that the portrait is not of a single person's idiosyncratic way of procedure but that it is a self-portrait of rational thought wherever it occurs. Of course, this move to the universal is not warranted by any finite number of corroborating experiences; and it is not taken to be invalidated by contrary claims about reason's manner of operation. For example, Descartes would be quite unperturbed by contrary claims which Aristotelians might make—as is clear from what he says in the second of the *Rules for the Direction of the Mind*. The universality of reason, with reason's mode of procedure as that described by Descartes, therefore remains an assumption. It is an assumption which comes to the fore in all of Descartes' works, but most especially in the *Rules*, the *Discourse*, and the *Meditations*.

Descartes did not deny the existence of relativism, nor did he deny the existence of what might seem to provide grounds for such a position, namely, widespread divergence of opinion on almost anything worth having an opinion about. But he did not take the existence of relativism and of its apparent grounds to be a consequence of epistemological and methodological tenets like his own. Instead, he explained all controversy as the result of prejudice, and prejudice he explained as flowing from wrong habits.

In the Preface to the *Principles* Descartes writes that "the principles are clear and nothing must be deduced from them but by very evident reasoning" and anyone has "sufficient intelligence to comprehend the conclusions that depend on" these principles (HR1, 210; AT9–2, 12). If that is so why did not all who read the *Principles* and reflected on the issues which Descartes raised come to the foundations and the conclusions he himself reached? He points to the permeating influence of habit and prejudice on the one hand, and the pervasive absence of method on the other. One way of introducing his answer is to consider what Descartes took to be the conditions for doing scientific work. Going this way will lead us back to the notions of objectivity and absolute truth, and will allow some further discussion of one of Descartes' fundamental assumptions, that of the universality of a rational faculty which is held to function only in the ways described through Descartes' methodological principles.

As stated at the end of the second part of the *Discourse*, the prerequisites for doing scientific work are: (i) overcoming partiality, (ii) observing life, and (iii) obtaining facility in the method. Overcoming partiality focuses especially on the task of freeing oneself from philosophical preconceptions. But, in general, overcoming partiality results in the kind of disinterestedness which enables one to distinguish between opinions or beliefs held because of the cultural epoch or geographical area in which one happens to live, and beliefs or items of knowledge accepted on rational grounds. Observing life has a double reward. It is, first, an aid to overcoming partiality. The experience that manners, customs, and opinions which in one country may be signs of sophistication are elsewhere deemed inconsequential or even silly is an important step on the way towards disinterestedness. Second, and at least as important, the observation of life provides one with a stock of experiences which can become starting points for analysis at various stages in one's scientific work. Finally, facility in method is needed for the simple reason that method is necessary for finding out the truth.[5]

5. The heading of the fourth of the *Rules for the Direction of the Mind* states this

Observing life is a prerequisite for doing scientific work. On the other hand, the very fact that we must observe life in order to overcome partiality is an indication that life itself has spoiled our ability to do scientific work. We need to observe life in order to recognize that the very process of growing up in a certain place at a certain time has saddled us with attitudes and beliefs peculiar to that place and time:

Since we have all been children before being men, and since it has for long fallen to us to be governed by our appetites and by our teachers (who often enough contradicted one another, and none of whom perhaps counselled us always for the best), it is almost impossible that our judgments should be so excellent or solid as they should have been had we had complete use of our reason since our birth, and had we been guided by its means alone. (HR1, 88; AT6, 13)

Our teachers "often enough contradicted one another." In this they themselves reflect the world around them, in which there are "many conflicting opinions . . . regarding the self-same matter, all supported by learned people"; a world in which philosophy, though "it has been cultivated for many centuries by the best minds that have ever lived" is nevertheless a discipline in which "no single thing is to be found . . . which is not subject of dispute, and in consequence which is not dubious" (HR1, 86; AT6, 8). Descartes' observation of life, his confrontation with a bewildering variety of opinion and conflict in doctrine, rather than leading him into thorough-going scepticism or relativism, instead prompts him to assert the absoluteness and universality of truth: never mind "how many conflicting opinions there may be regarding the self-same matter . . . there can never be more than one which is true." If only we had possessed "complete use of our reason since our birth" so that we would not have been ensnared by the bias of our teachers and the controversies of our tradition, we would not now have our natural light obscured and would live in the realm of truth. For, as he writes somewhat later in the *Discourse*, since there is "but one truth to discover in respect to each matter, whoever succeeds in finding it knows in its regard as much as can be known." To illustrate his point he introduces the example of a child "who has been instructed in Arithmetic and has made an addition according to the

unambiguously. The Haldane and Ross translation introduces ambiguity where none exists in the original: "There is need of a method for finding out the truth"; "Necessaria est methodus ad rerum veritatem investigandam."

rule prescribed; he may be sure of having found as regards the sum of figures given to him all that the human mind can know." Crucial, however, is that the addition be made "according to the rule prescribed." This rule is a specific application of the general method, of "the Method which teaches us to follow the true order and enumerate exactly every term in the matter under investigation" and which, if followed, gives "certainty" in the sciences. (HR1, 94; AT6, 21).

At the very end of the first part of the *Discourse*, that is, immediately prior to turning his attention to the articulation of the methodological precepts in the second part, Descartes writes:

> . . . I learned to believe nothing too certainly of which I had only been convinced by example and custom. Thus little by little I was delivered from many errors which might have obscured our natural vision and rendered us less capable of listening to Reason. But after I had employed several years in thus studying the book of the world and trying to acquire more experience, I one day formed the resolution of also making myself an object of study and of employing all the strength of my mind in choosing the road I should follow. This succeeded much better, it appeared to me, than if I had never departed either from my country or my books.

Study of the book of the world helped to overcome partially, a victory which made his natural vision clear. This, in turn, allowed him to succeed much better in studying himself. The outcome of this self-study is presented in the *Discourse*'s second part: the method which is to be used to gain truth in whatever area man believes he can obtain the truth. Clearing the natural vision, or releasing reason from the bondage of habit rooted in sense and in education, is to lead reason to become conscious of its own operations unhindered by sense or prejudice. The cause of relativism is uncritical acceptance of the data provided through one's cultural context. The consistent use of reason gives objectivity and truth in spite of the fact that through the operation of analysis it involves rejection of whatever is given through one's context. Because the use of reason leads to objectivity and truth it bears important additional "fruits."

One result of the consistent application of the method is the *Principles of Philosophy*. A "fruit" born of these principles is "that the truths which they contain, being perfectly clear and certain, will remove all subjects of dispute, and thus dispose men's minds to gentleness and concord" (HR1, 213; AT9-2, 18). This is in sharp contrast to "the controversies of the Schools" which "by insensibly making those who practice themselves in them more captious and self-sufficient [*plus pointilleux et plus opiniastres*]" are therefore "possibly the chief causes of the heresies and dissensions which now exercise the world" (ibid.). Gentleness and concord will be the lot of those who practise the use of Descartes' principles; the employment of reason carries the promise of healing for broken communities. The context of this passage emphasizes the point that such practice consists in working methodically at the foundation of the sciences.

The emphasis on method is not surprising for, according to Descartes, only the unhampered exercise of reason can lead to truth and hence to concord, and only methodic procedure allows (or better: *is*) the unhampered exercise of reason. Practice in working methodically, that is, learning to think reductionistically, leads to peace and tranquillity rather than dissension and opinionated conceit. Although unanimity is not a criterion for truth, it may function as a mark indicating its presence;[6] unanimity can come about once the method for gaining truth becomes available to man.

Overcoming partiality and obtaining facility in the method is to allow one to break through cultural relativism into the realm of absolute truth. But one cannot break into the realm of truth without "stripping oneself of all opinions and beliefs formerly received." That revolutionary act is not at all easy to carry out, for the "received opinions" are so firmly rooted in the mind that they hold reason captive.

II. THE LIBERATION OF REASON THROUGH DOUBT

In the Preface to the *Principles* we read that the "sovereign good, considered by the natural reason without the light of faith, is none other than the knowledge of the truth through its first causes, i.e. the wisdom whose study is philosophy" (HR1, 205; AT9-2, 4). It may at first sight look contradictory for Descartes to assign this role to philosophy for, as he continues, "experience . . . shows us that those who profess to be philosophers are frequently less wise and reasonable than others who have never applied themselves to the study." However, those to whom he refers are merely followers, some of Plato, most of Aristotle, and therefore their lack of wisdom ought to be no

6. See Kenny, *Descartes, Philosophical Letters*, p. 66; AT2, 597-98.

marvel. First, they have never thought for themselves and therefore have no right to "profess to be philosophers." Second, neither Plato nor Aristotle, though acute thinkers, did what Descartes holds philosophers ought to do; they failed "to seek out the first causes and the true principles from which reasons may be deduced for all that we are capable of knowing" (ibid.).

In fact Descartes believes that, with only one exception, up to his time no one has done the philospher's work, for "I do not know that up to the present day there have been any in whose case this plan [of seeking out the true principles] has succeeded" (HR1, 206; AT9-2,5). Despite not having done the philosopher's work, Plato and Aristotle were held in high esteem; their very "authority" was such "that those who succeeded them were more bent on following their opinions than in forming better ones of their own" (ibid.). Plato and Aristotle inspired timidity and, as we have seen, philosophy is not for the timid. Descartes identifies himself as the one exception; timidity was not one of his vices. As far as most other philosophers were concerned, Descartes held them to be in bondage to prejudice. First, we should see clearly why Descartes believed *reason* to be mostly *in bondage*. After that we can discuss his proposal for *the liberation of reason*.

Philosophers, says Descartes, are to live by the evidence of reason, not by the weight of authority. But "the greater part of those in later times who aspired to be philosophers, have blindly followed Aristotle," and even "those who have not followed him (amongst whom many of the best minds are to be found) have yet been imbued with his teaching in their youth, for it forms the sole teaching in the Schools; and these minds were so much occupied with this, that they were incapable of attaining to a knowledge of true Principles" (HR1, 207; AT9-2, 7). Descartes himself was amongst those who, though not followers of Aristotle, had in their youth become well acquainted with Aristotelianism. The fact that in spite of it he was capable of "attaining to a knowledge of true Principles" gives him hope for his contemporaries. For not all of them had been steeped in the doctrine of the ancients, and "those who have learned least about all that which has hitherto been named philosophy, are the most capable of apprehending the truth" (HR1, 208; AT9-2, 9). They, as well as those acquainted with but not blind followers of the ancients, could move towards independent thought with fresh help provided by Descartes' *Discourse, Meditations,* and *Principles*. For

those who are imbued with my doctrines have much less trouble in understanding the works of others and in recognizing their true value than those
who are not so imbued; and this is diametrically opposite to what I have just
said of those who commenced with the ancient philosophy, i.e. that the more
they have studied it the less are they fitted rightly to apprehend the truth.
(HR1, 209; AT9-2, 11)

As we have seen Descartes offers his own position as a new beginning. He takes his beginning to be new because it is meant to be a
rejection rather than transformation of the past. Its newness is guaranteed because the position cannot be taken up apart from a new
method. In that method the principle of doubt plays a dominant role,
for this new method requires that each of its users make the attempt
to doubt everything and, through this doubt, to reject all that is past
and all that is present.

Descartes has no illusions about the difficulty of this task of rejection. He knows that life itself militates against it. He knows that, as
we were brought up by our elders and educated by our teachers, the
parent-child and the teacher-student relationship demanded from us
closeness, trust, and the willingness to follow. He knows that as sentient beings we have the world thrust upon us regardless of our wishes
and desires. He is keenly aware of the fact that we have acquired the
near-ineradicable habits of trusting what we have learned from others
and trusting what our senses teach us, and that these habits have led
us to accept innumerable prejudices, that is, beliefs whose acceptance
reason has not authorized. During the course of life these habits and
many of these prejudices have come to be riveted to our minds so
that we are almost incapable of questioning, let alone rejecting, them
if "the evidence of reason" requires such rejection. Worse, these habits
are so deep-seated that they tend to preclude reason from presenting
evidence in the first place. Nevertheless, rejection of these habits is
necessary. Only through their rejection can we gain a radical distance
from our former beliefs, and allow reason to give its evidence. The
radical distance created in the *Meditations'* realm of theory—where, in
words from the *Discourse*, "I rooted out of my mind all the errors
which might have formerly crept in " (HR1, 99; AT6, 28)—frees reason
from bondage to habit and prejudice and is the prerequisite for its
mastery in the realms of both theory and practice.

Descartes holds that reason is ordinarily in bondage to prejudice.

And as is clear from the *Meditations*, one major prejudice has so far gone unmentioned. In the first Meditation, for example, we read:

these ancient and commonly held opinions still revert frequently to my mind, long and familiar custom having given them the right to occupy my mind against my inclination and rendered them almost masters of my belief; nor will I ever lose the habit of deferring to them or of placing my confidence in them, so long as I consider them as they really are, i.e. opinions in some measure doubtful, as I have just shown, and at the same time highly probable, so that there is much more reason to believe in than to deny them. That is why I consider that I shall not be acting amiss, if, taking of set purpose a contrary belief, I allow myself to be deceived, and for a certain time pretend that all these opinions are entirely false and imaginary, until at last, having thus balanced my former prejudices with my latter . . . my judgment will no longer be dominated by bad usage or turned away from the right knowledge of the truth. (HR1, 148; AT7, 22)

The ancient and commonly held opinions which are here rejected as entirely false because they are in some measure doubtful are, first, those expressing our habitual trust in the senses to give us our every-day, non-scientific, yet dependable knowledge of our surroundings. And, second, they are those expressing our habitual trust in the understanding or reason to give us scientific knowledge in the applied sciences such as medicine, as well as in what Descartes considers to be purely theoretical sciences, such as mathematics. Everyday sense-based knowledge, and especially scientific knowledge gained through the understanding, hardly seem candidates for the label "prejudice." One would be more inclined to oppose them as knowledge to the prejudice or opinionated folly of those who blindly accept the tradition. But the very fact that without more ado, we are inclined to accept as knowledge the givens of the senses and the products of the understanding, is in itself proof of the power of uncritically held beliefs over us. For if we are asked why we place this trust in sense and in reason, our answer is apt to take this form: everyone does it; or, my parents and teachers taught me so. Since neither of these answers contains or even points to clear and indubitable principles, their assertion merely betrays dogmatic conceit. Their very matter-of-factness is to be taken as an indication of the extent to which reason is in bondage to prejudice. Even the belief that reason is to be the arbiter of what is and what is not to be accepted as truth, though it is supported by the approval of the greatest thinkers of the past, is a belief which is to be questioned. And therefore even the definition of "prejudice"—a "prejudice" is any belief whose adoption reason has not authorized—is a definition which itself needs justification.

What has been introduced into the mind by reason and is known to have been introduced by reason, need not be rejected, provided, of course, that we have good grounds for trusting reason. The questions which naturally arise are: how do we know whether something has been introduced by reason? and how do we know that reason is trustworthy? What test can we apply to settle these questions and how do we go about applying that test? With these questions we enter the realm of methodology; moreover, as we shall see, these questions explicitly introduce the idea of a freedom. With method and free will combined we have the condition which allows for the liberation of reason. This *liberation of reason* is the second main theme of this section.

It is free will and method combined which are to bring about the revolution in the sciences. Through exercise of our freedom we are to attempt to extricate ourselves from the web of prejudice. That much is stated in the above quotation from the first Meditation, where we read that "I shall not be acting amiss if, *taking of set purpose* a contrary belief, I allow myself to be deceived." The "taking of set purpose a contrary belief" is an act of freedom. It results in the balance of former prejudices with this new one and so creates a situation which is to neutralize them both. Free will alone, however, cannot create this balance. For we may try by using will to bring this balancing act about, but mere use of will is not enough; we need a means of creating this balance. To extricate ourselves from prejudice, we need method as well as freedom. The use of method is as indispensable for doing away with the old as it is for establishing the new.

From the time he first wrote about the "reformation of science," Descartes regularly reiterated this point about the co-operation of free will and method. In the *Discourse* he writes "I did not wish to set about the final rejection of any single opinion which might formerly have crept into my beliefs without having been introduced there by means of Reason, until I had first of all employed sufficient time in . . . seeking the true Method of arriving at a knowledge of all the things of which my mind was capable" (HR1, 91; AT6, 17). And in his last work, *The Passions of the Soul*, he provides a "general remedy for all the disorders of the passions," disorders which, stemming from passions like pride or vicious humility or cowardice, strengthen all sorts of prejudice. In Article CLXI he writes that although "all the souls that God places in human bodies are not equally noble and strong . . . it is yet certain that good instruction serves much in correcting the faults of birth, and that, if we frequently occupy ourselves in the consideration of what free-will is, and how great are the advantages which proceed from a firm resolution to make good use of it . . . we may . . . acquire a general remedy for all the disorders of the passions" (HR1, 406; AT11, 453-4). From the time of the composition of the *Rules for the Direction of the Mind* "good instruction" refers to instruction in which practice in the method is the chief part, and "to make good use of free-will" consists in part in "carefully to avoid precipitation . . . in judgements" (as the first precept of the method later articulated in the *Discourse* has it). Thus whether the old (to be swept away) and the new (to be established) are in the realm of science or of personal conduct, freedom joined with method is a prerequisite for such action in either case.

A new attitude of mind is to be adopted, an attitude which, although it is to become a habit, results in what according to Descartes ought not to be called prejudice. Of the *Principles of Philosophy* Descartes writes: "in studying these Principles, we shall little by little accustom ourselves to judge better of all things with which we come in contact, and thus to become wiser" (HR1, 213; AT9–2, 18). Studying the *Principles* demands that we go through them from beginning to end, working ourselves through the material in the way in which Descartes presented it, which is in the order dictated by method. That is, studying the *Principles* is itself an exercise in method. But it is equally an exercise in freedom. For if we truly follow Descartes, making his arguments our own, we have to adopt as guides to our practice his contentions that we cannot accept or build on "judgments . . . precipitately formed," that it is therefore "necessary once in one's life to doubt of all things, so far as this is possible"; that we ought "to reject as false all these things as to which we can imagine the least doubt to exist." We have to agree with him that we can perform this act of rejection because we "experience freedom through which we may refrain from accepting as true and indisputable those things of which we have not certain knowledge" (*Principles* I, 1, 2, 6). Such action is to instil in us a new habit which will be the source of wisdom. Wisdom has its root not in tradition, culture, or community, but in individually experienced freedom and individually practised methodic procedure. Wisdom has its roots in egocentricity, in an individual's epistemic

7. This individual epistemic autonomy presupposes, for Descartes, that everyone

autonomy.[7] It is an epistemic autonomy which initially brands as "prejudice" even the trust in reason as the arbiter of truth and error. The first three of the *Meditations* are meant to show that this trust is justified and that reason neither needs nor can be given an authorization except that which it gives itself. It is, furthermore, an epistemic autonomy which, for Descartes, is sanctioned, perhaps even commanded, by God. "For since God has given to each of us some light with which to distinguish truth from error, I could not believe that I ought for a single moment to content myself with accepting the opinions held by others . . . " (HR1, 98; AT6, 27).

Descartes practised what he preached, sometimes even before he had formulated the precepts he was later to proclaim. His vision of how to go about "reforming" the sciences came to him away from schools and books, away from his native country, "in a quarter where . . . I found no society to divert me . . . shut up alone in a stove-heated room" (HR1, 87; AT6, 11). And as the opening paragraph of the *Meditations* tells us, his second sustained attempt at "reformation of the sciences"[8] begins under similar circumstances. It takes place away from his native land, on a day on which he could say "I have delivered my mind from every care and am happily agitated by no passions and . . . I have procured for myself an assured leisure in a peaceable retirement." Under such conditions he is ready "seriously and freely" to "address myself to the general upheaval of all my former opinions."

The liberation of reason from prejudice calls for the co-operation of free will and method. This co-operation of free will and method or, more particularly, of free will and methodic doubt, now needs more discussion. Let me begin with a passage from the fourth Meditation.

however probable are the conjectures which render me disposed to form a judgment respecting anything, the simple knowledge that I have that those are conjectures alone and not certain and indubitable reasons suffices to

equally possesses reason. This assumption he articulates in the opening paragraph of the *Discourse*: "the power of forming a good judgment and of distinguishing the true from the false, which is properly speaking what is called Good sense or Reason, is by nature equal in all men" (HR1, 81; AT6, 2). Arblaster has characterized this assumption as the "egalitarian faith in the universal possession of reason"; perceptively, he writes that "In his faith in the rationality of the independent individual, and his corresponding lack of faith in tradition, Descartes is the exact opposite of a thoroughly conservative thinker like Burke . . . " in *The Rise and Decline of Western Liberalism*, p. 128.

8. Here Descartes attempted both to sweep away the old ("I must once for all seriously undertake to rid myself of all the opinions which I had formerly accepted") and to establish the new ("and commence to build anew from the foundation").

occasion me to judge the contrary. Of this I have had great experience of late when I set aside as false all that I had formerly held to be absolutely true, for the sole reason that I remarked that it might in some measure be doubted. (HR1, 176; AT7, 59)

In this passage we again have the connection between freedom and method. Method comes to the fore in the act of doubting. For it was the exercise of *methodic* doubt (pushed beyond its normal limits to become metaphysical doubt) which, in the first three of the *Meditations*, cast "some measure" of doubt on "that which I had formerly held to be absolutely true."[9] And freedom comes to the fore in "setting aside as false" whatever is a conjecture. For with respect to what is dubious any one of three actions is possible: one can accept it as true, reject it as false, or suspend judgment with respect to it. But there is nothing automatic about the acceptance or the rejection or the suspension. In each case an act of will is required.

The connection between freedom and method appears repeatedly in this fourth Meditation. It is, we read, "in the misuse of the free will that the privation which constitutes the characteristic nature of error is met with" (HR1, 177; AT7, 60). Misuse of freedom occurs when we affirm or deny what is not clear and distinct, that is, what has not been subjected to thorough methodic doubt. Judgments made under such conditions are judgments not based on "real knowledge" and hence judgments which may be erroneous. But no judgments need be made under such conditions, for one could have exerted one's free will in the acts of suspending judgment and of submitting to methodic doubt the opaque complexity which confronted the mind. It is therefore within each person's power whether or not he will in fact err. So whether one continues in prejudice or falls into further error depends upon a deliberate choice.

It could have been otherwise. "God could easily have created me so that I never should err, although I still remain free, and endowed with a limited knowledge, viz. by giving to my understanding a clear and distinct intelligence of all things as to which I should ever have to deliberate" (HR1, 177; AT7, 61). This would obviate the need for method. To be more precise, it would eliminate the need for the analytical part of the method, for method to the extent that the prin-

---

9. In *The Imposition of Method*, chapters 4 and 5, I have given an account of how, precisely, method is involved in the first three of the *Meditations*.

ciple of doubt plays a role in it. God has not created me this way.[10] Alternatively, God could also have made it impossible for me to err "simply by His engraving deeply in my memory the resolution never to form a judgment on anything without having a clear and distinct understanding of it, so that I could never forget it" (ibid.). This would leave the use of method, including the principle of doubt, as a necessary condition for obtaining knowledge. But God has not done that either. Instead, a variant of this second possibility pertains. It is not God who has engraved this resolution deeply on my memory. This He has "left within my power." It is my duty "firmly to adhere to the resolution never to give judgement on matters whose truth is not clearly known to me." In this way I shall acquire a new habit; I shall "acquire the habit of never going astray." It is in acting out this duty "that the greatest and principle perfection of man consists" (HR1, 178; AT7, 62).

For Descartes it is not just freedom which is one of man's positive attributes; doubt also occupies that position. Only the exercise of free will and doubt together is the condition which allows for reason's liberation. Doubt is, therefore, not a defect. When at the beginning of the fourth Meditation Descartes writes that "I doubt, that is to say . . . I am an incomplete and dependent being," this presence of doubt is not a negative quality like, for example, evil or error. It is the presence of method; doubt, in this context, is methodic doubt. It is a doubt which is to be pursued and used while, to the contrary, error and evil are to be shunned. This doubt plays a positive role in that it is the road to freedom from prejudice. Once a person is free from prejudice, the use of doubt is the means to avoid subsequent error and renewed prejudice, both of which might without the presence of doubt result from precipitate judgment. Only when doubt is confused with irresolution does it become a defect. For as *The Passions* tells us, irresolution is "a species of fear" which proceeds "from a feebleness of understanding, which, having no clear and distinct conceptions, simply has many confused ones" (Article CLXX). Rather than fear, doubt is firmness of purpose. It proceeds from the state of mind determined not to accept as a primary given whatever may come to

---

10. If I had been so created I should, presumably, be quite a different being from what I am now. For it is not easy to see how a being composed of soul and body, and therefore subject to the "fluctuating testimony of the senses," could from the start have "a clear and distinct intelligence of all things as to which I should ever have to deliberate."

confront it, but to resolve such givens into a multiplicity of items which are clear and distinct. The practice of doubt is to liberate reason from prejudice by expelling from the mind all "knowledge" which I have not myself constructed upon my own unshakeable foundation. Thus it is the practice of doubt which allows for the manifestation of an individual's autonomy. For doubt clears the slate and thus makes it possible for a person to have only such beliefs as his own self-authenticated reason has authorized. Fundamentally, the exercise of doubt is what constitutes revolutionary activity.

Methodic doubt involves the exercise in freedom which liberates reason from bondage to prejudice. As we shall see, Descartes holds that, once liberated, reason is able to develop the knowledge which is to give us mastery over nature. The exercise of methodic doubt is therefore a prerequisite for acquiring mastery. Both the *Meditations* and the *Principles* begin with doubt but end with knowledge; the first with knowledge which is foundational to the sciences, the second with scientific knowledge proper. The "last and principal fruit" of the *Principles* is "that by cultivating them we may discover many truths which I have not expounded, and thus, passing little by little from one to the other, acquire in time a perfect knowledge of the whole of philosophy and attain to the highest degree of wisdom." Once doubt has set reason free, we are at liberty to progress indefinitely in our pursuit of mastery. The practical difference between the Cartesian master and the Aristotelian follower is striking: "there is no way in which we can better prove the falsity of those [principles] of Aristotle, than by pointing out that no progress has been attained by their means in all the centuries in which they have been followed" (HR1, 214; AT9-2, 18).

In his Introduction to *Descartes, Philosophical Writings* Alexandre Koyré aptly contrasts Descartes and Montaigne. Montaigne "abandons the external world—uncertain object of uncertain opinion—and tries to fall back upon himself in order to find *in himself* the foundation of certainty, the firm principles of *judgment*—that is, of a *discriminating discernment between the true and the false.*" Montaigne "looks for a firm foundation" and "finds nothing but perpetual change, instability, void." He "acknowledges his failure" and "fearlessly" faces up to the fact that "we have to accept things as they are," that "we have to renounce the hope with which we started," the hope of finding in ourselves the foundation of certainty. And so Montaigne's *Essais* are "a treatise of renunciation," a statement that "the last word of wisdom" is: "We have to abide by doubt" (p. x). Descartes would align Montaigne's doubt with irresolution and see it as fear. For Descartes doubt is merely the first word of wisdom. As methodic doubt it becomes the key to the passage beyond renunciation, the passage of hope and self-affirmation, of freedom and progress. Koyré nicely catches this contrast: "whereas Montaigne stopped at the finitude of the human soul, Descartes discovered the fullness of spiritual freedom, the certainty of intellectual truth." And so Koyré labels the *Discourse on Method* "the Cartesian *Confessions*" or Descartes' "*Itinerarium Mentis in Veritatem*," the story of Descartes' "successful breakthrough," the reply to the *Essais*." "To the sad story told by Montaigne, the story of a defeat, Descartes opposes his own, the story of a decisive victory" (p. xiv). Whereas Montaigne "*submits* to doubt as its slave, through weakness . . . Descartes employs doubt as his tool, or, if one prefers, as his weapon" (pp. xxii-iii).

In his juxtaposition of Descartes to Montaigne Koyré articulates the position I presented: freedom and doubt work together for Descartes. But Koyré's analysis stops short of the final truth about Descartes' freedom and doubt. At one time he calls him a revolutionary (p. xiii) and at another he describes him as a thinker who accepted the Christian gospels and allowed himself to be taught by St Augustine (xxxiv-v). The Christian gospels, especially as they were interpreted in the various traditions in which St Augustine remained influential, speak of a truth which confronts man from without, a truth that "will make you free" if without qualification you submit to it. For St Augustine, freedom is a gift from God. Koyré has rightly connected Descartes' method, doubt, and freedom. As he says, Descartes sets himself "the task of re-ordering all our mental activities on a new plan . . . and it is through freedom that we shall reach the truth, i.e. those clear and distinct ideas which our reason is unable to doubt." For Descartes, acts of free will precede the attainment of truth, and the truth attained is truth given by the individual to himself. Of course Descartes often professed his adherence to Christianity; and a recent commentator may well be right when he remarks that "To the end, Descartes remained a devout Catholic."[11] Nevertheless his philosophy was quite opposed to it. At least in practice Descartes' revolution in the sciences was accompanied by a revolt against the traditional Christian view of the place of man. For Descartes, man has the first word and the last

11. Blom, *Descartes, His Moral Philosophy and Psychology*, p. xiv.

in the matter of determining what is and what is not to be accepted as truth. In the end, the spirit of Descartes' philosophy is caught better by a writer like Vrooman than by Koyré when Vrooman speaks of "Descartes' faith in human reason" as giving him "a non-Christian . . . conception of man" and invokes "the fundamental principles and method of Descartes" "in order to restore faith in the human condition and in the possibility of man's being able to govern . . . his own destiny."[12]

12. Vrooman, *René Descartes, A Biography*, pp. 260-61.

II

Reason and Free Will

THE DESCARTES portrayed in chapter 1 held both that reason is in bondage and that it can be set free. This second chapter begins my exploration of the role and nature of the freedom which Descartes ascribes to a person even when he holds that person's reason to be in bondage. I start this exploration by considering the role which free will plays for Descartes in liberating and validating reason.

In this opening section I expose and begin to resolve the chief issue which underlies the first chapter, that of the relation between free will and reason. It is the main issue in this chapter, and it will also be central to chapter 4. This section is therefore the first of several in which I argue that Descartes takes free will, not reason, to be primary.

A rationalist position like Descartes' is usally taken as one in which reason is primary. Hence my thesis, that in important respects Cartesian free will possesses this primacy, will be quite controversial to a number of philosophers. But it is not that alone which warrants its examination. In this and in the next section I give grounds for the thesis of the primacy of free will. Some serious objections will need to be met. So in the fourth chapter protests will be considered and, I trust, decisively answered. In the course of answering them, we shall also find the tools which we need to deal with the other two concepts of prime interest: mastery and progress. This extended consideration of the place and (especially in the fourth chapter) of the nature of Cartesian free will is therefore warranted by the dividends it yields. It pays them in addition to the profits of obtaining clarity about the role and nature of free will in Descartes' position. These dividends are the tools which, in the fifth chapter, allow for an in-depth discussion of mastery and progress.

At the foundation of Descartes' system is the *cogito*. In the second part of this second chapter, I continue to discuss the relationship between free will and reason by means of an argument which confirms the conclusion that reaching the *cogito* requires an exertion of free will. In addition, I shall argue that the *cogito* itself incorporates a sustained exercise of free will in addition to that of reason.

The cumulative result of my first two chapters is that we find the most fundamental aspect of Descartes' position in his notion of freedom. For Descartes holds that reason is in bondage and is to be liberated and validated; that it can be liberated and validated only through the use of methodic doubt; and that such doubt does not come into play unless a person *wants* it to come into play. He is therefore committed to saying that, in spite of restrictions by prejudice, man is ultimately characterized by the possession of freedom. This gives freedom a place even more basic than that of the *cogito*, for we cannot reach the *cogito*, nor attain the liberation and validation of reason, apart from acts of free will.

Once it is clear how basic a role free will plays for Descartes, we will have an indication of a strong measure of affinity between the Cartesian position and that of eighteenth-century Enlightenment thinkers. However, after these two chapters we are ready to see that this affinity between Descartes and the *philosophes* can be stated in terms other than these very general ones. Therefore, before continuing my discussion of the nature of freedom and of the relation between free will and reason I shall, in my third chapter, turn to consider some of the details of this affinity between Descartes' thought and that of the eighteenth century.

I. THE PRIMACY OF FREE WILL

To defend the thesis that free will rather than reason is primary for Descartes, let me begin by examining an issue underlying my previous discussion of bondage and liberation. Recalling three major points, we can see at once the underlying issue which needs discussion.

(i) Descartes takes reason to be in bondage to prejudice. As we read in the first Meditation, "ancient and commonly held opinions still revert frequently to my mind, long and familiar custom having given them the right to occupy my mind against my inclination and rendered them almost masters of my belief" (HR1, 148; AT7, 22). Descartes therefore holds that his judgment is "dominated by bad usage" and "turned away from the right knowledge of the truth" (ibid.). (ii) If we are to gain (or regain) use of our reason, if we are to be able to give our unquestioning trust to what we take to be reason's deliverances, then, says Descartes, we must first dispel the mastery of the "commonly held opinions" and break the dominion of "bad usage." (iii) It is Descartes' belief that methodic doubt can deliver us from this bondage. Both the decision to adopt the method and the actual use of method are themselves exercises in freedom. In other words, no use of method is possible apart from the exercise of freedom. Unless the underlying issue is now made explicit, one might charge Descartes with confusion. For if we cannot liberate ourselves except through the employment of our freedom, then it might be said that either we need no liberation or we cannot liberate ourselves. We need no liberation if we are already free. We are unable to liberate ourselves if, lacking freedom, we can only gain freedom through putting our freedom to work. Since Descartes holds that it is the free use of methodic doubt which delivers us from bondage to prejudice he may seem to be saying that through our freedom we deliver ourselves from bondage.

The underlying issue which forestalls confusion consists in the important distinction in Descartes' concept of freedom. It is a distinction which places on one side free will as it functions, for example, in judgment: that is, when we make judgments on that which we perceive clearly and distinctly. In such a case we have the conformity or submission of the will to the truth. Such freedom is traditionally called the "liberty of spontaneity." On the other side there is set free will as it comes to the fore very clearly in acts like those of deciding to adopt the method, of suspending judgment, of rejecting as false whatever is dubious, and of making an effort to pay attention. All of these activities may be called acts of self-determination. In the *Meditations* at least, Descartes has no name for acts like these. (It will become clear enough in my fourth chapter that they cannot be put on a par with those acts which, in the fourth Meditation, he attributes to "liberty of indifference".) For reasons which will become apparent in a moment, I shall use the label "liberty of opportunity" for these manifestations of freedom. Descartes maintains that a human being always possesses liberty of opportunity and hence, in that respect, is always free. He also maintains that to the extent that reason is not liberated, a human being lacks liberty of spontaneity. The exercise of liberty of opportunity can co-exist with the absence of liberty of spontaneity. (In fact, the former may be the cause of the latter: one may *want* to accept what one's reason has not authorized and so one may *want* to remain in bondage to prejudice.) Since Descartes teaches that it is through the exercise of liberty of opportunity that we can attain the experience of liberty of spontaneity, there is no confusion in doctrine.

I can now restate my thesis with greater precision. In some[1] of the acts of will which are expressions of the liberty of opportunity, we find what Descartes takes to be a fully self-determined or autonomous will; it is in these autonomous acts that the will plays a role which is more fundamental than that which Descartes assigns to reason. In brief, support for my thesis can now be expressed as follows.

In the first three of the *Meditations*, the liberation of reason is to be achieved; and its trustworthiness and autonomy are to be established in an argument which stretches from the articulation of the *cogito* near the beginning of the second Meditation to the end of the third. Because the path one has to travel in order to liberate reason and to establish its trustworthiness cannot be entered except through acts of will which are expressions of the liberty of opportunity, it follows that such acts of will must be found at the basis of reason's liberation and validation. The will is not determined by anything beyond itself in acts like these. So it must be said to be self-determined or autonomous. It now remains to show that the texts bear this out.

Since in the *Meditations* he does not even give a name to what I have called the "liberty of opportunity," does such liberty really exist for Descartes? And, if it exists, is it really as important for him as I claimed? I shall answer these quesions, first, by showing that for Descartes free will is not limited to expressions of liberty of spontaneity, that is, to its legitimate functioning in acts of judgment where will conforms to the truth. Second, I shall do so by discussing the distinction between liberty of spontaneity and liberty of opportunity in terms of the determination by the truth in the former case and in terms of self-determination in the latter case. This stress on determination and

---

1. I say "some," because not all acts of will which are to be classified under "liberty of opportunity" are acts in which the will is fully self-determined. Proposing hypotheses in the development of science calls for acts of liberty of opportunity rather than of liberty of spontaneity. There are grounds for proposing one hypothesis rather than another, but since the hypothesis proposed may turn out to be false, the proposal is not an expression of liberty of spontaneity. The liberty in question is that of opportunity. Since it functions in a context where particular grounds determine one way rather than another, there is in this case no total self-determination. For background to this point, see my "Peirce and Descartes," pp. 88-104, especially pp. 95-103.

self-determination or autonomy is no more than an amplification of the point that for Descartes the legitimate use of free will is not confined to the area of correct judgment.

First, *free will and conformity to truth*. Although the will plays its role in judgment, that is, in affirming or denying a claim on the basis of knowledge,[2] acts of will are not limited to contexts of either judgment or knowledge. This point is clear from Descartes' argument in the first Meditation. There the decision to reject as false whatever is doubtful, the decision to become free from prejudice, is not the assertion of will as one finds it in the judgment that two plus two equals four. It is instead a resolve in which freedom asserts itself at a more fundamental level than that of judgment. It is an assertion of freedom, in which the will is not determined by reason or truth, and thus it is a manifestation of liberty of opportunity. One can, of course, also in judgment assert one's freedom while the will is not determined by truth. Such acts occur when we make judgments in the absence of clarity and distinctness. But as the argument of the fourth Meditation makes abundantly clear, Descartes considers such acts illegitimate. It is precisely because such illegitimate acts can and do occur that prejudice exists and reason is in bondage. I am now concerned with some of the manifestations of free will which are legitimate, but not determined by reason.

Grounds for the distinction between these different acts of will are clearly present in Descartes' practice as a philosopher, as portrayed in his *Meditations*. I shall turn to that in a moment. First I should like to point out a passage in the third Meditation where Descartes himself makes the distinction, without arguing for it or discussing it. He writes that "in willing, fearing, approving, denying, though I always perceive something as the subject of the action of my mind, yet by this action I always add something else to the idea which I have of that thing; and of the thoughts of this kind some are called volitions or affections, and others judgments." (HR1, 159; AT7, 37). Kenny writes in his commentary on the passage that here "judgments are contrasted with volitions rather than classified as a species of volition." The contrast "makes clear that Descartes uses 'volition' in a narrow sense as well

---

2. In "Will and Reason in Descartes' theory of Error," Caton argues convincingly against Kenny's claim that it is *only* in the later works (from the *Meditations* onwards) that judgment is an act of will rather than one of reason. See Kenny's "Descartes on the Will," pp. 1-17, and Caton, pp. 88-89 and pp. 100-03.

as in a broad sense, volitions strictly so called being a species of a genus of acts of will which includes also judgments."[3] Descartes' practice in the *Meditations* support Kenny's conclusion.

In terms of the practice of the first Meditation we can say: making the resolution to reject as false whatever is doubtful and implementing that resolution are acts of freedom but not acts of judgment, acts of liberty of opportunity rather than experiences of liberty of spontaneity. Such acts of freedom are not limited to the first Meditation; they are also found in the fourth. In the fourth Meditation the decision not to judge unless that on which we pronounce judgment is clear and distinct is an act of freedom but not an act of judgment. We can say, in addition, that faithfully implementing such a decision is also an act of freedom distinct from its exercise in judment. In both cases we exercise freedom. But in neither case do we experience liberty of spontaneity because in neither case do we submit ourselves to truth. Again, we can say in terms of the first Meditation that methodic doubt cannot deliver us from bondage to prejudice unless we exercise our freedom by willing to use this doubt. And of the fourth Meditation's argument we must say that having the criteria of clarity and distinctness, having the method to lead us to items which are clear and distinct, and having the will operate in judgment are not enough. We also need the will to implement the method, and the will to resolve successfully not to judge unless we have gained clarity and distinctness through the use of method. All of these are manifestations of the liberty of opportunity. Thus, in the first Meditation it is, fundamentally, our freedom as liberty of opportunity which is to deliver us from the bondage imposed on us by our "commonly held opinions." In the fourth it is the exercise of this liberty which guarantees our continuance in freedom. For acting on the resolve not to exercise the will in judgment unless that which we judge is clear and distinct has obvious consequences. It prevents us from accepting what is false as true, and so keeps us from renewed bondage to prejudice.

Thus Descartes believes he can make these moves of liberation, and can perform these acts which guarantee continuation in liberty, because of the distinction he introduces within his concept of freedom. It is a distinction which allows for a freedom, that of opportunity, beneath the freedom legitimately enjoyed in judgment, that of spontaneity. It is this freedom of opportunity whose exercise is a necessary

3. Kenny, "Descartes on the Will," p. 12.

condition for reaching the foundations of knowledge. This freedom, therefore, is more fundamental for Descartes' position than even the *cogito* itself. It is a freedom which for him is a necessary condition for philosophizing, a freedom without whose exercise we cannot hope to liberate and validate reason. Hence without it we cannot expect to reach the foundations of knowledge, and we cannot come "to establish any firm and permanent structure in the sciences" (HR1, 144; AT7, 17). It is, therefore, a freedom without which we cannot possibly achieve progress in any area of life. On these grounds it is appropriate to call it "liberty of opportunity."

Unless we reach the *cogito* we cannot hope to validate reason. Unless we can validate reason we cannot accept as trustworthy anything which reason presents to the mind. Lacking both of these, we cannot make progress in the pursuit of truth. But, as Descartes makes abundantly clear, we cannot reach the *cogito* unless we suspend judgment and unless we use the method. Both activities involve acts of freedom. The freedom involved in acts like these, one must conclude, plays for Descartes a role more fundamental than that of the *cogito*. To this point I shall return in my next section.

I shall further pursue the distinction between these two kinds of freedom by looking again at Descartes' practice in the *Meditations*. I shall discuss this distinction in terms of *self-determination* in the case of liberty of opportunity and in terms of *determination by the truth* in the case of liberty of spontaneity. This, it will be remembered, is the second approach to answering the questions whether the liberty of opportunity actually exists and is as fundamental for Descartes as my thesis maintains.

In the *cogito* we obtain our first item of knowledge. When the understanding pays attention to anything that is clear and distinct then reason or truth determines the will. As we read about the *cogito* in the fourth Meditation, "I could not prevent myself from believing that a thing I so clearly conceived was true . . . because from great clearness in my mind there followed a great inclination of my will . . ." (HR1, 176; AT7, 58–9).[4] No such determination of the will by reason

---

4. See also Descartes' letter to Mesland of 2 May 1644. After he has quoted the passage from the fourth Meditation now under consideration, he writes that "if we see very clearly that a thing is good for us it is very difficult—and, in my view, impossible, as long as one continues in the same thought—to stop the course of our desire" (Kenny, *Descartes, Philosophical Letters*, p. 149; AT4, 116).

can occur in the *Meditations* before the moment when we reach the *cogito*. Nevertheless the will has been exercised prior to that moment. Descartes' practice therefore shows that it is not as if the truth always dominates or always ought to dominate the will.

Reason or the truth dominates the will when we pay attention to what is clear and distinct. But as we have seen, in order to get ourselves in the position where the truth can thus dominate through clear and distinct perception, we have first to exert the will in acts of deciding to use the method, in the actual use of the method, and in the act of paying attention[5] to that to which methodic procedure leads us. If we want to speak of the will as determined in these acts, we have to conceive of it as self-determined and not as determined by the truth or by reason. In this case the will cannot be determined by clear and distinct knowledge because no such knowledge is as yet before us. All we have before us is the possibility of coming to such knowledge. In this situation we may determine ourselves to follow the road (adopt the method) which will place us where we might obtain a clear and distinct perception. We may do this, but equally we may not. In this situation we are free, since it is in our power to follow or not to follow that road. Whichever choice we make in this situation, it is one which clearly shows our self-determination. It clearly discloses the will engaged in autonomous action.

The objection might be made that after all the will is determined here by something else and so there is not the kind of freedom which I hold to be present. One might say that we know we are able to obtain the truth only if we go about our business methodically, that this is a clear and distinct item of knowledge, and that the will is thus determined by this clear and distinct knowledge. But that will not do as an objection in these early Meditations. It will not do at the time when we are still trying to free reason from bondage and to validate reason, for in these Meditations it must still be asked whether reason itself is reliable; whether any clarity and distinctness can be attained; whether clarity and distinctness can in fact function as criteria of truth. It cannot be stipulated *a priori*, therefore, that method will lead us to the truth.[6]

---

5. The act of "paying attention" is crucial in the process of the validation of reason. See, e.g., the last full sentence of HR1, 165 (AT7, 45) and the last full paragraph of HR1, 167 (AT7, 47-8). That it is an act of will is stated explicitly in the letter to Mesland from which I quoted in the previous footnote.

6. If in the first Meditation Descartes had stipulated in an *a priori* manner that the

Let me put this differently. A statement of right methodic procedure may be said to be a description of the way the mind works in its successful pursuit of truth. But in these Meditations we need to establish whether the mind can ever work in a way (and can be known to work in a way) which leads to truth. The method itself needs to be shown to be effective; its success cannot be presupposed. Accordingly we may, but need not, determine ourselves to follow this road. If we decide to use the method—as Descartes does in the *Meditations*—it is meant to be a case of pure self-determination. It is an instance of exercising one's freedom in the form of liberty of opportunity.

The conclusions I now take to be established are: (i) that for Descartes, freedom is a necessary condition for obtaining the foundations of knowledge; (ii) that this freedom differs from the legitimate use of free will in judgment; (iii) that it is a more basic feature of Descartes' position than even the *cogito* in the following way: it is a necessary condition for philosophizing itself and thus for reaching the *cogito* at all. Hence (iv) it is a necessary condition for procuring the liberty and confirming the validity of reason. Most, if not all, of what I have just said is at least implied by what Descartes wrote in the Synopsis of the *Meditations*. I have quoted part of its second paragraph earlier, but should now introduce all of it:

In the second Meditation, mind, which making use of the liberty which pertains to it (*propria libertate utens*), takes for granted that all those things of whose existence it has the least doubt, are non-existent, recognizes that it is however absolutely impossible that it does not itself exist. This point is likewise of the greatest moment, inasmuch as by this means a distinction is easily drawn between the things which pertain to mind—that is to say the intellectual nature—and those which pertain to body.

Note how the liberty of opportunity and methodology are here connected. All prejudice is to be removed through doubt. The existence of mind is to be established through doubt. The grounds for the distinction between mind and body (a distinction which underlies the entire metaphysics and thus all the other sciences) are to be provided through doubt. Thus, since the doubt in question is methodic doubt, method is to clear our mind from prejudice. It is to allow us to reach our first certainty, and is to give us grounds for our first and most

---

use of method will lead to the truth, that would have involved circularity. See *The Imposition of Method*, chapter 4, section 3.

fundamental distinction. It is doubt activated by the mind's liberty of opportunity which is to accomplish all this. It is a liberty which "pertains" or "is proper to" the mind. But method is also proper to the mind. Without methodical doubt being activated by the mind's liberty of opportunity, however, we cannot arrive at freedom from prejudice; we cannot use the mind to understand; we lack something about which we can form judgments.

Even when methodical doubt is pushed beyond its limits to become what Descartes calls "metaphysical" doubt (HR1, 159; AT7, 36), this move depends on an act of liberty of opportunity. For it is through the introduction of the evil genius that methodical doubt becomes metaphysical doubt. Doubt is then turned towards questioning the trustworthiness of reason in all its modes of operation. But the evil genius can be brought upon the stage of consciousness only through an act of man's will. When, in the first Meditation, the evil genius is brought on the scene, Descartes writes "I shall then *suppose* . . . that . . . some evil genius not less powerful than deceitful, has employed his whole energies in deceiving me" (HR1, 148; AT7, 22). For Descartes, making a supposition always involves an act of will. Since it is only a supposition that is summoned up, the act cannot be determined by the truth. The supposition in question may well be false. Hence the liberty involved is that of opportunity, not that of spontaneity. It again follows that a use of the freedom of the will as an act of liberty of opportunity is necessarily presupposed in the exercise of attempting to demonstrate the absolute trustworthiness of reason. This pertains also to that part of the exercise which consists in the introduction of the evil genius.

The autonomy of the will is fundamental for Descartes. Free will rather than reason is primary. Unless we presuppose the existence of an autonomous will expressing itself as liberty of opportunity, reason cannot be liberated and its trustworthiness cannot be established.

II. THE ARCHIMEDEAN POINT

Much more needs to be said about the thesis that free will is primary in Descartes' position. There are passages in Descartes' works which appear to conflict with this thesis; these will have to be taken into account. What I have called the "liberty of opportunity" will have to be related to what, in the fourth Meditation, Descartes calls "liberty of indifference." And the important implications of this thesis for the Cartesian view of mastery and progress need to be made explicit. I shall deal with these aspects in later chapters. I shall use this section to relate the thesis of the primacy of free will to Descartes' *cogito*.

If the liberation of reason cannot be brought about and its trustworthiness cannot be established except through free acts of an autonomous will, then what is the nature and place of the *cogito*? The *cogito* is generally taken to be the most fundamental aspect of Descartes' position. But the argument of my previous section has established that free will occupies the more fundamental place: the occurrence of acts of freedom is a necessary condition for the liberation of reason, for coming to the *cogito*, for constructing systematic knowledge. This conclusion calls for re-consideration of the nature and place of the *cogito*. If the outcome of this discussion confirms my earlier conclusion then I shall have achieved my major objective for this chapter: placing beyond doubt the fact that free will is fundamental to Descartes' position.

Perhaps we can best deal with this question of the nature and place of the *cogito* if we approach it by means of the opening paragraph of the second Meditation:

The Meditation of yesterday filled my mind with so many doubts that it is no longer in my power to forget them. And yet I do not see in what manner I can resolve them; and, just as if I had all of a sudden fallen into very deep water, I am so disconcerted that I can neither make certain of setting my feet on the bottom, nor can I swim and so support myself on the surface. I shall nevertheless make an effort and follow anew the same path as that on which I yesterday entered, i.e. I shall proceed by setting aside all that in which the least doubt could be supposed to exist, just as if I had discovered that it was absolutely false; and I shall ever follow in this road until I have met with something which is certain, or at least, if I can do nothing else, until I have learned for certain that there is nothing in the world that is certain. Archimedes, in order that he might draw the terrestrial globe out of its place, and transport it elsewhere, demanded only that one point should be fixed and immovable; in the same way I shall have the right to conceive high hopes if I am happy enough to discover one thing only which is certain and indubitable.

This passage is fraught with difficulties, not all of which need concern us here. It is clear enough that we are to continue on the path of freedom and doubt; that no firm foundation or even part of a firm foundation for science has yet been reached; that consequently we still lack all systematic knowledge; that more than free will and doubt seem to be required if we are to save ourselves from the worst form of scepticism. What is needed is an Archimedean point.

In an attempt to explain the principle of the lever, Archimedes is reputed to have said to Heiro ii, ruler of Syracuse, "Give me a place to stand, and I will move the world." Descartes believes that he will be right to hope for success in the enterprise of providing a firm foundation for the sciences if he can "discover one thing only which is certain and indubitable." This "one thing" seems intended to be the equivalent of what Archimedes demanded, "that one point should be fixed and immovable," that he be given "a place to stand."

It has generally, and correctly, been assumed that the *cogito* is meant to be Descartes' Archimedian point. The assumption has helped to fix both the nature and place of the *cogito*. Exploration of this notion of an Archimedian point through examining what Descartes took to be its nature and function, and comparing that with the nature and role of free will and doubt, should help us to determine the relationship that exists between free will and the *cogito*.

This exploration should confirm that, in his *system of knowledge*, the *cogito* is indeed Descartes' Archimedian point. The *cogito* is the "fixed and immovable point" which is to allow for the kind of systematic or scientific knowledge which the opening paragraph of the *Meditations* characterizes as a "firm and permanent structure." But it will also lead us to the re-affirmation that the *cogito* is not the most basic aspect of Descartes' *position*. That role is played by free will. The existence of free will is necessary if Descartes' systematic knowledge, including its "fixed and immovable point," is to be possible. The place of the *cogito* will therefore be seen to be basic to Descartes' system, but not to his position. We might say that in Descartes' thought the *cogito* takes a position of epistemic priority, but free will occupies a position of metaphysical or ontic priority.

My exploration will also draw attention to a feature concerning the nature of the *cogito* which commentators tend to neglect. It will become clear that, in addition to the activity of reason, the *cogito* itself also incorporates a sustained activity of the will.

I shall begin my exploration with a comparison of Archimedes' and Descartes' "place to stand." Second, I shall examine in some detail what is involved in Descartes' own use of the concept of an Archimedian point. And, third, I shall draw three conclusions from this exploration. These include the two mentioned above, namely, (i) that the *cogito* is Descartes' Archimedian point and (ii) that free will is the most basic aspect of Descartes' position. The third (a conclusion which my analysis seems to make inescapable) is that in spite of the prominence of talk about God in the third Meditation, as far as philosophizing is concerned it is, for Descartes, irrelevant whether or not God exists. God neither provides, nor guarantees the "fixedness" of, Descartes' Archimedean point.[7]

First, *Descartes and Archimedes*. It should strike us immediately that the comparison Descartes draws between Archimedes and himself is incongruous in at least one crucial respect. The "place to stand" which Archimedes demanded was meant to be a place apart from himself and the world which was to be moved. That Descartes understands this is clear from his formulation: "the terrestrial globe" is to be "drawn out of its place and transported elsewhere" and for that a "fixed and immovable point" is needed. If this fixed and immovable point were to be found in the world to be transported, the example could not possibly be a coherent illustration of the principle of the lever. I shall assume that Archimedes' example is coherent in this respect, so that it is essential to his illustration that the "fixed and immovable point" be outside the thing to be moved. It is precisely in this essential respect that Descartes' comparison is incongruous. Alternatively, perhaps we should say that Descartes is aware of this incongruity and that for his purposes the notion of an "outside" is not essential to that of an "Archimedean point." For in these early Meditations there is no "outside" for Descartes: in the world of spirit there is no god whom we can trust, and in the world of time there is neither space nor matter to fill it. The "place to stand" will therefore have to fall within the "world" we experience as existing, a "world" composed so far only of freedom and doubt. Must we then conclude that one of these is Descartes' Archimedian point? And if it is one of these, which is it? Consideration of a passage from the *Discourse* parallel to that which we are considering from the *Meditations* will help to answer these questions.

After the statements "I rejected as false all the reasons formerly accepted by me as demonstrations" and "I resolved to assume that

7. God is irrelevant for reaching foundation of Descartes' system. But (as I have argued in *The Imposition of Method*, chapters 4 and 5) God is also irrelevant for providing a validation of reason. Reason validates itself; that is precisely why reason is for Descartes autonomous. If these two factors together do not make God irrelevant for Cartesian philosophers, they certainly go a long way towards His expulsion from their philosophizing. (See also footnote 17 of this chapter.)

everything that ever entered into my mind was no more true than the illusions of my dreams," the *Discourse* continues:

But immediately afterwards I noticed that whilst I thus wished to think all things false, it was absolutely essential that the 'I' who thought this should be somewhat, and remarking that this truth "*I think, therefore I am*" was so certain and so assured that all the most extravagant suppositions brought forward by the sceptics were incapable of shaking it, I came to the conclusion that I could receive it without scruple as the first principle of the Philosophy for which I was seeking.

   And then, examining attentively that which I was, I saw that I could conceive that I had no body, and that there was no world nor place where I might be; but yet that I could not for all that conceive that I was not. On the contrary, I saw from the very fact that I thought of doubting the truth of other things, it very evidently and certainly followed that I was; on the other hand if I only had ceased from thinking, even if all the rest of what I had ever imagined had really existed, I should have no reason for thinking that I had existed. From that I knew that I was a substance the whole essence or nature of which is to think, and that for its existence there is no need of any place, nor does it depend on any material thing . . . (HR1, 101; AT6, 32)

   This passage appears to identify the "fixed and immovable point" with the *cogito*. For it is of "this truth *I think, therefore I am*" that he says it "was so certain and so assured that all the most extravagant suppositions brought forward by the sceptics were incapable of shaking it." However, the "I think, therefore I am" here appears as a condensed formulation of a statement which, among others, includes the concepts of freedom and of doubt: "I noticed that whilst I thus wished to think all things false, it was absolutely essential that the I who thought this should be somewhat."[8] From this statement it might seem as if there are five possible candidates for identification with that which is incapable of being shaken. All of these are in some way related to the *cogito* but not all include the concepts of both freedom and doubt. There is, first, the noticing that while wishing to think all things false, the I that thinks must exist; second, the noticing; third, the wishing to think all things false, or (to use a more explicit alternative formulation) the wishing to reject as false all things I can doubt; fourth, the wishing or willing; fifth, the thinking all things false, or

   8. The concept of freedom is present in "I . . . wished" (*je voulois*), that of doubting in "to think all things false."

the doubting. But three of these, namely the second, fourth and fifth can immediately be ruled out as viable candidates since they all suffer from incompleteness. The second can be ruled out because no noticing can occur unless there is something to be noticed. The fourth can be disregarded for the same reason; as Descartes says in the third Meditation, "in willing . . . I always perceive something as the subject of the action of my mind" (HR1, 159; AT7, 37). Also the fifth, the doubting, can be ruled out. For the doubt in question is methodic doubt, and no methodic doubt can occur apart from an act of will. This leaves the first and third as possible candidates for Archimedean point. Before I consider them, something more should be said about this concept of an Archimedean point.

"Archimedes, in order that he might draw the terrestrial globe out of its place, and transport it elsewhere, demanded only that one point should be fixed and immovable." The basic incongruity between Descartes and Archimedes I have already pointed out: for Archimedes the "point" must be "without," for Descartes it can only be "within." But let us assume that the reference to Archimedes is not entirely inept. We should then look for ways in which congruity may be found. Descartes of course knew that "the place to stand" to "move the world" functioned in an illustration of the principle of the lever. Neither Descartes' nor Archimedes' formulations list all the necessry ingredients for such an illustration. There is the "world," the thing to be moved. And there is "the place to stand" or the "fixed and immovable" "one point." Implicit is the presence of the lever. There is also the hand or person to press the bar of the lever ("Give *me* a place to stand, and *I* will move the world"; "Archimedes, in order that *he* might draw . . . "). But if all that is asked for is a place to stand for the person who handles the bar of the lever, then we still lack the crucial point or fulcrum. Therefore the "place to stand" must itself include the fulcrum—which may be implied in Descartes' formulation of "Archimedes . . . demanded only that one point should be fixed and immoveable." A fulcrum placed on quicksand will not do. Thus for minimum completeness the picture demands (i) a thing to be moved; (ii) an instrument with which to move it (the lever, including both bar and firmly fixed fulcrum); (iii) the power to be exerted on the bar, a power which must itself be sufficiently "firmly fixed" to be able to provide the needed pressure.

Let us now return to the two items from the *Discourse* which remain as candidates for the "fixed and immovable point." This will allow a more careful examination of what is involved in *Descartes' own Archi-medean point*—which is the second main issue for this section. These two items are the first (the noticing that while wishing to think all things false, the I that thinks must exist) and the third (the wishing to think all things false, or the wishing to reject as false all things I can doubt). One of these may perhaps be related as congruent with the second and/or third of the three ingredients just listed as ingredients necessary for minimum completeness of Archimedes' illustration. Neither of them can be so related to the first, to the thing to be moved, although both of them contain a reference to the thing to be moved in the phrase "all things false." For we do know what Descartes intends to be his counterpart to Archimedes' "world." It is all so-called knowledge, all supposed knowledge which is even in the least uncertain or doubtful as well as that about which this "knowledge" purports to be. That we must take all so-called knowledge and its object as the equivalent of Archimedes' "world" is clear from Descartes' own words: Archimedes' challenge is to "draw the terrestrial globe out of its place" and, says Descartes in the same paragraph, his own task is "setting aside all that in which the least doubt could be supposed to exist."

However, "setting aside all that in which the least doubt could be supposed to exist" is an incomplete expression for the task Descartes has set himself. When the expression is completed, it appears that once again the analogy with Archimedes breaks down. The "setting aside" is only the first part of his task. It is the revolutionary activity of "completely sweeping away" all opinions and beliefs, the activity I have discussed in the first chapter. Such "setting aside" or "sweeping away" is the first or preparatory part of a task. The major part of that task is to establish a "firm and permanent structure in the sciences." Fulfilment of that task presupposes a "firm foundation" on which to build this structure if there is to be any hope of "permanence"—as Descartes also states in the opening paragraph of the first Meditation. In the second Meditation it is still this task, rather than that of rejecting all that is doubtful, which remains of prime importance. And thus the first paragraph of the second Meditation expresses the task again in terms which go beyond rejection of what is doubtful: "to discover one thing only which is certain and indubitable."

At this point the positions of Descartes and Archimedes are, as it were, the reverse of one another. Archimedes needs a place to stand to move the world. Descartes' world is "moving," in fact it is disintegrating. It is Descartes himself who "moves" his world, who through reductive analysis pushed by doubt takes it apart and throws the parts away. Therefore his question is: where is it that I stand, since I am moving the world? As he does not know where he stands, he is not even certain that he stands. Hence the statement "just as if I had all of a sudden fallen into very deep water, I am so disconcerted that I can neither make certain of setting my feet on the bottom, nor can I swim and so support myself on the surface." Nevertheless, he must be standing somewhere and he must be handling the right tool, for the world is being moved. What then is congruent with the remaining two aspects of Archimedes' illustration: the firmly placed lever as instrument with which to move the world, and the power which is to activate the lever? Can we align with these two the two remaining items from the *Discourse*?

One of these is the wishing to think all things false, or the wishing to reject as false all things I can doubt. "To reject as false" is what is happening; the world is moving. Rejection is taking place because "the principles upon which my former opinions rested" (HR1, 145; AT7, 18) cannot withstand the force of doubt. Doubt, therefore, is the lever, bar and fulcrum included and, because doubt is successful, the fulcrum must be fixed and immovable. Because (apart from the will) nothing else exists, doubt is itself this firm place. But no methodic doubt occurs unless there is the will to engage in such doubt. The willing or wishing part is therefore essential as the power which activates the doubt, as the equivalent to the force which presses the bar to move the world. In this statement from the *Discourse* we therefore cover the remaining aspects of Archimedes' illustration: the place to stand, the tool to use, and the force needed for its use. Doubt activated by will is Descartes' Archimedean point.

This conclusion is corroborated by what we read in a re-cast form of this part of his argument in *The Search after Truth*. There, through his mouthpiece Eudoxus, Descartes says: "I am going to conduct you further than you think. For it is really from this universal doubt which is like a fixed and unchangeable point, that I have resolved to derive the knowledge of God, of yourself, and of all that the world contains" (HR1, 316; AT10, 515).

If it is correct to draw the conclusion that doubt activated by will is Descartes' Archimedean point, then it is wrong to say, as I did earlier,[9] that more than free will and doubt are called for if we are to save ourselves from the worst form of scepticism, that in addition to free will and doubt we need an Archimedean point. Doubt activated by free will is the Archimedean point. Because doubt activated by free will may appear to be an activity which is not a source of knowledge, however, this conclusion may seem to introduce a problem.

The problem to which I am alluding arises from the truth that knowledge is to be "founded on" or "derived from" something. Once Descartes' system is being developed, once, for example, he is constructing his mechanics, there is no difficulty in speaking of knowledge as "founded on" or "derived from" an activity. For at that stage knowledge may be "derived from" the activity of observation or "founded on" that of experimentation. And in either case we can speak of that activity as a source of knowledge. At the point where Descartes is still in search of a foundation for the sciences, the activity is that of doubt, of the kind of doubt which attempts to "set aside" rather than to convey "knowledge." The problem then lies in how to move from that activity to knowledge or truth. If it is a problem at all, it is not one which seems to bother Descartes. As we just saw, he writes that "from this universal doubt . . . I have resolved to derive the knowledge of God, of yourself, and of all that the world contains." To see how "knowledge" is taken to be "derived from" this activity we should consider the remaining item from the *Discourse* which I introduced as a candidate for the Archimedean point. That item is the first, the noticing that while wishing to think all things false, the I that thinks must exist.

Because the expression "I think, therefore I am" is a condensed form of the statement "I noticed that whilst I thus wished to think all things false, it was absolutely essential that the I who thought this should be somewhat," doubt activated by free will is the activity designated by the concept *cogito*. But, says Descartes, this thinking that is going on involves self-consciousness: it includes awareness of the fact that there is thinking going on. The "noticing" of the truth that there is an activity which doubt cannot shake is therefore essential as part of the Archimedean point. That is to say, the Archimedean point involves self-consciousness. It is self-conscious doubt self-consciously activated by free will that is the foundation from which building the

9. See the end of the third paragraph of this section.

"firm and permanent structure in the sciences" is to commence. What is "noticed" first is that doubt necessarily involves existence, that there can be no thinking apart from being. From that point on, it will be "noticed," that since "I" exist, God exists, and, given the nature of the "I" and of God, a "world" exists apart from the "I" and apart from God. The *cogito*, therefore, is an activity which is a source of knowledge.

Archimedes had to be given a secure place to stand, a place of which he would have to have knowledge and in which he would be able to position himself. The Cartesian thinker who wants absolute certainty has no tool for attaining such certainty except the kind of thought which consists in doubt activated by free will. At this stage in the *Meditations*, at the very foundation of systematic knowledge, self-conscious doubt activated by self-conscious free will is all that constitutes the thinker,[10] and is all that is known to exist. Thus this thinker *qua* thinker or this doubter *qua* doubter is himself the Archimedean point. The thinker recognizes this once doubt or thought—the "tool" used to "move the world"—cannot reject the existence of thought. For Descartes, the Archimedean point is the thinker's recognition of the absoluteness of thought, of free will pushing doubt. In the Archimedean point we have, for Descartes, the revelation of the autonomy of man *qua* thinker. What is taken to be absolutely firm and trustworthy even if "whoever turns out to have created us .. should . . . prove to be all-powerful and deceitful" (*Principles* I, 6) is the intellectual intuitive power to grasp the truth of self-evident items. This "intuiting" is the "noticing" which appeared in the formulation of what I called the *first* candidate for the status of Archimedean point. A chief objective of the argument of the *Meditations* is to establish the fact that even if the ultimate power in the universe (assuming such a power to exist) were against me, I can nevertheless trust this intellectual function of mine. In this respect, therefore, reason is absolutely trustworthy. And since its trustworthiness is not bestowed on it from "without," it is autonomous. The *Meditations* then continue by arguing that all of reason can be shown to be absolutely trustworthy by means of the use of that feature of reason which has already been identified as trustworthy. And so reason (in its intuitive function) validates rea-

---

10. And it is all that is and remains essential to a *res cogitans*. Again, *Principles*, I, 32: "in us there are but two modes of thought, the perception of the understanding and the action of the will."

son (in its deductive function)—a procedure which is to guarantee all of reason's activities.[11]

If this section's prime concern were with the validation of reason, much more should be said on this score. But I have already done so elsewhere.[12] Moreover, since my main interest is in the role of freedom in this validation of reason, rather than in this validation *per se*, these few comments will now suffice. It only remains for me to draw *three important conclusions*. Such is the role of the third and final part of this section.

The first is that we may, and indeed we must, call the *cogito* Descartes' Archimedean point. As we do so, we should remember that in this thinking-which-is-going-on we have more than the activity of reason or the understanding. The thinking takes the form of doubting, and doubting (like all thinking) cannot occur apart from an act of free will. To think is an exercise in freedom. Within the *cogito* neither free will nor understanding has priority one over the other. At the basis of Descartes' *system*, free will and understanding are co-present and equally necessary.

My second conclusion concerns the dilemma of this section's second paragraph. The dilemma is this. First, let it be claimed that the *cogito* is the most basic aspect of Descartes' system. How can that claim co-exist with the assertion that the occurrence of acts of free will is a necessary condition for coming to the *cogito*? This latter assertion would seem to make certain acts of free will more fundamental than those which help constitue the *cogito*. I believe this apparent dilemma allows a solution which permits the statement of both claims without contradiction.

For Descartes, philosophizing in the sense of constructing a philosophical system must start with the *cogito*. The *cogito* is basic to his philosophical *system* and therefore to all his systematic knowledge. Nevertheless, the conclusion reached in the preceding section must be retained: free will was active before we reached the *cogito*. Before intuitive knowledge became a reality in the cognition that doubting necessarily implies existence, free will was engaged in its constant

11. Since, for Descartes, reason is man's essence, the phrases "the autonomy of reason" and "the autonomy of man" may be used interchangeably. The same may be said for the phrases "the autonomy of will" and "the autonomy of man." This is shown nicely by Broadie, *An Approach to Descartes' Meditations* pp. 130, 135-38.

12. For an adequately detailed discussion of this validation of reason see my *The Imposition of Method*, chapter 2, part 3, and chapters 4 and 5.

pushing of doubt to reduce to ever greater simplicity the complex items which confronted the understanding. It is only in retrospect, once we have attained the state of the *cogito*, that this activity of free will can be recognized as efficacious. So what kept free will active? Why did it continue to push the doubt before a successful outcome to this activity could be known? Nothing but hope or faith or trust that there would be a succesful outcome—a hope, faith, and form of trust which could only be generated by and rest in the doubter himself. For, at this stage of the argument, nothing exists except the doubter. Perseverence on the way of doubt is meant to be pure self-determination.[13] Thus the main conclusion of the previous section must be upheld: underneath the *cogito* is the freedom of self-determination which leads to it.

It is nevertheless the *cogito* rather than that freedom which is to be called Descartes' Archimedean point, because it is not until we reach the *cogito* that we "discover" the "one thing . . . which is certain and indubitable." For the construction of systematic knowledge the *cogito* is the "one point" which is "fixed and immovable." It therefore remains the most basic constituent of Descartes' *system* if by "system" we refer to the body of knowledge presented in the *Meditations*, *Principles*, and *Passions*. But it is not the most basic aspect of Descartes' *position* if, by use of the term "position," we intend to account for the condition which, though not itself a part of the system, is held to be necessary to the system. That condition is the self-assertion of the *res cogitans* in acts of will which are taken to be fully autonomous.

13. None of this is to say that in this exercise the understanding is absent. There is, for Descartes, no "hope" except in the awareness of a good or of an evil, more particularly, in the "consideration" that there is some "prospect that we shall obtain what we desire" (cf. *The Passions of the Soul*, art. LVIII). In the case at hand, the "consideration" is of the perceived evil of reason's bondage and of the expected good of establishing reason as absolutely trustworthy. Hope clearly permeates the *Meditations* from the very beginning—again using phrases from *The Passion's* art. LVIII—in what one might deem a form which is "excessive," so that it is to be called "confidence or assurance" (hence my use of "faith or trust"). The will does not act randomly. But since the hope is one that reason be freed from prejudice and be found trustworthy, and the willed action is directed to establish this freedom and trustworthiness, the "consideration" cannot itself at this point have any truth value attached to it derived from reason. As Professor Elmer Kramer put it in his comments on this argument at the 1985 meetings of the Canadian Philosophical Association in Montreal, it is "worth emphasizing that all acts of free will have reasons." I agree. What also needs emphasis is that for Descartes not all *reasons* are authorized by *reason*.

The *cogito* cannot be reached apart from the doubt which requires firmness of purpose, apart from the freedom to sweep away all beliefs in the revolutionary activity of their reduction to elements of utter epistemic simplicity. It was failure of nerve which kept Montaigne from finding in himself the foundation of certainty. It was Descartes' unrelenting exercise of free will which for him established the autonomy of reason.

A third conclusion, one with which I shall bring this section to a close, is that Descartes' position tends towards making God irrelevant for philosophizing. Let me approach that conclusion by way of a quotation from Hiram Caton's *The Origin of Subjectivity, An Essay on Descartes*:

The Cogito brings thought to consciousness of its nature . . . In that moment the mind apprehends an objective limit upon deception, for the Cogito exhibits to thought a limit upon omnipotence circumscribed by thought itself, indeed, *my* thought.

By bringing reason to consciousness of its inner nature . . . the Cogito emancipates reason from all restraints of piety: it empowers a self-consciously secular reason . . . An unshakeable and immutable will is the basis of the autonomy of reason. "Self-consciousness constitutes itself in defiance of all omnipotence . . . Here begins in philosophy as such the rebellion against Christianity that we call Enlightenment."[14]

This "rebellion against Christianity" which here "begins in philosophy as such" is neither timid nor half-hearted, for it is unequivocally reason's unilateral declaration of independence. In emancipating itself "from all restraints of piety," reason has rejected its most powerful "prejudice." Descartes the man may say and probably mean what he says in the closing paragraph of the third Meditation:

it seems to me right to pause for a while in order to contemplate God Himself, to ponder at leisure His marvellous attributes, to consider, and admire, and adore, the beauty of this light so resplendent, at least as far as the strength of my mind, which is in some measure dazzled by the sight, will allow me to do so.

Nevertheless, there is no doubt whatsoever that Descartes the philosopher means it when he writes:

14. These last two sentences Caton quotes from Krüger, "Die Herkunft des philosophischen Selbstbewusstseins," p. 246.

But meanwhile whoever turns out to have created us, and even should he prove to be all-powerful and deceitful, we still experience a freedom through which we may abstain from accepting as true and indisputable those things of which we have not certain knowledge, and thus obviate our ever being deceived. (*Principles* I, 6).

And (if I may continue my use of this artificial distinction for a moment) it is not Descartes the notably pious man, but Descartes the free thinker when philosophizing, who helped shape the modern mind.

The third Meditation closes with a statement which invokes the medieval attitude of contemplation. But it opens with a statement to the effect that the only ground for doubt of the absolute trustworthiness of reason in all affairs of life is the supposed existence of an evil genius. Rejection of that ground for doubt entails the removal of God from philosophy. It makes the call to contemplation an anachronism within the *Meditations*. The only ground for doubting reason is the supposed existence of the evil genius. But, says Descartes, if God exists, God cannot be a deceiver, for it is contradictory to hold that deception and perfection can co-exist in the same being.[15] Therefore, if God exists there cannot be such doubt and reason can be taken as trustworthy. But similarly: if God does not exist there cannot be an evil genius, for the evil genius is stipulated to be supremely powerful, that is, must be God, who has been said not to exist. And since the evil genius's supposed existence is said to be the only ground for distrusting reason, we can therefore trust reason. Thus whether or not God exists, we can trust reason.

This is not to say that Descartes recognized where his position really led him on the point of the relevance of God for philosophy and science. He believed in the existence of God, and in the importance

15. Cf. Cottingham, *Conversation with Burman*, pp. 2, 6. Also HR2, 78; AT7, 195.

16. Apart from the example of the atheist's knowledge which follows in the text, Descartes' references to divine voluntarism in both the *Replies to Objections* and the *Correspondence* are cases in point. It is perhaps telling that Descartes seems not at his philosphic best when he attempts to make God relevant to his philosophy: he appears oblivious to the fact that the atheist can be a better Cartesian than the theist, and he appears unaware of the problem which extreme divine voluntarism poses for the argument about deception in mathematics in the first of the *Meditations*—an argument which would seem to require a (platonic) realistic background for it to be coherent. Perhaps Turgot was correct when he wrote that Descartes dared not make the irrelevance of God explicit because "he was frightened by the solitude in which he had put himself . . . " (Cf. Meek, editor and translator, *Turgot on Progress, Sociology and*

of God's existence for the possibility of systematic knowledge.[16] In the
Reply to Objections VI he asserts that, strictly speaking, the atheist cannot
have systematic knowledge "unless he first acknowledges that he has
been created by the true God, a God who has no intention to deceive"
(HR2, 245; AT7, 428). Nevertheless, my argument shows that the atheist
can quite consistently be a Cartesian. The atheist is entirely capable
of entertaining the *hypothesis* that there exists an omnipotent God who
constantly tricks him. He is equally capable of showing that, on Descartes' grounds, this hypothesis is self-contradictory. Hence the atheist
is as able to provide an argument for the validation of reason as is the
theist. The Cartesian atheist's position is stronger than the Cartesian
theist's. They share the conclusions that the Cartesian position allows
no room for a God who deceives. Only the atheist recognizes that the
Cartesian position has no need for the concept of a veracious God.

Pascal's complaint was to the point: "I cannot forgive Descartes. In
all his philosophy he would have been quite willing to dispense with
God. But he could not help granting him a flick of the forefinger to
start the world in motion; beyond this he has no further need of
God."[17] We need not wait for either "the English" (as Brinton supposed[18])
or for the *philosophes*[19] to see deism practised in philosophy.

Economics, p. 94.) If Descartes dared not make God's irrelevance explicit even to himself,
then Maritain goes too far when he attributes to Descartes knowledge of "the profound
incompatibility of his philosophy with the whole authentic tradition of Christian wisdom" (*The Dream of Descartes*, p. 44.) That is not to say that Maritain is wrong in his
assessment of the nature of Descartes' philosophy: in this respect my conclusions place
me firmly with Maritain rather than with Koyré (compare the final paragraphs of
chapter 1).

17. Pacal, *Pensées*, Section 2, 77, p. 26.

18. See my Introduction.

19. That deism or (depending on what Cartesian texts are selected and which *philosophes* taken for comparison) naturalism characterizes Descartes' work as much as that
of the *philosophes* is argued convincingly by Vartanian in his *Diderot and Descartes*. Vartanian makes his case in terms of Descartes' physics, drawing especially upon the
unpublished early work *Le Monde* but supporting his argument with judicious references
to the *Principles*. See especially Vartanian's conclusions on pp. 106-07 and 314. For the
fact that the *philosophes* themselves treated Descartes as a supporter of deism, see Grimsley, *Jean-Jacques Rousseau*, pp. 58-59.

III

Descartes and the Enlightenment

THE CONCLUSION of the first two chapters is that freedom is the fundamental feature of Descartes' position. This emphasis on free will is itself a strong indication of affinity between Descartes' thought and that of the eighteenth-century Enlightenment. But this affinity exists not only in such a general way. I can now begin to relate some of the important specific issues discussed in these two chapters to features characteristic of eighteenth-century thinkers.

In the Introduction I stated it as my thesis that Descartes was chief amongst those who brought the modern mind into being, while the *philosophes* were representative of those who developed its implications and extended its influence. I also said that the spreading of the Enlightenment was to a large extent the growing acceptance of that part of Descartes' position imbued with the concepts freedom, mastery, and progress. Mastery and progress have not so far been much in the picture—they will come more to the foreground later on—as I have focused on freedom and will continue to do so in this first of three chapters in which I explicate the relationship between Descartes and the Enlightenment.

This will not complete my discussion of freedom. Instead, it will re-introduce a central concern (that of the relationship between free will and reason) for further discussion in the next chapter. Such discussion will, in turn, allow the portrayal of an affinity between Descartes and the *philosophes* greater than that which can be drawn here.

In the meantime the resemblance which I am able to draw at this point should be sufficiently strong to lay to rest whatever qualms there may have existed about presenting a study of Descartes as a means of illuminating the Enlightenment. This judgment I shall support by considering the *philosophes'* view with respect to the following closely related theses: (i) that man is in bondage to prejudice, (ii) that he is able to liberate himself from prejudice, (iii) that he is able to liberate himself because he has available to him the method by which liberation can be effected, (iv) that this method is universal in its application, (v) that the method's application occasions revolution, and (vi) that this revolution is desired for the sake of progress both in the attainment of greater freedom and in the increase in mastery. With each of these six points I shall now deal in turn. Taken together they express an important and substantial part of the *philosophes'* view. But it is clear that they can just as well be considered as a concise summary of Descartes' position as I have presented it in the preceding chapters. Even a brief consideration of these various points will reveal that the affinity between the two positions is anything but superficial.

(i) *Prejudice.* Until the beginning of the modern period "the whole of Europe," says Condorcet in his *Sketch for a Historical Picture of the Progress of the Human Mind,* was submerged in "the shameful slumber into which superstition had plunged her" (106).[1] This wholesale dormancy seemed beyond danger of interruption, for each new generation, each new child was immersed in the prejudice of its surroundings and seemed to have no avenue of escape. The prejudiced older generation "exercised control" over the new generation "during the years of childhood and youth when the flexible intelligence and uncertain, pliant soul can be shaped at will" (118). "Teaching . . . was everywhere in a state of bondage and everywhere exercised a corrupting influence, crippling the minds of children with the weight of religious prejudices and stifling the spirit of liberty in older students with political prejudices" (119). Because of the pliable nature of youth the "fallacies which are imbibed in infancy" come to be "in some way identified with the reason of the individual . . . " (100).

Statements like these, clearly echoing Descartes', are certainly not limited to Condorcet. De Condillac is equally explicit: "While we are yet in the state of childhood . . . we fill our heads with such ideas and maxims as chance and education offer. When we come to an age in which the mind begins to arrange its thoughts, we continue to see

1. Throughout this chapter all my quotations from Condorcet are from his *Sketch for a Historical Picture of the Progress of the Human Mind,* translated by Barraclough. The page number in the text, in brackets, is at the end of each quotation.

only those things with which we have been long acquainted."[2] And in *Émile*, Rousseau inimitably puts it in these words: "Our widsom is slavish prejudice, our customs consist in control, constraint, complusion. Civilised man is born and dies a slave. The infant is bound up in swaddling clothes, the corpse is nailed down in his coffin. All his life long man is imprisoned by our own institutions."[3]

Descartes and the *philosophes* were at one on the point that a person's cultural context burdens him with the kind of prejudice which seems to make progess nigh impossible. They were agreed, furthermore, that it was especially early education that riveted prejudice to the mind in a way which seemed to preclude its deracination. And most agreed that this bondage to prejudice was "unnatural." If a person were to be allowed to develop "naturally," that is to say, away from the various pressures which a cultural context imposes, then his reason would by itself lead him to the conclusions which were those of the unprejudiced. Descartes believed that "the light of nature" would lead such a person to accept the conclusions which he himself had embraced. Most *philosophes* held that if someone grew up "naturally" then that person's mind would be filled with only such unprejudiced opinions as also they had made or could make their own. The image of a person developing "naturally," away from all cultural contexts, the image of a person growing up, say, on a desert island, was an image which haunted the eighteenth century. It is an image of which it is usually said that it is typically eighteenth century, and that it has its roots there. It is, nevertheless, an image which has its roots in the seventeenth century. For it is an image which is also Descartes'. As he writes in *The Search after Truth*: "a man with a healthy mind, had he been brought up in a desert and never received more than the light of nature to illuminate him, could not if he carefully weighed all the same reasons, adopt an opinion different from ours" (HR1, 311; AT10, 506).

(ii) *Liberation.* As for Descartes, so for the *philosophes* there is no contradiction in speaking of bondage—of universal bondage even—and of a liberation from it effected by the very ones who are in bondage. Though man is tyrannized by error, prejudice, and superstition, his free will is not taken to be totally destroyed. Essentially,

2. De Condillac, *An Essay on the Origin of Human Knowledge*, p. 301.
3. Jean-Jacques Rousseau, *Émile*, translated by Foxley, p. 10.

man is held to be free, or free enough to rouse himself to do battle with authority and fanaticism, free enough to free himself. In the Introduction I drew attention to the high praise accorded by Turgot and d'Alembert to Descartes: he "destroyed the tyranny of error" and shook off "the yoke of prejudice and barbarism." They praise him for beginning a task which they see themselves as continuing, the task of doing battle with all forces they considered to be anti-rational. The language of battle recurs in all the *philosophes* and, with Descartes, most of them firmly trust that reason will be victorious: "So we shall see reason triumphing ... overcoming ... bracing ... resisting ... crushing under its all-powerful hand, first, religious hypocrisy ... then ... political hypocrisy ... " (*Sketch*, 102-03). "Everywhere ... we see reason and authority fighting for supremacy, a battle which prepared and anticipated the triumph of reason" (*Sketch*, 117). Man is free enough to free himself once he knows how reason functions and applies its rule to all of life.

(iii) *Method*. The *philosophes'* aim—in Diderot's words: to "change the general way of thinking"—was that of Descartes. For neither of them did this change depend upon the acquisition and use of a new power. Instead it demanded the release of something taken to be as ancient as it was modern: human reason had to be liberated. Reason unbound, reason free to function in accordance with its own rules, would make for the kind of change in the general way of thinking that would overcome prejudice and would allow the successful pursuit of greater freedom and mastery. For the *philosophes*, reason free to function in accordance with its own principles is reason functioning as described by Descartes in his *Rules* and in his *Discourse*.

There is, then, strong continuity on this point between Descartes and the *philosophes*. Some recent writers would accept this statement about continuity as correct (e.g., Robert Butts, Kathleen Hardesty,[4] Ronald Grimsley,[5] D. M. Robinson[6]). Others perhaps more influential—like Isaiah Berlin and Peter Gay—reject it.

4. Butts speaks of d'Alembert's method as "Cartesian," and Hardesty generalizes Butts's statement by applying it to "most successful scientists" of the eighteenth century. For both of these, see Hardesty's *The Supplément to the Encyclopédie*, pp. 21-22.

5. In his *Jean D'Alembert*, Grimsley writes that "in taking over the Cartesian methodology" d'Alembert "also accepted another premise implicit in the Cartesian outlook—that doubt was a mere preliminary to establishment of rational truth; scepticism was but a stage on the way to ultimate certainty." He then quotes d'Alembert as saying about Descartes that "His method alone would have been enough to make his name

Like Berlin,[7] Gay urges a case for discontinuity. He contrasts Descartes and the *philosophes* when he writes that "the Enlightenment was not an Age of Reason but a Revolt against Rationalism." According to Gay, the Enlightenment's claim "was in no way a claim for the omnipotence of reason" but was, instead, "a political demand for the right to question everything, rather than the assertion that all could be known or mastered by rationality."[8] The grain of truth implicit in this statement—that the *philosophes* rejected Descartes' style of metaphysics—is used to deny the more important truth concerning their closeness on the matter of methodology. Gay fails to recognize that talk of the "omnicompetence of criticism" is itself a manifestation of the "omnipotence of reason," at least in its analytic function. That is, with respect to the relation of reason and whatever is inherited from the past, of reason and whatever is proposed for acceptance by others past or present. To "shake off the yoke of authority," whatever the nature of authority as long as it is not that of the individual's reason, is to be accomplished through "analysis" or "criticism" according to the *philosophes*, and through "analysis" or "doubt" according to Descartes.

Sometimes the *philosophes* themselves discuss their method in terms which are explicitly Cartesian. Condorcet speaks of Descartes as the one who "brought philosophy back to reason." Descartes was able to do so, says Condorcet, because he had the only right method for doing so: "he had understood that it must be derived entirely from those primary and evident truths which we can discover by observing the operations of the human mind" (132). This "metaphysical method" was a "universal method" and was therefore "applied to all the various undertakings of the human understanding" so that "every branch of knowledge" was "subjected to analysis."[9] For criticism, for liberation,

---

immortal . . . " (pp. 270–71). Earlier in this work he describes d'Alembert's and the other *philosophes*' procedure in terms of Cartesian methodic practice (albeit in part in Lockean language). Cf. p. 229.

6. Robinson, in *Significant Contributions*, writes of Condillac's *Logique* as a work which conveys "the deeper and more pervasive sources of Enlightenment thinking" because we find in it "the quiet acceptance—the Cartesian acceptance—of reason." He adds that "It is a treatise on how we ought to think and on the risks of going about thought in any other way. It is a little handbook of right reason whose debts to Descartes . . . are acknowledged only between the lines," (p. xxv).

7. I shall deal with Berlin's opposition more appropriately in my final chapter.

8. Gay, *The Enlightenment, 1: The Rise of Modern Paganism*, p. 141.

9. "Every branch" is to be taken literally: "analysis" is to be used in arithmetic, but also in the evaluation of a work of art. D'Alembert, in his Encyclopedia article on "Taste,"

and for continuation in freedom Condorcet placed his full confidence
in this method. Descartes' articulation and first self-conscious use of
this method he called a "new step in philosophy," a step whose consequences were momentous, for it

> imposed a barrier between mankind and the errors of its infancy, a barrier
> that should save it from relapsing into its former errors under the influence
> of new prejudices, just as it should assure the eventual eradication of those
> that still survive unrecognized, and should make it certain that any that may
> take their place will exercise only a faint influence and enjoy only an ephem-
> eral existence. (132)

From the details of Condorcet's own argument, it is clear that his was
no shallow admiration of Cartesian methodology. His admiration is
particularly well expressed in his utilization of its details. Let me illustrate this by reference to the concept of "balance." It is a concept
of whose relevance to the eighteenth century Gay is quite clearly
convinced, but whose historical origins he fails to recognize.

Descartes uses "balance" explicitly and deliberately as an ingredient
in the process of analysis. His own words from the first Meditation
best support this claim:

> I consider that I shall not be acting amiss, if, taking of set purpose a contrary
> belief, I allow myself to be deceived, and for a certain time pretend that all
> these opinions are entirely false and imaginary, until at last, having thus
> balanced my former prejudices with my latter so that they cannot divert my
> opinions more to one side than to the other, my judgment will no longer be
> dominated by bad usage or turned away from the right knowledge of the
> truth. (HR1, 148; AT7, 22)

And Descartes' practice further strengthens the claim. Consider the
following statements. *I can trust my senses to give me reliable knowledge*

---

invokes Cartesian "analysis" in the context of Lockean "sensibility": "The true philosopher proceeds more or less in the same way whether he is criticizing or creating; at
first he gives himself over to the keen and lively pleasure of receiving impressions;
however, because he is convinced that true beauty always gains upon examination, he
soon retraces his steps, goes back to the causes of his pleasure, analyzes them, separates
the elements which deceived him from those which impressed him deeply, and by
means of this analysis puts himself in a position to render sound judgment on the
entire work." (Quoted from Hoyt and Cassirer, *Encyclopedia Selections*, p. 371.)

of the world about me contracticts *what the senses give me "are nought but illusions and dreams."* Again, *I am in the hands of a "God who is supremely good and the fountain of truth"* contradicts *I am the victim of "some evil genius not less powerful than deceitful."* Statements like these are crucial to the argument of the *Meditations.* Descartes introduces them immediately after he gives notice of the fact that "balance" is going to be one of the tools through which he can generate and continue the doubt which, rather than land him in scepticism, frees him from prejudice and leads him into truth.

The establishment of such "balance" is part of his manner of procedure. It is part of a methodology through which one consciously attempts to relativize the truth of whatever comes before the mind with a claim to be accepted as true. It is part of the intellectual style that Gay says retained its influence in the eighteenth century. But Gay does not recognise that this "balance" also is a crucial part of Descartes' "style" or methodology. He is acutely aware, however, that it is part of the intellectual style of the eighteenth century. Indeed it is no exaggeration to say that although he does not employ this term, the concept of balance is one of the keys Gay uses in his interpretation of the Enlightenment. Consider these statements. "The philosophes' experience, I discovered, was a dialectical struggle for autonomy, an attempt to assimilate the two pasts they had inherited—Christian and pagan—to pit them against one another and thus secure their independence." This "assimilation" and "pitting against one another" Gay calls "eclecticism," and of it he says that "this, for the Enlightenment, was the triumph of criticism over theory, the symbol of its intellectual independence." He calls Diderot's article on the eclectics in the Roman empire "a virtual self-portrait of the eighteenth century philosophe"— and this is the article in which Diderot describes the eclectic as one who preaches and practices autonomy, as one who "is a philosopher who tramples underfoot prejudices, tradition, antiquity, universal assent, authority, in a word, everything that overawes the mass of minds, who dares to think for himself . . ."[10]

That Gay is correct in his "discovery" about the *philosophes'* use of "balance" (or to use his own phrase, "pitting one against the other") and that this use of "balance" is just as much an application of method

10. These statements are all from *The Enlightenment, 1: The Rise of Modern Paganism,* pp. xiii, 160.

in their works as it is in Descartes', may both be illustrated from Condorcet's *Sketch*. In it, examples of the use of this tool and of Condorcet's praise of its efficacy are quite conspicuous.

Take what Condorcet says about "scholarship." "Scholarship . . . seemed doomed by its respect for the past and its deference towards authority always to lend its support to harmful superstitions." It "nevertheless contributed to their eradication" for it "knew how to weigh up authorities and compare them . . ." (168). So when Greek philosophical manuscripts became available in the early Renaissance, for example, a person could pit Aristotle's actual claims against "what had officially passed for the doctrine of Aristotle"; and against Aristotle he now also had Plato to "set up in opposition." He could not without contradiction accept both Aristotle and the tradition, or both Plato and Aristotle. Reason compelled him to choose to escape contradiction. Hence, "Once people felt that they had the right to choose their master, they had already begun to throw off the yoke" (103). But scholarship did not merely pit Plato against Aristotle, or weigh the traditional interpretation of Aristotle against other newly available sources. Scholars were now aware both of the ancient doctrines of the Greeks and of the modern dicta of priest and king. These were now put in the balance together and this juxtaposition of contradictory opposites "fanned the all but extinguished notions of the ancient right of human reason" (ibid.). When, therefore, "reason . . . at last found a sure method of discovering and recognizing truth" this method demanded the juxtaposition of "the superstitions of antiquity" to "the abasement of reason before the transports of supernatural religion," a juxtaposition in which both opposites undermined each other and "disappeared from society as from philosophy" (136).

(iv) *Universality of method*. The method through which Descartes "brought philosophy back to reason" was the method shared by the *philosophes*, in general and in most of its details, because they took it to be the universal method. They took it to express the workings of each person's reason and to be applicable to all subject-matter. We had clues of both these aspects of its universality in Condorcet's statements about Descartes bringing philosophy back to reason. As we saw, Condorcet said of Descartes that he "had understood" that method "must be derived entirely from those primary and evident truths which we can discover by observing the operations of the human mind," and that it was a method to be "applied to all the various undertakings of the human understanding." He agrees with Descartes that the method articulated presents a picture of "the operations of the human mind," that it is meant to be a picture of the workings of *any* human mind in its successful pursuit of truth, and that no knowledge of any subject-matter can be obtained apart from precisely these "operations of the human mind."

Condorcet is quite explicit about the universal applicability of Cartesian methodology. He speaks of Descartes' who "announced in advance" that the methodological principles "would be applied with equal success to all the objects whose relations are capable of precision . . ." (148). That "announcement" he calls "this great discovery, showing for the first time this final objective of the sciences, which is to subject all truths to the rigour of calculation . . ." (ibid.). Of these methodological principles he writes that "they compare with the natural workings of the human understanding . . ." (149). The method therefore "contains within it the principles of a universal instrument, applicable to all combinations of ideas" (ibid.). (See also 134 and 168.)

Condorcet's statements about method explicitly acknowledge their Cartesian source. Others present the same doctrine in Lockean language (with or without acknowledgement of Locke). Others again present it in Cartesian terms without acknowledging Descartes. But apart from these variations in expression, the doctrine presented is essentially one and the same, and essentially Cartesian. In the *Discours préliminaire* d'Alembert writes about Locke as one who, in studying the human mind, contemplated his own mind's procedures and, in the *Essay*, holds up to mankind the mirror in which each can see the operations of his own mind reflected.[11] And Condillac, in his *Essay*

---

11. Cf. Lough, *The Encyclopédie*, p. 143. That d'Alembert's evaluation does justice to Locke's intentions is clear from what Locke writes to Edward Stillingfleet, Bishop of Worchester. Stillingfleet had condemned the *Essay concerning Human Understanding* as "a new way of reasoning; new hypothesis about reason; new sort of certainty; new terms; new ways of ideas; new method of certainty." In addition, he accused Locke of presenting as his own "invention" that which, according to the *Essay* itself, should have been presented as "common" to all men. Locke replies: "But as to the way your lordship thinks I should have taken to prevent the having it thought my invention, when it was common to me and others; it unluckily so fell out, in the subject of my Essay of Human Understanding, that I could not look into the thoughts of other men to inform myself. For my design being, as well as I could, to copy nature, and to give an account of the operations of the mind thinking, I could look into nobody's understanding but my own, to see how it wrought . . . All therefore I can say of my book is, that it is a copy of my own mind, in its several ways of operation." These passages are from p. 137 and pp. 138-39 of *John Locke, Works*, vol. 4.

Concerning the Origin of Human Knowledge, speaks about the mind's operations in terms straight from Locke's *Essay*. For example, Part I, section II, chapter 6 has as its heading "Of the operations which consist in distinguishing, abstracting, comparing, compounding, and decompounding our ideas." But when he comes to speak about the relation between these operations and the right method, the echoes from Descartes' *Rules* (notably Rule 8) are unmistakable: "Our first aim, which we ought never to lose sight of, is the study of the human understanding; not to discover its nature, but to know its operations; to observe . . . how we ought to conduct them, in order to acquire all the knowledge of which we are capable" (5-6). That a statement of method is a functional definition of reason is a theme which comes to the fore again and again in this work: "From the knowledge we have acquired of the operations of the mind . . . we are now to learn the conduct which ought to be observed in the investigation of truth. Before this it was impossible to frame a good method; but now it seems to present itself, and to be a natural consequence of our researches" (300).

Because reason was taken to be universally the same and because Descartes' description of its operation (though sometimes presented in Lockean terminology) was accepted as correct, the shared picture includes the belief that there can be no access to truth except through analysis or reduction. It includes, therefore, the doctrine of radical epistemic individualism. It is that doctrine which dictates the need for revolution. Hence it is no surprise that someone like Condillac advocates such a revolution, a Cartesian revolution recommended in Lockean language: the right method of acquiring truth requires "a new stock of ideas" and hence rejection of all those we already possess for these are "but very indeterminate."[12] Since, like Descartes, they assumed that reason is universally the same, their advocacy of this revolution did not make them relativists. This assumption did not of course entail for them the non-existence of relativists. But they explained relativists' views, and the tell-tale signs of their presence, namely, divergence of opinion and controversy, as caused basically by prejudice.

We can now see better why they held the prejudices acquired in childhood to be especially pernicious: these become unquestioned habits of mind which prevent one from becoming conscious of the

12. *Ibid.* p. 301.

mind's mode of operation in its successful pursuit of truth. These, in fact, present a false account or picture of the human mind's mode of operation. In the words of Condorcet, quoted earlier under the heading "prejudice," the "fallacies which are imbibed in infancy" come to be "in some way identified with the reason of the individual." In none of this did the *philosophes* go beyond the boundaries of Descartes' position; in all of it they unmistakably echoed his views.

(v) *Revolution*. That the eighteenth-century Enlightenment is a revolutionary movement is a statement which needs no support, for almost everyone who has written on that epoch has made this point. A contention which does call for support is that at the basis of this movement's revolutionary outlook is Cartesian doctrine. Condillac's statement quoted in a preceding paragraph is one of many which can provide this support. And Condorcet's *Sketch* contains enough material by itself to make the point undeniable. Let me therefore turn to it again.

It was, Condorcet writes, "the genius of Descartes" which "gave men's minds that general impetus which is the first principle of a revolution in the destinies of the human race . . ." (147). From earlier statements concerning prejudice, liberation, epistemology and methodology, one would expect this statement *not* to be a general statement with a connotation of "revolution" so broad that just about anyone who had anything new to say would qualify for the label "revolutionary." Like Descartes, Condorcet uses "revolution" in a radical sense. Mere reformation will not do. Speaking about reformers like Luther, Condorcet says "The spirit that animated the reformers did not lead to true freedom of thought. Each religion allowed, in the country where it dominated, certain opinions only" and so they "refused to give reason its full freedom" and "the chain was not broken" (110).

Reformers are too timid to effect the revolution required. And since anything short of revolution results in sectarianism, the reformers only succeeded in multiplying sects. However, "All sects and governments and every authoritarian body were in accord on this alone: that they were against reason." Even after the reformer's work "Reason had to be covered with a veil which hid it from the gaze of tyrants but let it be seen by philosophy." Hence "it became necessary to retire once more into . . . timid reserve . . ." (109). Until "Descartes, a bold and clever philosopher," arose to give mankind "that general guidance of which it seemed to stand in need" through providing "a method for finding and recognizing truth." There was no timidity here: "He

wished to extend his method to all the subjects of human thought;
God, man and the universe . . ." "He stimulated men's minds, and
this all the wisdom of his rivals had never done. He commanded men
to shake off the yoke of authority, to recognize none save that which
was avowed by reason . . ." (122). None, that is, save that which was
avowed by each person's own reason. For, ascribing to Bacon a doctrine which he then proceeds to identify as Descartes', Condorcet
writes: "He asked that the philosopher, cast into the middle of the
universe, should begin by renouncing all the beliefs that he had received and even all the notions he had formed, so that he might then
recreate for himself, as it were, a new understanding admitting only
of precise ideas, accurate notions . . ." (121).

Not just the philosopher, but everyone who pursues truth in earnest
must recreate for himself a new understanding: "Every man had to
begin by recognizing his own errors before he could dispel those of
others, and before wrestling with the natural difficulties placed in the
way of truth he had as it were to refashion his own intelligence" (119).
And as the opening words of the Introduction to the *Sketch* tell us, to
refashion one's own intelligence calls for the reduction of the complexity of our sentient states into the epistemic atomic units which
these states were assumed to contain.

Descartes' call for revolution was heeded. "He was obeyed, because
he won men by his boldness and led them by his enthusiasm" (122).
The revolution spread and "At last man could proclaim aloud his
right, which for so long had been ignored, to submit all opinions to
his own reason . . ." (136). The *philosophes* arose, and observing what
they took to be the absurdity and intolerance of religion, the despotism
and tyranny of politics, proceeded by "laying their axes to the very
roots of these sinister trees" all the while "never ceasing to demand
the independence of reason . . . as the right and the salvation of mankind" (137). As for Descartes, so for the *philosophes*: not the reformer's
work of restoration or improvement but revolutionary deracination
is a necessary condition for progress.

(vi) *Revolution and mastery.* We have seen that, for Descartes, no
validation of reason can occur without prior acts of will, that reason
cannot be liberated and its trustworthiness cannot be established without presupposing the autonomy of will. The *philosophes* took a similar
position: without boldness there will be no battle to liberate reason
from prejudice. With respect to Descartes I should now draw attention
to one important implication of this position. If the autonomy of

reason cannot be established without presupposing the autonomy of will, moreover—as we saw as well—if one cannnot even reason without involving acts of will, then in what sense can Descartes speak of the autonomy of reason? Or, for that matter, how can the *philosophes* speak of the independence of reason? For they also presuppose free will in the liberation of reason.

They can speak of reason's autonomy or independence only in the sense that reason neither needs nor can possibly be given an external guarantee for its trustworthiness. Neither church nor state, neither God nor devil can detract from or add to reason's trustworthiness; neither can nor needs to vouch for the validity of reason's products. By its nature reason is independent in the sense that it vouches by itself for the soundness of its products. It cannot lose that nature and that nature cannot be restored to it. It can, however, be imprisoned, and then its nature cannot express itself or can do so only in a limited manner; then truth eludes man or can only be seen dimly. If imprisoned it can be liberated; once free it can function to its full extent. But no liberation occurs and no free functioning takes place apart from acts of will. It is the will which both allows and instigates reason to function, which motivates a potentially rational being to begin its own liberation and to enjoy the subsequent functioning of reason.

But this means that Descartes shares a further important doctrine with the *philosophes*: the doctrine that reason alone is not a power sufficient to motivate a person to take action, at least not to take upon himself the actions of liberation or revolution—or even the activity of thought itself. The revolution is desired for the sake of attaining greater freedom and becoming one's own master. Apart from the desire for freedom, no revolution would take place, and apart from the desire for increase in mastery, no reasoning would take place. Condorcet proclaims that "The time will therefore come when the sun will shine only on free men who know no other master but their reason" (179). Here he presupposes that men will freely want to place themselves under reason's compulsion for the sake of achieving greater freedom and mastery. For Descartes, as for the *philosophes*, no one is going to be compelled by reason unless his own will places him under such compulsion.

If it is really Descartes' position that reason by itself does no compel then this brings him far closer to another doctrine which is often said today to be present only from the middle of the eighteenth century onwards. That is the doctrine which receives perhaps its most famous statement in David Hume's *Treatise of Human Nature*. Hume wrote: "We speak not strictly and philosophically when we talk of the combat of passion and of reason. Reason is, and ought only to be, the slave of the passions, and can never pretend to any other office than to serve and obey them."[13] As we shall see, Descartes also holds that reason is to serve the passions. It is to serve what might be called a human being's "chief" or "master" passion: his strong desire for mastery.

The discussion of reason in the service of the desire for mastery will constitute important parts of both chapters 5 and 6. These chapters presuppose a further (somewhat technical) discussion of the relation of free will and reason in Descartes' thought. To that discussion I shall now turn in the next chapter.

13. *A Treatise of Human Nature*, Book II, Part III, Section III.

IV

Autonomy and Spontaneity

AN ACCOUNT of human freedom is fundamental to Descartes' position. This account stipulates that human freedom consists in the exercise of an autonomous will. An "autonomous" will, for Descartes, is guided or determined neither by human reason, nor by something apart from the person who originally does the willing, such as God or an independently existing truth or good. Absence of such determination does not make this notion of autonomy sterile, for it does not render autonomous action directionless or pointless. The will is taken to be self-directed; and to say that it is not directed by reason is meant to emphasize this notion of self-directedness. If it were directed by reason, the will could be seen as originally other-directed, if only because reason is the faculty through which man grasps truth which exists apart from himself. Such other-direction does take place but, as I shall make clear in the second part of this chapter, only when it is allowed to take place by an autonomous or self-directed act of will.

Through the power of his autonomous will a person is taken to be capable of liberating himself from prejudice. Such liberation, says Descartes, is necessary for the development of science and the realization of mastery. This process of liberation I have examined at length in the first two chapters. But I have so far said nothing about the transition from the stage of being free from prejudice to the stage of achieving mastery; from the stage of autonomous action to that of action which is directed by reason. No mastery can be attained except through the development of science, and no science is developed except through the exercise of reason. It is therefore only through the use of his reason that man can achieve mastery. But not just through its use. For he must submit to reason in order to become a master and so, for the sake of achieving mastery, it seems that reason must become the master's master. This mastery or compulsion by reason is not, for Descartes, meant to conflict with the autonomy of the will. Nevertheless, determination by reason is involved. In a sense which I shall make clear later, it is correct to say that the progress of science which is to lead to mastery and hence to an increase in one kind of freedom is bought at the price of banning another kind of freedom. Descartes attempts to protect this part of his position from paradox by drawing upon the distinction between liberty of indifference and liberty of spontaneity. Descartes' use of this distinction is thus central to my discussion in this chapter.

In the first two chapters it was necessary to neglect the idea of the determination of the will by reason in order to maintain the right emphasis on autonomy. In the first section of the present chapter there is also selective emphasis, namely on the determination of the will. We shall be looking at some passages in which it even appears that Descartes rules out the notion of an autonomous will. These passages contain a comparison of the divine will (which Descartes holds to be fully autonomous) and the will of man. That comparison seems to rule out the ascription of autonomy to human will. A consideration of those passages will also allow me to present Descartes' accounts of free will in terms both of liberty of indifference and liberty of spontaneity. After looking at these accounts, Descartes' contention that the compulsion of reason does not conflict with the autonomy of the will seems plausible. However, more careful reflection will lead us to recognize that there is an underlying, unresolved tension at this point.

Such reflection is postponed until the first part of chapter 5, for it presupposes work awaiting in the second part of the present chapter. That part introduces major details of the relationship between a compelling reason and an autonomous will, through an enumeration of a variety of possible contexts. In some a person experiences only liberty of indifference. In others he possesses liberty of indifference together with liberty of spontaneity. This enumeration is somewhat technical, but it clarifies matters. It will allow me to relate clearly Descartes' notion of the liberty of indifference to what I have called the liberty of opportunity. It will also allow me to correct an important shortcoming in what is probably the best of all recent accounts of Cartesian free will, to be found in Anthony Kenny's essay "Descartes on the Will." Most important, this enumeration provides the ground needed for the argument of the fifth chapter, which deals with the transition from autonomous action to action determined by reason. There we shall find that it is precisely the co-existence of autonomy and determination which is to make possible both progress and mastery. We shall find there too the tension of which I have just spoken.

I. AUTONOMY AND DETERMINATION

There are many passages in Descartes' writings which seem to be in direct and open conflict with the doctrine of the autonomy of the will. In the fifth Meditation, for example, we read that ". . . I cannot conceive God without existence," and from this fact "it follows that existence is inseparable from Him." This is not because my thought can "impose any necessity on things, but, on the contrary, because . . . the necessity of the existence of God determines me to think this way. For it is not within my power [I am not free] to think of God without existence (that is, of a supremely perfect being devoid of a supreme perfection) though it is in my power [I am free] to imagine a horse either with wings or without wings" (HR1, 181–82; AT7, 67).[1] Why am I not free to think of a supremely perfect being devoid of a supreme perfection while I am free to think of a horse with or without wings, of the earth as larger than the sun, even (under the conditions of metaphysical doubt) of two plus three not being equal to five? What is it that constrains me in the first instance, if constraint it is? And how, if at all, does such constraint fit with the doctrine of human autonomy?

Answers to these questions call for the consideration of liberty of indifference and liberty of spontaneity, and of the ways in which these two kinds of liberty are said or implied to pertain to man and to God (assuming for the moment that Descartes holds both of these to pertain to God). We have to tread with considerable care here because this part of the Cartesian doctrine is obscured by two factors. First, Descartes employs the phrase "liberty of indifference" in a way which deviates from its use in the medieval tradition. Second, he allows certain differences of context to lead him to use the term in two quite different senses.

Although Descartes uses the phrase "liberty of indifference," I am

---

1. The Latin is important: *neque enim mihi liberum est Deum asbque existentia cogitare, ut liberum est equum vel cum alis vel sine alis imaginare.* The bracketed words which I introduced in the text do greater justice to the original.

not aware of his using "liberty of spontaneity." But since the doctrine covered by this traditional label is very much present in his works, I have no qualms about using both these scholastic phrases in my discussion. In doing so I am following the practice of commentators such as Anthony Kenny. In his essay "Descartes on the Will" Kenny presents a helpful discussion. (In spite of my disagreement with some of its conclusions, I remain much indebted to it.) Kenny analyses a sentence like "we have liberty of indifference with regard to doing x" as meaning "we are free in doing x if and only if it is in our power not to do x." There is an alternative formulation which he gives elsewhere: "to act freely is to act in possession of the power to act otherwise."[2] And "we have liberty of spontaneity with regard to x" is analysed as "we are free in doing x if and only if we do x because we want to do x."[3] I shall use these phrases with this, their traditional meaning. As my discussion develops it will become clear that the strong difference between Kenny and myself does not call for a new account of "liberty of indifference." This difference only concerns the extent of what counts as the liberty of indifference in Descartes' works.

In an important paragraph of the fourth Meditation, Descartes gives two accounts of free will. One is in terms of liberty of indifference, the other in terms of liberty of spontaneity. When he presents these accounts he compares man's will with that of God.

It is free-will alone or liberty of choice which I find to be so great in me that I can conceive no other idea to be more great; it is indeed the case that it is for the most part this will that causes me to know that in some manner I bear the image and similitude of God. For . . . the faculty of will consists alone in our having the power of choosing to do a thing or choosing not to do it (that is, to affirm or deny, to pursue or to shun it), or rather it consists alone in the fact that in order to affirm or deny, pursue or shun those things placed before us by the understanding, we act so that we are unconscious that any outside force constrains us in doing so. For in order that I should be free it is not necessary that I should be indifferent as to the choice of one or the other of two contraries; but contrariwise the more I lean to the one—whether I recognize clearly that the reasons of the good and true are to be found in it, or whether God so disposes my inward thought—the more freely do I choose and embrace it. . . . Hence this indifference which I feel, when I am not swayed to one side rather than to the other by lack of reason, is the lowest grade of liberty, and rather evinces a lack or negation in knowledge than a

2. Kenny, *Will, Freedom and Power*, p. 122.
3. "Descartes on the Will," p. 17.

perfection of will: for if I always recognized clearly what was true and good, I should never have trouble in deliberating as to what judgment or choice I should make, and then I should be entirely free without ever being indifferent. (HR1, 175; AT7, 57–58)

The various parts of this definition, and the comments on it contained in this passage and in others related to it, will be part of the discussion through most of this chapter. To begin with I shall single out the implicit comparison between man's will and that of God.

Descartes makes explicit this comparison in his reply to objections to the passage. The authors of the sixth set of objections in the *Objections and Replies*, reading "indifference" with the meaning it traditionally possessed, find that a

difficulty arises from the indifference of the judgment or liberty which you refuse to allow to the perfection of choice, but ascribe to an imperfect will alone, thus removing the indifference as often as the mind clearly perceives what ought to be believed or performed or left undone. But do you not see that by positing this you destroy the liberty of God, from Whom you remove that indifference as to whether He will create this world rather than another or any world at all? Though yet it belongs to the faith to believe that God has from eternity been indifferent as to whether He would create one, or many, worlds, or no world. But who doubts that God has at all times had the clearest vision of all things that were to be done or left undone? Therefore the clearest vision and perception of things does not annul the indifference of choice; and if it cannot harmonize with human liberty, neither will it be compatible with the divine, since the essences of things are, like numbers, indivisible and unchanging. Wherefore indifference is included no less in the divine than in human freedom of choice. (HR2, 237; AT7, 416–17)

Descartes could reply that, indeed, "the essences of things are . . . indivisible and unchanging," and that he has given an incorrect account of man's free will to the extent that he spoke of it in terms of indifference where the use of "indifference" is meant to "evince a lack or negation in knowledge." Alternatively, he could deny his critics' premise, and point out that "indifference" is used multivocally and so refers to distinct essences when applied to God as compared to when it is applied to man. Descartes explicitly argues the latter, and he therefore responds as follows:

the indifference which attaches to human liberty is very different from that which belongs to the divine. Neither does it here matter that the essences of things are said to be indivisible: for firstly no essence can belong in a univocal sense both to God and his creatures; and finally indifference does not belong to the essence of human liberty, since we are free not only when our ignorance of the right renders us indifferent, but also, and chiefly, when a clear perception impels us to prosecute some definite course. (HR2, 248–9; AT7, 443)

Regarding indifference as ascribed to the will of God, Descartes is quite straightforward in his reply. The doctrine he presents he states without variation in several other places.[4] The doctrine is this:

it is self-contradictory that the will of God should not have been from eternity indifferent to all that has come to pass or that ever will occur, because we can form no conception of anything good or true, of anything to be believed or to be performed or to be omitted, the idea of which existed in the divine understanding before God's will determined Him so to act as to bring it to pass. Nor do I here speak of priority in time; I mean that it was not even prior in order. . . . Thus, to illustrate, God did not will to create the world in time because He saw that it would be better thus than if he created it from all eternity; nor did he will the three angles of a triangle to be equal to two right angles because he knew that they could not be otherwise. On the contrary, because he worked to create the world in time it is for that reason better than if he had created it from all eternity; and it is because he willed the three angles of a triangle to be necessarily equal to two right angles that this is true and cannot be otherwise; and so in other cases . . . Thus that supreme indifference in God is the supreme proof of his omnipotence. But as to man, since he finds the nature of all goodness and truth already determined by God, and his will cannot bear upon anything else, it is evident that he embraces the true and the good the more willingly and hence the more freely in proportion as he sees the true and the good the more clearly, and that he is never indifferent save when he does not know what is the more true or the better, or at least when he does not see clearly enough to prevent him from doubting about it. (HR2, 248; AT7, 431–2)

"We are free . . . chiefly, when a clear perception impels us . . ." Since God is never "impelled" by clear perceptions, that in which our freedom differs from God's seems to be precisely that in which the essence of our freedom is here said to consist. God's freedom is one of indifference, where "indifference" is to indicate that there is no

4. It is also expressed, for example, in the letter of 2 May 1644 to Mesland. This letter is printed in translation in Kenny's *Descartes, Philosophical Letters*, pp. 146-52. The relevant passage is on p. 151. (In the AT edition this letter is in vol. 4, pp. 110ff.)

determination whatsoever of the divine will. Man is also free when he is indifferent. But this human "indifference" is not that in which human freedom is here said to consist "chiefly." Rather it is an "indifference" which results from ignorance. If we would judge or act in spite of ignorance, this involves a precipitate use of the will and constitutes the kind of affirmation or denial which may result in error, the kind of pursuing or shunning which may lead into sin. In either case, for man to act when he is free because he is indifferent carries the risk of entrapment in bondage to prejudice or superstition.[5] It is clear that "chiefly" man's liberty is here said to be that of spontaneity, although it is also the case that man possesses liberty of indifference, namely, when he is ignorant.

It is not easy to see what remains of the force of the Fourth Meditation's statement that in my free will "I bear the image and similitude of God." If any similitude remains it is in terms of a shared "infinity" of will. That, however, seems not much of a likeness. For although, like God, I can will whatever I want, unlike God I lack the power to make such willing always efficacious, let alone necessarily efficacious. As Descartes himself puts it, God's will "does not seem to me greater" than man's only "if I consider it formally and precisely in itself" (HR1, 175; AT7, 57). If we compare the two wills in terms of the consequences of their exercise, almost all likeness seems to evaporate. In terms of an exercise of liberty of indifference, man's willing either is in vain because of his lack of power, or it is efficacious but tends to lead him into bondage because of lack of knowledge. In whatever way we consider it there seems no similitude at all. God never possesses liberty of spontaneity, for his nature precludes his wanting to do something because clear and distinct perception compels him. Neither does God ever possess liberty of indifference in the sense that man is here said to possess it, for God never acts out of ignorance or out of partial knowledge. On the other hand, the passages I introduced from the *Objections and Replies* were directly precipitated by the account of freedom in the fourth Meditation, an account presented in the very same paragraph where Descartes posited the "similitude" of the will of God

5. Because this kind of exercise of will is not essential to man, involves no compulsion of reason, and tends to lead into bondage and thus to inhibition of rational action, Descartes sometimes says of such an exercise that it is not a human activity at all and hence no real exercise of human willing. As he wrote to Regius, "no actions can be reckoned human unless they depend on reason" (Kenny, *Descartes, Philosophical Letters*, p. 102; AT3, 371).

and of man. It would therefore seem premature to jettison the idea of such a similitude. Instead, we should remember that Descartes' response is to a very specific objection, made against what he takes to be one very specific use (among other possible uses) of the phrase "liberty of indifference." The objection to which he responds is one which his critics couched in the words: "indifference . . . you . . . ascribe to an imperfect will alone."

The phrase "imperfect will" is that of Descartes' critics; it is not Descartes'. But the passage to which they object in the fourth Meditation makes use of this phrase appropriate. For Descartes speaks there of an exercise of will which (in the words from a subsequent paragraph of the same Meditation) consists in "the misuse of the free will," a misuse in which "the privation which constitutes the characteristic nature of error is met with" (HR1, 177; AT7, 60).[6] It makes sense to say that this misuse of the will as liberty of indifference does not belong to the will essentially. But it also makes sense to assume that just because a particular exercise of will which is a misuse of the liberty of indifference is said not to belong to free will essentially, this does not necessarily imply that other kinds of exercise of liberty of indifference are not essential to man's free will. Can Descartes provide some content for the notion of similitude through other acts that he would allow to come under the umbrella term "liberty of indifference"?

If some other expression of liberty of indifference were not essential to human free will, then the conclusion of my first two chapters would be that man liberates himself from bondage through an exercise of the kind of free will of which he could be deprived without detriment to his nature. Such a conclusion would conflict with that part of my earlier argument which led to the affirmation that the free will used in man's liberation is fundamental to human nature.

It is therefore likely that Descartes uses "indifference" equivocally even when he applies it only to man. When applied to God it is applied

---

6. The use of the word "privation" is important. It tells us that for Descartes ignorance and error are not "real," just as blindness is not "real." They indicate a lack of power as distinct from the actualisation of a human faculty. In error, therefore, a human being does not actualise any of his powers. This further explains why the use of will in asserting or denying in a context of ignorance should not really be counted as an instance of human willing (compare footnote 5 above). And it further weakens talk of similitude between the human and the divine will in terms of "infinity." Descartes also articulates this doctrine of privation in his reply to Hobbes. Cf. HR2, 74-75; AT7, 190-91.

to a Being whose will is neither imperfect not determined by prior considerations of truth or goodness. When applied to man it is applied to a being whose will may be determined by truth or goodness (and who then enjoys liberty of spontaneity) and whose will, when not determined by truth or goodness, may be called "indifferent." But in this latter case further distinctions must be drawn about Descartes' applications of "indifferent." One use is that which belongs to the subject of discussion at this point between Descartes and his critics. It concerns the misuse of liberty of indifference which occurs when a person fails to heed the maxim "that the knowledge of the understanding should always precede the determination of the will" (HR1, 176; AT7, 60). Such an exercise of will ought not to occur. Here Descartes intends to discuss the kind of act of liberty of indifference which is not essential to human freedom. There are, however, other kinds of acts which he would also call acts of liberty of indifference and which are essential to human freedom. There are other kinds of acts which are in man's power to perform. They are not determined by prior knowledge, but they are nevertheless not the expression of an "imperfect will." Among these are the acts I discussed in my first chapter. Descartes did not deal with these in his reply because his critics made no mention of them in their objection. These acts are crucially important for Descartes, because on their possibility rests man's presumed capacity for self-liberation, for achieving mastery, for progressing in freedom. As we shall see in the next chapter, their existence is required if Descartes is to be able to reach another goal. They are needed to give content to the notion of similitude between the divine and human will to the extent that such similitude goes beyond the vacuousness of a "formal" definition.

These are assertions which need support. A systematic statement of what for Descartes constitute the major types of human acts of volition should reveal whether these assertions are warranted.

II. INDIFFERENCE AND SPONTANEITY

Before I list the major types of acts of will, we should recall the account of free will which Descartes gives us in the fourth Meditation:

the faculty of will consists alone in our having the power of choosing to do a thing or choosing not to do it (that is, to affirm or deny, to pursue or to shun it), or rather it consists alone in the fact that in order to affirm or deny, pursue or shun those things placed before us by the understanding, we act so that we are unconscious that any outside force constrains us in doing so.

In the part which precedes the "or rather," Descartes presents an account of willing in terms of liberty of indifference; in that which follows it, he gives an account in terms of liberty of spontaneity. In both he says that the faculty of will "consists alone in." The presence of this phrase, coupled with the use of "or rather," gives this definition the initial appearance of very confused thinking on Descartes' part.

My main purpose in recalling these statements at the outset is to drive home the point that Descartes unmistakably speaks of willing in terms both of power, and of wanting; in other words, Descartes speaks of acts of will both in terms of indifference and of spontaneity. As I list the major types of acts of will I intend to characterize each of them in terms of indifference and spontaneity.

Through this enumeration I shall reach a number of objectives. I shall establish beyond doubt that, as he applies it to man, Descartes does not use the phrase "liberty of indifference" univocally. I shall begin to dispel the appearance of contradiction in the account of freedom. And I shall identify those crucially important acts of liberty of indifference which allow for self-liberation, for mastery, and for progress. This will provide the chief ingredients I need for the accounts of mastery and progress to be given in the next chapter.

(*a*) I am free to judge when I see things clearly and distinctly, that is, I am free to exercise my will in affirming the truth of that which I see clearly and distinctly to be true. Such judgment takes place when, for example, I affirm that two plus three equals five. Similarly, I am free to deny the truth of what I see clearly and distinctly to be false, as when I deny that it is true that two plus three does not equal five. It is the understanding which places before me whatever is clear and distinct. Of items like these Descartes says that the more I recognise such "reasons," "the more freely do I choose and embrace them." The liberty experienced in this context is that of spontaneity. Since the knowledge in question involves judgment, the object of knowledge is characterized by complexity. It is derived knowledge or knowledge *per aliud*, rather than self-evident knowledge or knowledge *per se*.

(*b*) With respect to items which Descartes takes to be self-evident and therefore known *per se*, or known without affirmation or denial (items such as the *cogito*), the situation is like that just described concerning what is clear and distinct but not self-evident. That is, if a self-evident item is before my mind and I am paying attention to it, then I experience liberty of spontaneity. (I separate *a* from *b* not because in the first case the object is known *per aliud* and in the second it is known *per se*. Instead, I separate them because, once I introduce the notion of metaphysical doubt, a difference will arise between these two cases with respect to the kind of liberty which is then said to be experienced.)

(*c*) I am free to suspend judgment, that is, free not to exercise my will through affirmation or denial, whenever that on which I might pronounce judgment, is not, or does not seem to be, clear and distinct. I might, for example, judge that apples are really red and lemons really sour. In such cases I judge that what I subjectively experience through sensation is "similar to" what exists objectively. Descartes holds that I have no grounds for such a judgment (*cf.* HR1, 192; AT7, 81). In situations like these I can, through suspension of judgment, save myself from ever erring. Since the understanding placed before me nothing that is, or is seen to be, clear and distinct, it did not determine my will through knowledge.[7] The liberty exercised is therefore not that of spontaneity but that of indifference. Moreover, since I am suspending judgment, that is, since I am *refusing* "to affirm or deny, to pursue or to shun," the liberty is not that to be described in *d*, which is that of indifference as balance.

(*d*) I am free to judge when that on which I might pronounce judgment is not, or is not seen to be, clear and distinct. I might, for example, affirm that lemons are really sour. But equally I might affirm that there is nothing "similar to" sourness in the lemon itself. According to Descartes, I have no clear and distinct ideas to serve as grounds for either judgment. Since I am nevertheless free to make either judgment, and since one of them must be false, I am free to err. Again, the understanding has placed before me nothing that is

---

7. But I do then act in accordance with the rule which says that I must not judge unless that on which I judge is clear and distinct. I may be acting on that rule because I recognize the truth of the statement that I ought not to judge precipitously if I want to stay free from error. However, that there is no inescapable compulsion to obey this rule is clear from the fact that it can be disregarded. Although the fact that it can be disregarded by persons who are cognizant of it may be explained by what I shall say under *g*, the considerations under *h* are of greater weight in this matter. (This note is equally relevant to *e*.)

seen to be clear and distinct. The relevant type of freedom is therefore that of indifference. And since I "affirm or deny," "pursue or shun" in spite of "a lack or negation in knowledge," the liberty of indifference must in this instance be qualified as that of "balance."

In his comment on the statements quoted at the beginning of this section, it is of this liberty of indifference that Descartes says "this indifference which I feel, when I am not swayed to one side rather than to the other by lack of reason, is the lowest grade of liberty." It is this indifference which is said to be "not necessary" to human freedom. The "or rather" in the statement is to this extent a retraction: freedom consists in indifference, but to the extent that indifference is that of balance, of acting while "not swayed to one side rather than to the other by lack of reason," indifference does not constitute the essence of free will. It is this sense of indifference which was the object of discussion in the sixth of the *Objections and Replies*.[8]

(*e*) The experience of liberty of indifference as balance involves my freedom to affirm as true or as false whatever I do not see clearly and distinctly, that is, whatever is doubtable. Anything which Descartes takes not to be self-evident (for example, that the square root of 13689 is 117, or that there exists a world of material things) is to some extent doubtable for him. It is doubtable because, at best, it is known *per aliud*; and one may wonder whether what one claims to know *per aliud* is in fact known. One may wonder whether it has in fact been derived ultimately from what is known *per se*. This wondering about that which is not self-evident constitutes placing it in some measure of doubt. And once in doubt I may exercise the liberty

---

8. The denigration of liberty of indifference as balance dovetails with the importance assigned to "balance" as an aspect of Descartes' methodic procedure (see chapter 3, part iii). The creation of balance as part of Cartesian methodic procedure aims at facilitating the act of liberty of indifference as suspension; it is meant to prevent judgment in ignorance, that is, it is intended to forestall the exercise of liberty of indifference as balance. Both suspension of judgment and judgment in spite of ignorance, are acts of liberty of indifference. The former extricates us from prejudice or prevents us from falling into it; the latter entraps us in prejudice, in irrational action. Since "no actions can be reckoned human unless they depend on reason" (see footnote 5), it is clear why Descartes would hold that liberty of indifference as balance—which is exercised when we judge in spite of ignorance—is a liberty not essential to human freedom. It is, for him, a liberty of which it must be said that we are better off without it.

of indifference as balance, covered in *d*, or the liberty of indifference in suspension, covered in *c*.

If I do the latter a new course of action becomes available to me. For I am free to take that which is not known *per se* and is now no longer taken as clear and distinct, and reduce it to its self-evident basis (if it has such a basis). In the performance of this action the understanding does not yet have the truth before it and therefore knowledge does not determine the will. Hence the liberty exercised is that of indifference (but not that of balance). As I exercise my will in the act of reduction, I shall find that what is not self-evident but nevertheless at least a candidate for knowledge either does or does not have a self-evident basis. In either case, what is before me at the end of this process of reduction is something clear and distinct, but complex. Either it is an item which I now recognize as not grounded on what is self-evident and therefore deserving to be rejected. Or it is an item which I now see to be grounded on what is self-evident and therefore meriting acceptance. Under normal circumstances, that is to say, under circumstances which exclude metaphysical doubt, this exercise of the liberty of indifference accordingly leads me into the following situation:

(*f*) I am not free, in the sense that I do not possess the liberty of indifference, to affirm the truth of what I see clearly and distinctly not to be grounded in what is self-evident. Neither am I free to deny the truth of what I see clearly and distinctly to be grounded on what is self-evident. I possess neither this liberty to affirm nor this liberty to deny, as long as I pay attention to these clear and distinct items. But under these circumstances I am free in the sense that I enjoy liberty of spontaneity. I am free in that sense because it is in the nature of the will to be guided by the understanding when an attentive understanding confronts what is to it clear and distinct.[9] Thus the liberty of indifference exercised in the process of reduction has led me into the enjoyment of liberty of spontaneity. This is only part of the picture. Another part is that which involves the act of paying attention.

---

9. That in cases like these it is the nature of the will to be guided by the understanding is, of course, a doctrine not confined to the fourth Meditation. For a statement at least as clear, see the seventh axiom of the *Arguments drawn up in geometrical fashion*: "The will of a thinking being is borne, willingly indeed and freely (for that is the essence of the will), but none the less infallibly, towards the good that it clearly knows" (HR2, 56; AT7, 166).

(*g*) I am free to pay attention or not to pay attention. Paying attention is an exercise of liberty of indifference, for that to which I am about to pay attention cannot determine the will through its truth before attention comes to be paid to it. The consequence of paying attention to what is clearly and distinctly before the mind is that I enjoy liberty of spontaneity.

It is vital to note and to remember that, for Descartes, a situation in which I enjoy liberty of spontaneity (and cannot enjoy liberty of indifference as balance) occurs only if I want it to occur. For it depends on two distinct acts of liberty of indifference, the performance of either of which is entirely in my power. Also, both of them are necessary conditions for this situation to occur. One of these is present in the process of reduction, the other in that of paying attention. The important conclusion is that, for Descartes, a person is free to have or not to have his will determined by his understanding.

Paragraphs *f* and *g* deal with situations which pertain under normal conditions. There is one situation pertaining only under an abnormal condition which is of great interest to Descartes. This situation arises when there is what Descartes calls "metaphysical doubt." The condition of metaphysical doubt demands that the trustworthiness of reason itself be questioned. But why is it a condition of such great importance for Descartes? It is because he believes that it allows him to establish that reason is absolutely trustworthy. It is nevertheless an abnormal condition because, as the opening sentence of the *Principles of Philosophy* has it, "in order to examine into the truth, it is necessary once in one's life to doubt of all things, so far as this is possible." If we have just once placed ourselves under metaphysical doubt, and if we have then come to see reason as absolutely trustworthy, then it becomes the norm to use and trust reason. It is crucial to note the context in which Descartes' statements about freedom occur in both the *Meditations* and the *Principles*. The context is that of the attempt at a validation of reason. It is important to deal with this abnormal case. It is essential to see how free will functions under the condition of metaphysical doubt, that is, at the time when the trustworthiness of reason itself is in question.

(*h*) Under metaphysical doubt I cannot experience liberty of spontaneity with respect to that which is complex and which is under normal circumstances taken to be true because of its clarity and distinctness. I cannot experience liberty of spontaneity even with respect to such relatively uncomplicated judgments as: two plus three makes five (cf. HR1, 159; AT7, 36). My will cannot then be determined by the understanding. This is the case even when I then pay full attention to that which is before the mind. In other words, it is the case even though I would enjoy liberty of spontaneity if these were normal circumstances, rather than those brought about by metaphysical doubt. Under the condition of metaphysical doubt, suspicion is directed to the supposed trustworthiness of all mental faculties, and even the criteria of clarity and distinctness are put in question as criteria of truth. Therefore what is compound and clear and distinct can no longer determine the will, and I cannot experience liberty of spontaneity.[10] In the context of such an unusual plight I do, however, possess liberty of indifference. In fact, this situation came about precisely because I exercised my liberty of indifference: I am capable of doubting to this extent only through bringing in the hypothesis about the evil genius. I myself introduced this hypothesis of my own free will and—since I was not determined by the understanding to do so[11]—the freedom exercised in this act is the liberty of indifference.

This employment of my liberty of indifference is then the very act which expels liberty of spontaneity from my experience. As the Synopsis of the *Meditations* states, "In the second Meditation, mind, which making use of the liberty which pertains to it, takes for granted that all those things of whose existence it has the least doubt are non-existent . . ." It is through acts of liberty of indifference that I free

10. In a sense the doubt is not internal to that which is before the mind; hence it appears just as clear and distinct as it did before metaphysical doubt was brought to bear on it. And so we read in the third Meditation that Descartes cannot see how it could be true "that two and three make more or less than five, or any such thing in which I see a manifest contradiction" (HR1, 159; AT7, 36).

11. I could not in this instance be determined by the understanding, for the understanding only determines the will through presentation of the truth. The hypothesis about the evil genius, being a self-contradictory hypothesis, is by definition devoid of truth. (For the self-contradictoriness of this hypothesis, see Cottingham, *Descartes' Conversation with Burman*, pp. 4, 9.) I should here add that whenever a hypothesis is introduced, liberty of indifference must be to some extent involved. For we then assert the provisional truth of a statement which may turn out to be false. Certainly we do not know whether it is true or false at the time when we make the assertion. I say "to some extent," since a hypothesis is not just any statement: disciplined action of the mind is involved in its advancement. But it is only once the hypothesis is seen clearly and distinctly to be the truth that liberty of spontaneity takes over with respect to it. For the discipline of the mind which is involved in the proposing of hypotheses, see my article "Peirce and Descartes: Doubt and the Logic of Discovery," pp. 88-104.

myself from bondage to my culture and tradition. Hence Descartes can say in the opening paragraph of the Synopsis that "the utility of a Doubt which is so general . . . is . . . very great, inasmuch as it delivers us from every kind of prejudice." We may wonder whether the exercise of liberty of indifference in the imposition of metaphysical doubt does not accomplish more than Descartes wants it to. The outcome of this exercise seems to leave nothing which might determine the will. Thus I appear to ban my liberty of spontaneity forever, and with it the possibility of science and hence of progress to greater mastery. But this is indeed only appearance. For this assertion of my liberty of indifference allows for the possibility of reinstatement of my liberty of spontaneity: "it delivers us from every kind of prejudice, and . . . makes it impossible for us ever to doubt those things which we have once discovered to be true" (HR1, 140; AT7, 12).

Liberty of spontaneity is reinstated because not all presumed knowledge is of a deductive or composite nature. That is, not all presumed knowledge is of the kind which I introduced in *a* above. There remains the class of non-deductive, non-compounded knowledge. This is the class of items known *per se*, the class I introduced in *b*. It is the class which includes the *cogito*. In contexts of metaphysical doubt, the situation is as follows with respect to this class:

(*i*) I enjoy liberty of spontaneity when an item knowable *per se* is before my mind and I pay attention to it. The understanding then fully determines the will. I have no liberty of indifference as balance which would allow me to deny the truth of that which is so before the understanding. But this situation pertains only when the mind is attentive. And it is in my power to be or not to be attentive. Once I decide to pay attention and succeed in doing so (acts and results of acts of liberty of indifference) the understanding fully determines the will and I enjoy liberty of spontaneity. This is so in spite of the fact that I here operate under the abnormal condition of metaphysical doubt, for no metaphysical doubt can enable me to reject as false that to which I am now paying attention. Thus it is an act of liberty of indifference which reinstates the enjoyment of liberty of spontaneity. It does so not only with respect to what is knowable *per se*, but also with respect to what is knowable *per aliud*. It is this act of paying attention which has as a result the cancellation of the consequences of an earlier act of liberty of indifference, namely, that which through the introduction of the hypothesis about the evil genius brought metaphysical doubt upon the scene. The cancellation of those consequences removes all questioning of the trustworthiness of reason.

There is one more type of act of will which I want to introduce. But first I wish to draw a major conclusion from the material now before us: that the liberty of indifference—but not as "balance"—plays a crucial role throughout the Cartesian system. In the account of free will which opened this section, Descartes begins by explicating freedom in terms of indifference, while in the sentences that follow he says that liberty of indifference is not essential to human freedom. The liberty thus declared non-essential is that of indifference as balance. In the cases I have listed, indifference as balance only makes its appearance in *d*. Forms of liberty of indifference which cannot be characterized as ones of balance appear in all the other cases. In some of them each appears by itself. In others the form appears in conjunction with the liberty of spontaneity. Thus it is clear that "indifference" is not used univocally as it applies to God and as it applies to man. This we saw in this chapter's first section. But also we encountered the much more important theme that "indifference" is not used univocally even when it applies to man only. There is far more to "indifference" than what may be subsumed under "balance." Descartes hardly hides the fact that it is liberty of indifference which is fundamental to his entire program—something which cannot of course be said of the indifference which consists in balance. The passages from the Synopsis which I quoted in *h* would by themselves go a long way to establish this point.

Works other than the *Meditations* support this interpretation. In the *Principles*, for example, it is the liberty of indifference (but not of indifference as balance) rather than that of spontaneity which is the first to be brought upon the scene (in I, 6) and which continues to play a dominant role in its later parts. (See, for example, I, 34 and 37.) What comes through clearly in the articulation of these principles is that I need not be bound by error and prejudice, and that I will not be bound by them only if I do not want to be. These principles make it very clear that I am indeed determined by the truth (and thus can enjoy liberty of spontaneity) but only if I want to be so determined (through acts of liberty of indifference).

Descartes also states explicitly in his correspondence that there is an important use of liberty of indifference which cannot be assimilated to the notion of balance. The letters of 2 May 1644 and of 9 February

1645 are particularly relevant.[12] As far as their importance for the present discussion is concerned, the upshot of the position stated in these letters is that one more item needs to be added to my enumeration of acts of will.

(j) When I pay attention to an item like the *cogito*, which is an item knowable *per se*, I then enjoy liberty of spontaneity but not liberty of indifference as balance. The will is then fully determined by the understanding. But this is the case only as long as I pay attention. A situation like this can, therefore, exist only through the co-presence of two distinct forms of liberty. The first of these is characterized by autonomy, the second by determination. The first is the liberty of indifference present in the act of paying attention, the second is the liberty of spontaneity which I experience when I pay attention to an item knowable *per se*. The co-presence of the autonomous action in this exercise of liberty of indifference, and of the reason-determined experience in the enjoyment of liberty of spontaneity made possible through this autonomous action, necessarily excludes the existence of liberty of indifference as balance.

In the second of the letters just mentioned, Descartes writes about two types of liberty of indifference. One of these, the indifference as balance, he again describes as "the state of the will when it is not impelled one way rather than another by any perception of truth or goodness." As in the *Meditations*, so also in this letter he calls it "the lowest degree of liberty."[13] This liberty of indifference as balance he explicitly contrasts with another type of liberty of indifference. The latter he describes as "a positive faculty of determining oneself to one or other of two contraries." It is a "positive faculty" which we can exercise "with respect to all other actions," that is, with respect to all actions other than those "to which it is not pushed by any evident reasons on one side than on the other."[14] That is, it is a "positive faculty" which is exercised in all free acts other than those in which

---

12. They are printed in translation in Kenny's *Descartes, Philosophical Letters*, pp. 146-54, 159-61. I accept the interpretation of these letters, especially of the controversial second letter, which Kenny advances in "Descartes on the Will." For the second of these letters Kenny provides an incorrect reference. Instead of AT4, 218, it should read AT4, 172).

13. Kenny, *Descartes, Philosophical Letters*, p. 159 (AT4, 173).

14. Ibid.

we exert our liberty of indifference as balance. Of this "positive faculty" he then writes that

when a very evident reason moves us in one direction, although, morally speaking, we can hardly move in the contrary direction, absolutely we can. For it is always open to us to hold back from pursuing a clearly known good or from admitting a clearly perceived truth, provided we consider it a good thing to demonstrate the freedom of our will by so doing.

What wins out in that case is not "truth" or "goodness." I thus override what would be of ultimate importance if I were "morally speaking." What wins out is my determination to show my independence, my ultimate autonomy. Since I can show my independence whenever I want to, I am, "absolutely speaking," never simply determined by the true or the good without my willing it. This is so even in the case of a "very evident reason," even in the case of a "self-evident truth." For I can always will not to pay attention. This takes me back to the final sentence of *h*. There I said that the exertion of my liberty of indifference leads to the reinstatement of my liberty of spontaneity. And I quoted from the Synopsis that this liberty of indifference "delivers us from every kind of prejudice, and . . . makes it possible for us ever to doubt those things which we have once discovered to be true." I have just argued that it is Descartes' position that unless I will to be, I need never be determined by the truth. In other words, it is always in my power "to doubt those things which we have once discovered to be true."

What may now appear to be a conflict in Descartes' position in fact is not a conflict at all. The *Meditations* are designed to show that there are no grounds whatsoever to doubt the trustworthiness of reason, that whatever reason discloses as true we can always absolutely trust to be true. No grounds adduced by the sceptics can ever shake this conviction. But that does not do away with the fact that each person is held to be thoroughly autonomous. Hence, indeed, it is "impossible" to doubt in terms of grounds not within my control. It is, for example, impossible for arguments adduced by the sceptics to shake my confidence. If, however, I "consider it a good thing to demonstrate the freedom of my will" then I can create the conditions which allow me to doubt whatever I wish to doubt.

I can therefore exercise my liberty of indifference at any time to bring home to me that, unless I will it, I need never nor ever can enjoy liberty of spontaneity. The truth can determine me only if I want it to do so. Only if I pay attention to what is clear and distinct, is it "impossible . . . ever to doubt those things" which I "have once discovered to be true." The decision whether to pay attention or not is mine, and mine alone. (Through emphasis on the power I possess of withdrawing attention from—rather than of paying attention to— that which I know clearly and distinctly and which thus determines my will, *j* is meant to be an amplification of what I said under *g*.)

Two final points remain to be made in this section. Both of them concern Kenny's work on Cartesian free will. First, although Kenny's "Descartes on the Will" is the best sustained examination of the nature and role of freedom in Descartes written in English during the past two or three decades, it suffers from a number of shortcomings. One of these is the "table" in which Kenny summarizes what he takes to be Descartes' position:

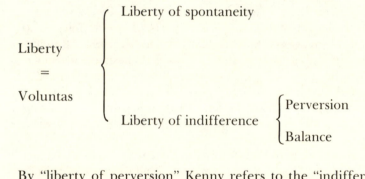

Liberty
=
Voluntas

Liberty of spontaneity

Liberty of indifference — Perversion / Balance

By "liberty of perversion" Kenny refers to the "indifference which consisted in the possibility of acting against the weight of reason," an indifference which Descartes "explicitly distinguishes from indifference in the sense of balance of reasons."[15] First, one could quarrel with the condemnative labelling of this activity as "perversion." I suspect Kenny so names it because of an evaluative clause that Descartes employs in the letter of 9 February 1645: "following the worse although we see the better." That is one way of speaking. Another way,

---

15. "Descartes on the Will," p. 28.

from the same letter, is: "it is always open to us to hold back from pursuing a clearly known good, or from admitting a clearly perceived truth, provided we consider it a good thing to demonstrate the freedom of our will by so doing." Descartes did consider it "a good thing" to "demonstrate the freedom of our will." If someone really wants to criticize Descartes on this point, though the context gives no indication that this was his intent, it is hardly proper for Kenny to label as "perverse" something that Descartes called "good"—and called "good" for reasons which Kenny would likely applaud as soon as he saw the point. That Descartes was in earnest about this application of that label may be said to be the theme of the first two of the *Meditations* as well as of the two first principles of the *Principles of Philosophy*. It was also the theme of my first two chapters.

Second, and more important, is the fact that in his article Kenny leaves the impression that his table is a complete summation of the basic elements of Descartes' view on free will. But it should be clear that in it Descartes' view is not adequately presented as far as "liberty of indifference" is concerned. For there is far more to "indifference" than can be placed under either "perversion" or "balance." "Balance," as I noted earlier, appears only in one item of my enumeration, in *d*. What Kenny calls "perversion" may be seen, for example, in *g*. But it does not appear in most of the other items. That is because it cannot account for the exercises of liberty of indifference as exemplified in the act of suspending judgment (as in *c*), or in the act of reducing what is complex to what is simple (as in *d*), or in that of paying attention (as in *g*), or that of introducing hypotheses (as in *h*). None of these are unimportant. In fact, all of these are crucial for Descartes. All of them present man with a challenge or an opportunity: not to err; to gain clarity and distinctness; to be determined by the truth; to show the trustworthiness of reason and to advance science. I therefore subdivide the liberty of indifference into that of balance and of what I named "opportunity." All the acts of will that ought to be subsumed neither under spontaneity nor under indifference of balance must be subsumed under indifference of opportunity. It will happily accommodate even the "indifference of perversion."

Before I proceed to use the data before us in a discussion of mastery and progress, let me give a summary outline of the various forms of liberty of spontaneity and of liberty of indifference which I have considered.

subspecies 1ₐ

This is the conformity of the will to reason, where the object of knowledge is knowable *per se* (as in *b*). This liberty one enjoys as long as one pays attention to underived, self-evident items like the *cogito*. No judgment is involved; one's understanding functions intuitively rather than deductively.

species 1
liberty
of
spontaneity

subspecies 1ᵦ

This is the conformity of the will to reason, where the object of knowledge can be known only *per aliud* (as in *a*). This liberty a person experiences in the cases of judgment, where that upon which he pronounces judgment is clear and distinct, and is perceived by him to be clear and distinct. This liberty one experiences in the development of the sciences.

genus
volition
or
liberty
or
freedom

subspecies 2ₐ

Here, there is no conformity of the will to reason. Judgments are made in spite of ignorance (as in *d*). It is the liberty of indifference which Descartes qualifies as 'balance'. Descartes calls it 'the lowest grade of liberty' and deems it 'not necessary' to human freedom.

species 2
liberty
of
indifference

subspecies 2ᵦ

Also here, there is no conformity of the will to reason. This is the freedom I call "liberty of opportunity," partly to allow for the will's demonstrating its autonomy (as in *j*, which is about acts of withdrawing attention, and thus includes Kenny's notion of "liberty of perversion"). The more important reason for this name is that this exercise of will is to free the mind from prejudice, and is to provide the condition for increasing mastery and freedom through the development of science. Its exercise in liberating the mind from prejudice is exemplified in *e*. Its employment in keeping the mind from renewed bondage to prejudice is exemplified in *c*. Its involvement in the development of science is exemplified primarily in *g*, in the act of paying attention (an act which is present also in *a*, *b*, and *i*). Its employment is necessary also in *h*. In fact, since the introduction of hypotheses always depends on acts of liberty of opportunity, this liberty is also in this respect crucially important for the development of science.

V

Freedom, Mastery, and Progress

IN THE FIRST PART of this chapter I shall discuss the transition from autonomous agency to action determined by reason. I shall show that, according to Descartes, the achievement of mastery is only possible if autonomous agency and action determined by reason are jointly present. There remains an unresolved tension in Descartes' position between, on the one hand, the doctrine of an autonomous will and, on the other hand, the dogma of an authoritative reason.

In the second part I shall deal with the concept of progress implicit in Descartes' writings. It should be said from the outset that if I were to speak of Descartes' *theory* of progress, this would be to exaggerate the care which he gives to the concept. It is true that Descartes regularly uses the word "progress." It occurs, for example, several times both in the *Discourse on Method* and in the Preface to the *Principles of Philosophy*. It is also true that an optimistic belief in progress permeates all of Descartes' works. Nevertheless, Descartes does not deal systematically with any of the various problems related to this concept. In fact, he does not even make his view on the nature of progress itself very explicit. There are, however, enough clear hints in his works to allow me to draw a coherent picture. The view of progress implicit in Descartes' works turns out to be the very one which was later on made most explicit by the *philosophes*. As we shall see in the next chapter, it is the view of progress which became commonplace in the second half of the eighteenth century.

My treatment of this implicit concept of progress is itself subdivided into three sections. In these I discuss: (i) the problem of the availability of a criterion which would allow for an objective or generally acceptable assessment of progress; (ii) the problem of the applicability of such a criterion when it is said both that progress is to be assessed in terms of advances made in science, and also that the object of the scientist's concern is an infinite universe; (iii) the framework within which Descartes can deal successfully with these two problems. The last of these three sections consists of a discussion of two issues. The first, (*a*), discusses whether, according to Descartes, the application of scientific knowledge is a sufficient condition for the achievement of mastery. The second, (*b*), asks whether the requirement implicit in Descartes' work, one which will supposedly enable us to detect whether mastery is being achieved, could form a criterion which might become generally acceptable.

I. FREEDOM AND MASTERY

As we saw at the end of the preceding chapter, Descartes takes it to be "a good thing to demonstrate the freedom of our will" by holding back "from a clearly perceived truth." This act of consciously averting one's attention from a truth is meant to bring home to his reader that he needs to be determined by that truth only if he wants so to be determined; such a truth will be his master only if he so desires.

But why should anyone ever want to submit to a truth? Why would it be a good thing to "pay attention"? Why should anyone deprive himself of any kind of exercise of liberty of indifference? In the words of the opening paragraph of the *Meditations*, why should I "seriously and freely address myself to the general upheaval of all my former opinions" in order "to establish" a "firm and permanent structure in the sciences"? That is to say, why should I place my liberty of indifference in the service of the liberty of spontaneity?

The answer to these questions derives from the human desire for mastery. The exercise of liberty of indifference frees a person from bondage to tradition. Freed from this bondage he is master of himself—except that he is still subject to the toil of providing for his daily bread, still in danger of bodily suffering, and still vulnerable to the quarrels of the passions (quarrels which tend to put a person at war with himself and with those around him).

It is Descartes' position that in each of these areas of subjection I can liberate myself if I want such liberty. He also holds that I would be foolish if I did not want such liberty. For since he takes me to be dominated in each of these areas by "nature," by something which in essence is non-human, I am other-dependent and hence deprived of autonomy to the extent that I lack this liberty. He holds that I can increase my autonomy if I gain mastery over "nature," if, on the foundation of metaphysics and physics, I develop mechanics, medicine, and morals and apply these sciences in my daily life. But the development of these sciences demands that I forgo all forms of liberty of indifference which do not lead to enjoyment of liberty of spontaneity.

What is there to be gained which Descartes now seems to consider as of far greater importance than what I can lose? This: as I obtain more knowledge and hence become capable of exercising greater mastery, I gain a greater measure of automony with respect to "nature." This process will not be gained at the expense of any measure of autonomy which I possessed in exercising liberty of indifference as opportunity. For it is precisely my persistent exercise of that liberty which allows me the enjoyment of liberty of spontaneity in the development of mechanics, medicine, and morals. All I lose is the exercise of liberty of indifference *as balance*. Descartes takes this to be a small loss. It is the loss of the liberty I exercise when I allow myself to be swayed one way rather than another by causes which are irrational (or at least by causes which, if they are rational, I do not recognise as rational). My loss is, therefore, taken to be the shedding of something which I, as a rational being, should not want to possess anyway.

It is through mechanics, medicine, and morals that I gain mastery over nature and so increase my autonomy. There are many passages in Descartes' works which make this point. Probably the best known of these is that of the *Discourse*, Part VI, in which we read that

so soon as I had acquired some general notions concerning Physics, and as, beginning to make use of them in various special difficulties, I observed to what point they might lead us . . . I believed that I could not keep them concealed without greatly sinning against the law which obliges us to procure, as much as in us lies, the general good of mankind. For they caused me to see that it is possible to attain knowledge which is very useful in life . . . a practical philosophy by means of which . . . we can . . . render ourselves the masters and possessors of nature. This is not merely to be desired with a view to the invention of an infinity of arts and crafts which enable us to enjoy without any trouble the fruits of the earth and all the good things which are to be found there, but also principally because it brings about the preservation of health, which is without doubt the chief blessing . . . in this life. . . . We could be free of an infinitude of maladies of both body and mind, and even also possibly of the infirmities of age, if we had sufficient knowledge of their causes, and of all the remedies with which nature has provided us.' (HR1, 119–20; AT6, 61–62)

The idea of mastery over the passions is not made explicit here but comes to the fore in the brief parallel passage at the beginning of the Preface to the *Principles of Philosophy*. In it, all three of the main branches of "physics" appear, in the order of morals, medicine, and mechanics: "philosophy signifies the study of wisdom, and . . . by wisdom we not only understand prudence in affairs, but also a perfect knowledge of all things that man can know, both for the conduct of his life and for the preservation of his health and the invention of all the arts" (HR1, 203-04; AT9-2, 2). And, of course, Descartes has much to say about the mastery over passions in *The Passions of the Soul*. (*The Passions* will be the focus of my seventh chapter.)

Knowledge, for Descartes, is not an end in itself. Knowledge serves the ends of acquiring facility in the "invention of all the arts," of obtaining the ability to conserve one's health, and of achieving control over one's own conduct. For knowledge to be able to "subsume these ends, it is essential that it should be derived from first causes," in other words, that it should be systematic or scientific knowledge. The end of science is to serve the cause of mastery. And the most basic desire or goal of man is to gain mastery. That desire is to rule all his other desires; it is to regulate all his actions. That is therefore the

---

1. Two statements here call for annotation. The first is: "the law which obliges us to procure, as much as in us lies, the general good of mankind." This statement may seem to imply that altruism overrules egocentricity, and that in this way bounds are set to individual autonomy. For Descartes, however, this law is to be acted out egocentrically. In his rational universe, procurement of the other's good is a necessary and automatic consequence of each individual's successful attempt to procure his own "supreme good." Hence Descartes can write to Queen Christina of Sweden that "the supreme good of all men together is the total or aggregate of all the goods, of soul, of body and of fortune, which can belong to any human being . . ." (Kenny, *Descartes, Philosophical Letters*, p. 226; AT5, 82). The second is the well-known statement: "we can . . . render ourselves the masters and possessors of nature." Through neglect of the word *comme* this well-known English sentence is possibly stronger than its French counterpart. Perhaps all the original warrants is: "we can . . . as it were render ourselves the masters and possessors of nature" (*nous rendre comme maistres et possesseurs de la Nature*). On the other hand, this stress on *comme* may well result in too literal a translation, one which shelters the reader from the force of the blow Descartes here aimed at the medieval tradition of "knowledge for the sake of contemplation." I shall therefore follow the majority of translators, and ignore this occurrence of *comme*.

desire which I identified as man's master passion.[2] It is for the ideal of mastery that man strives to leave behind all liberty of indifference which does not serve the liberty of spontaneity. Again, what Descartes leaves behind him he does not consider cause for lament. Suppose that I have freed myself from bondage to prejudice and have come to realize that it is up to me to decide whether or not truth shall be my master. Then I am free to use only such forms of my liberty of indifference as will serve to increase my experience of liberty of spontaneity. I am free to leave behind those forms of liberty of indifference which do not serve this cause. If I use only the former and always forgo the latter assertion of free will, then I am autonomously working at the realization of what Descartes takes to be my most basic desire: achieving mastery.

A necessary condition for the achievement of mastery is scientific knowledge. And no scientific knowledge is gained unless the understanding leads the will. This presupposes that the exercise of liberty of indifference will create the conditions for the experience of liberty of spontaneity. Because I desire mastery and see no other way of achieving it, I place my liberty of indifference in the service of liberty of spontaneity: I seek out and submit myself to the truth. Reason serves the passion for dominion; scientific knowledge is the instrument which is to make me master of my fate. It is my will, my profoundest desire, that I be truly a master. Hence, rather than doing violence to myself when I place my liberty of indifference in the service of liberty of spontaneity, this act is to be the way in which I am to realize my highest aspiration.

It is now possible to complete the discussion of two questions left over from the last chapter. One of these concerns the "incoherence" of the definition of freedom in the fourth Meditation. The other is the question of the content Descartes can give to the notion of "similitude" in his comparison of the divine and the human will. Because they share important elements, the answers to these two questions are interwoven.

The definition of freedom in the fourth Meditation may well give an initial impression of incoherence. The definition, it will be remembered, first states that free will "consists alone in" liberty of indifference, and then continues with the announcement that it "consists alone

2. See the closing paragraphs of my third chapter.

in" liberty of spontaneity. The two parts of the definition are connected with an "or rather," and so this definition seems altogether to remove liberty of indifference because it is said to be "not necessary" to human freedom. But we have already seen that the liberty thus withdrawn is not that of all indifference. It is only that of indifference *as balance*. More may now be said about the fact that this definiton does not deny that liberty of indifference in the sense of *opportunity* is necessary to human freedom. The role which Descartes assigns to this liberty of indifference as opportunity, a role which only such liberty of indifference can play, is essential to his system. It is the role of making possible the experience of liberty of spontaneity. Liberty of indifference is necessary for the development of science and hence for the achievement of mastery.

The goal of exercising such liberty of indifference is that of enjoying liberty of spontaneity. On Descartes' view, it is part of man's very essence to desire the enjoyment of liberty of spontaneity, for only through enjoyment of liberty of spontaneity can man begin to reach the fulfilment of his basic desire for mastery. Therefore, as well as telling us in this definition that liberty of indifference *in the sense of balance* is not essential to human freedom, the words "or rather" are meant to convey the ideal, indeed the essential, task placed before man. That task consists in constantly exercising the liberty of indifference in order to attain the state of liberty of spontaneity.

It is in terms of this task that it becomes meaningful to speak of the similitude of the divine and the human will. The aspect of similitude which Descartes stresses when he presents the definition of free will is the "formal" aspect that God's will is not greater than mine, that, in the words of *Principles* I, 35, both wills are "infinite," because "we perceive nothing which may be the object of some other will, even of the immensity of the will that is in God, to which our will cannot also extend." As I pointed out before, this is at once the least important and the most dangerous aspect of similitude. It is the least important because of its vacuity: like God, I can will whatever I desire, but unlike God, I often lack the power to make all or even most of such willing effective. And it is the most dangerous aspect of similitude for, like God, I can extend my will to any object of thought but since, unlike God, I lack clarity and distinctness with respect to most of these objects, this exercise of will tends to lead me into error or sin. In both these instances the liberty experienced is that of indifference. But this is not all that needs to be said. In terms of liberty of indifference there is a further aspect of likeness which is meant to be neither vacuous nor dangerous. This aspect is connected with the task of exercising liberty of indifference in order to secure liberty of spontaneity. Descartes believes it to be the case that in the execution of this task there are no restrictions placed upon man's liberty of indifference that would constrain or determine it externally. If there are any determinations, they are taken to be self-determinations. This is one way in which the similitude is realized.

Since man, a finite being with a finite understanding, lives in an infinitely large and complex universe, the pursuit of that full scientific knowledge which would give him complete mastery over nature involves an endless task.[3] Thus the exercise of liberty of indifference for the sake of winning liberty of spontaneity is a process that can last as long as man and the universe endure. For Descartes this entails man's mastery and autonomy growing indefinitely, moving forever along the way to a better life, a fuller humanity. But in whatever situation man may find himself, Descartes holds him always capable of self-determination, always able to set himself on or off the endless road to greater mastery and autonomy. He is able, so long as he is willing. And whether or not a person is willing, Descartes takes to depend on no one or nothing but that person himself. Like God, man has the power of self-determination even though, unlike God, man does not always make the best use of this power.

Man is a finite being, and his finitude shows in the very fact that he is "on the way." But man's finitude does not detract from this similitude between the human and the divine will. Man can exercise self-determination and enjoy autonomy, since he can determine himself to be on the way and can determine the way because he can determine its end. The origin of his action, says Descartes, lies in himself alone. Like God, in being self-determined, man is his own master. And as he experiences more and more liberty of spontaneity he becomes increasingly determined by reason and ever more human and autonomous because he is less and less determined by "nature."

3. Descartes is careful about the use of "infinite," for its use may imply comprehension of that which the finite human mind cannot comprehend, namely, an infinite universe. He therefore suggests the use of "indefinite" instead, where "indefinite" is meant to indicate that as far as man can comprehend, there is no end state to his knowledge of the universe. For my discussion at this point, it does not matter whether I use "indefinite" or infinite" and I shall therefore employ the latter term. About "comprehension" of the "infinite," cf. HR1, 166; AT7, 46.

"No master but his reason." Like his followers, such as Condorcet, Descartes holds that man will freely decide to place himself under the compulsion of reason for the sake of achieving greater mastery, greater self-realization. For man, whose nature it is to be rational, to allow himself to be compelled by reason can carry no threat of foreign imposition. And this leads me back for one last time to the "contradictory" definition of free will.

"For in order that I should be free it is not necessary that I should be indifferent"—"be impelled both ways"—"as to the choice of one or the other of two contraries." Freedom of indifference in terms of a balance of reasons is not to be preferred above the freedom of spontaneity which results from the freedom of indifference as opportunity. Not only is it not to be preferred, it should be categorically rejected. As man goes about exercising his liberty of indifference, for the sake of experiencing liberty of spontaneity in his development of scientific knowledge, he must use the method, for without method no science can be developed at all. And the very first methodological principle of the *Discourse* forbids the precipitous use of judgment. It forbids all exercise of liberty of indifference which does not lead to liberty of spontaneity. This principle enjoins me "to accept nothing as true which I did not clearly recognize to be so: that is to say, carefully to avoid precipitation and prejudice in judgments, and to accept in them nothing more than what was presented to my mind so clearly and distinctly that I could have no occasion to doubt it." Avoiding improper haste calls for suspension of judgment. That with respect to which judgment has been suspended then needs to be "divided up . . . into as many parts as possible." This is decreed by Descartes' second methodological precept. Both the suspension of judgment and the reduction to simplicity are acts which involve liberty of indifference as opportunity. Both acts presuppose the rejection of indifference as balance. By suspending judgment we are to stay free from prejudice; by achieving the reduction we are to gain clarity and distinctness. Ending up with mere freedom of indifference in terms of a balance of reasons would amount to a negation of the promise implied in the liberty of opportunity. For such indifference only evinces "lack . . . in knowledge" rather than "perfection of will," prejudice instead of clarity and distinctness, doubt of irresolution rather that the doubt which signifies firmess of purpose, impotence rather than self-realization. Fulfilment of the promise, or true realization of the potentiality, occurs only through the enjoyment of liberty of spontaneity. For "as to the choice of one of the other of two contraries . . . the more I lean to the one" because "I recognize clearly that the reasons of the good and the true are to be found in it . . . the more freely do I choose and embrace it. And undoubtedly . . . natural knowledge, far from diminishing my liberty, rather increase[s] it and strengthen[s] it" (HR1, 175; AT7, 157-58).

Descartes was convinced that each human being (and therefore all of mankind[4]) can progress indefinitely, that he can attain the ever greater autonomy which results from an expanding mastery over nature. He firmly believed in the possibility of man's indefinite progress because he was convinced that in making public his method he had made available to mankind both the instrument to bring about the revolution prerequisite for science's development, and the tool to develop science. The method articulated he took to be human reason's self-portrait. Reason, therefore, commands revolution and promises mastery. Descartes believed that because man is a rational being, he is born to be a revolutionary and a master.

Reason commands revolution and, if its command is obeyed, reason promises mastery. There is no clue in Descartes' writings to suggest that he was aware of the unresolved tension between his doctrine of a fully autonomous will and his equally firmly held doctrine of an authoritative reason. Nevertheless, the tension does exist and I shall conclude this part by bringing it into the open.

It is Descartes' position that, if I will it, I can achieve mastery through applying the sciences of mechanics, medicine, and morals. He holds that I would be foolish if I did not work to realize this mastery, for to the extent that I achieve such mastery, I free myself from domination by "nature." Through becoming a master I give concrete expression to my autonomy. Not to express my autonomy in this way would be foolish because it would be acting against my nature. This is one important dimension of Descartes' doctrine. But there is also another dimension which we have seen clearly stated as Cartesian doctrine, namely, that if I want to be, I can be foolish. It is, after all, part of my essence that I can demonstrate my independence over against goodness and truth whenever I want to do so. But it now appears that to do so would be foolish. I can express my nature by demonstrating my independence, but I ought not to do so, for doing

4. That progress made by each individual constitutes progress for mankind is a doctrine implicit, for example, in the letter to Queen Christina of Sweden, footnote 1.

so goes against the realization of my desire for mastery. My desire for mastery, in turn, expresses my very essence. So I can express one feature of my essence (that of a completely autonomous being) by thwarting the expression of another such feature (that of a being whose deepest desire is for mastery over nature).

Descartes believes that it is "a good thing to demonstrate the freedom of our will" by holding back "from a clearly perceived truth." He also holds that it is meritorious to work at achieving mastery. Both of these activities he pronounces to be good, because he believes that both are activities which express my essence. The problem is that the absolute freedom of the first act is incompatible with what is required in the second, that the pursuit of mastery is possible only if absolute freedom is sacrificed. An explicit choice is demanded: a choice for absolute freedom or for true mastery. Whichever choice is made, it will affect what is taken to be man's essence. Descartes never explicitly makes this choice. As a consequence, he never faces the fact that he has ascribed features to man's essence which cannot co-exist in it.

This problem is not peculiar to Descartes' position. It is the problem of "ultimacy," the question of "Who conforms to whom or to what?" Is it the will, the willing subject, which is ultimate? Or does ultimacy belong to nature, to reason, to God? When he faces this question, a moderate rationalist may become an extreme rationalist. He will then tend to safeguard the notions of universality, objectivity, law. And he will feel inclined to sacrifice the idea of autonomy, the notion of a totally free will. Alternatively, he may become an extreme voluntarist and, while safeguarding the subject's autonomy, tend to sacrifice the ultimacy of reason, or of a rational universe, of law, or of God. Descartes never squarely faces this problem of ultimacy. In the end, he never explicitly raises and never clearly answers the question of who conforms to whom or to what. My preceding chapters showed Descartes asserting the ultimacy of autonomy. It is now apparent that he asserts with equal force the necessity of submission to scientific truth. Because he never faces the question of who conforms to whom or to what, the unresolved problem of ultimacy continues to haunt his position. He never allows it to surface into clear view. But it nearly breaks through the surface more than once.

In this section, for example, it nearly surfaced in the passage from the *Discourse* which I quoted earlier. There, for the sake of mastery over physical nature, I am said to relinquish absolute personal autonomy—I am said to relinquish my freedom to do absolutely whatever I can efficaciously will to do. The "whatever" comes to be restricted through excluding from it the freedom to divert attention from what I clearly know to be true or good. I must relinquish this freedom if I want—as I should want—to be a master. I cannot both exercise this freedom and achieve mastery over nature. The point here is not that I cannot eat my cake and have it too. It is, instead, that I am forced to eat my cake rather than to have it. This point may be clearer when we focus on another place in which this tension nearly surfaces.

This happens when it becomes clear that, in the composite definition of freedom presented in the fourth Meditation, the "or rather" is meant to convey the essential task placed before man. Man is faced with the task of constantly exercising his liberty of indifference in order to attain for himself the state of liberty of spontaneity. He will only be able to become what he is meant to be, if he wholeheartedly accepts this task. How can one escape the implication that the very presence of this required task places a heteronomous limit on the human will, and that therefore the will cannot be autonomous? It may be true to say that in the execution of this task there are no restrictions placed on man's liberty of indifference that would constrain or determine it. But that does not touch the point that, unless man does choose to execute this task, he is foolish. In other words, it does not touch the point that, if he acts as a human being ought to act, he has no choice about whether or not to accept the task.

This submerged tension between autonomy and reason seems to reveal its outlines also in the conclusion that freedom of indifference as a balance of reasons is to be categorically rejected. It is to be rejected because the first methodological precept of the *Discourse* forbids it to play a role. The method is reason's self-portrait. Reason therefore forbids that there be room for liberty of indifference as balance. When Descartes holds that, in the banishment of this liberty of indifference, all I lose is something which as a rational being I should not want to possess in any case, he inclines towards extreme rationalism rather than to extreme voluntarism.

More often, however, he tends the other way. He usually stresses the primacy of human freedom, the ultimacy of autonomy. The tension which exists at a deep level between the autonomy of the will and the authority of reason remains submerged. The fact that it remains submerged gives the Cartesian position a semblance of coherence greater than that which it in fact possesses.[5]

5. In an underdeveloped passage, James Miller points at a similar tension in Rousseau's position. See his *Rousseau, Dreamer of Democracy*, p. 170.

II. MASTERY AND PROGRESS

Descartes is convinced that through science man can attain mastery. Such mastery will increase man's happiness because, as it progressively frees him from determination by "nature," it increases his autonomy and brings his human nature to greater perfection. This conviction is reflected in the lengthy title which he originally had in mind for the *Discourse on Method*: "The Plan of a Universal Science to raise our Nature to its Highest Degree of Perfection . . ."[6] It is reflected as well in the final paragraph of the Preface to the *Principles of Philosophy*. There he says that "the difference which is observable between these principles and those of all other men and the great array of truths which may be deduced from them" should lead people "to observe to what a degree of wisdom, to what perfection of life, to what happiness they may lead us" (HR1, 215; AT9–2, 20).

Happiness, for Descartes, is not to have to toil for daily bread, not to suffer from disease, not to be ruled by unregulated passions. That is putting it negatively. Positively, the words "freedom," "autonomy," "mastery," and "self-realization" each sum up equally well Descartes' idea of "happiness," of "perfection of life." None of this can be attained except through science. The growth of scientific knowledge is to allow for decrease in toil, for conquering of disease, for regulation of the passions. Only the growth of science allows for increase in mastery.

So far I have used the word "mastery" and I have avoided the word "power" (in spite of the fact that Bacon's dictum "knowledge is power" would naturally seem to sanction the use of that word). Through the juxtaposition of "mastery" and "power" I now want to draw an important distinction. Although Descartes does not explicitly address himself to it, his position allows this distinction to be drawn and invites its application.

There are many varieties of power. Brute force is power, but it need not be a manifestation of progress. For Descartes, only power which is an application of scientific knowledge can be an instance of progress. Even where scientific knowledge is applied, it need not be such an instance. I reserve the term "mastery" for the kind of power which is an instance of progress. A necessary condition for the correct

6. See Descartes' letter to Mersenne, March 1636. The translation is from Kenny, *Descartes, Philosophical Letters*, p. 28.

employment of "progress" is that it be used to stand for the application of scientific knowledge. Whether that is a sufficient condition depends on how we define "scientific." For the distinction between power and mastery parallels the distinction between "science" used in the narrow sense of that word (for example, when it refers to mechanics or medicine) and "science" used in the broader and also common seventeenth-century sense (when it refers to the systematic knowledge which, in the first of the *Rules for the Direction of the Mind*, Descartes calls "universal Wisdom"). We shall see that for Descartes the application of science in the narrow sense is not necessarily an instance of progress, as it may well constitute an exertion of power which is quite different from an achievement of mastery. By contrast, when "science" refers to an application of science in the broad sense, then what Descartes considers wisdom is itself built into this application. As we shall see, an application of this latter kind would, for him, always result in progress; it would always be an instance of mastery.

Let us consider the notion that for Descartes the basically trustworthy assessment of progress is to be found in science. That notion allows him to deal successfully with certain issues which often prove an embarrassment to some non-Cartesian views on progress. I shall focus on two of these issues: (i) the existence of a criterion which would allow for an objective or generally acceptable assessment of progress, and (ii) the applicability of such a criterion in spite of the fact that the object of the scientist's concern is an infinite universe. After that I shall discuss some aspects of (iii) the framework within which Descartes can deal successfully with these two issues. It is in this third part that the distinction between power and mastery, as well as that between science in the narrow and the broad sense, will play their important role particularly when I deal with the question whether the application of scientific knowledge is really a sufficient condition for the exercise of mastery. This third part also includes consideration of the question whether Descartes' criterion is in fact generally acceptable in judging whether a particular application of scientific knowledge is necessarily laudable.

(i) *The general applicability of the criterion.* If power were to be taken as the criterion of progress, it could not be an objective criterion. Take the increase in power of the dictator who, through his knowledge of human nature, strengthens his position by craftily playing on the frustrations and ambitions of the people. Depending on one's point of view, this could be seen as either an instance of progress or of retrogression. Descartes rejects the validity of the notion of "points of view." Here his absolutism (which I discussed in the second part of the first chapter) again presents itself. It is an absolutism which does not conflict with the belief introduced in the previous section, belief in man's potential for unlimited progress. Man is (or at least can be) forever on the way in his development of science and in gaining mastery through the application of science. Man is (or can be) forever engaged in raising his "Nature to its Highest Degree of Perfection" so that, in a sense, it may even be said that man himself is in the making. Nevertheless, this state of being does not involve for Descartes a creation but a liberation of man's rational nature. This nature, as we saw, he takes neither to differ from place to place nor to change over time. Moreover, as we read in the *Discourse*, "Reason is by nature equal in all men" and so "the diversity of our opinions does not proceed from some men being more rational than others, but solely from the fact that our thoughts pass through diverse channels and the same objects are not considered by all" (HR1, 81-82; AT6, 2). For a being to be human it must possess reason, and the essence of reason is eternally fixed. For human beings to progress they must use reason, and they must use it well. As the *Discourse* continues, "to be possessed of good mental powers is not sufficient; the principal matter is to apply them well" (ibid.). It is only through the proper application of his mental powers that man can develop scientific knowledge. And the only way to apply them well is that dictated by Descartes' method. For, as we have also seen, the method is taken to be simply a statement of how reason goes about its business in its successful pursuit of truth.

The method precludes the legitimacy of "points of view"; it necessarily leads whoever employs it to the same result. With respect to any problem which the human mind is capable of solving, its solution ultimately demands its decomposition into elements of utter simplicity and to first principles. This is then to be followed by careful composition into intelligible complexity. When a problem has been resolved into its simplest parts, these parts are clear and distinct (cf. *Rules*, Rule 12; also *Principles* I, 45). The clarity and distinctness attained at this level of utter simplicity can be reached because of two factors. The first is the nature of the human mind. Its universal nature is taken to be expressed as a functional definition in the articulation of the method, the method whose application leads to the recognition of items characterized by clarity and distinctness. The second is the nature of any complex object of knowledge, which is taken to be such that it is compounded out of and therefore reducible to epistemic atoms and to first principles, to unrelated bits of knowledge which are characterized by clarity and distinctness and knowable *per se*.[7] What is thus clear and distinct is indubitable.

It is therefore to this clarity and distinctness that Descartes relates the general acceptability of his criterion for progress, the possibility of public[8] verification and hence universal acceptability. And that not just at the level of foundations. For clarity and distinctness will continue to function as a criterion of truth in the process of increasingly complex deduction or composition. The application of this criterion determines what is and what is not science. And so all of science is clear and distinct. But it is only that for any being "in the least degree rational," for any being proceeding methodically.

Descartes rejects the notion of "points of view" because methodic procedure necessarily leads its practitioners to the same results. He holds that with respect to each matter there is only one truth; and reason used methodically[9] is adequate to lead to that truth if in principle it is a truth which man can come to know. His absolutism rules out the notion of "points of view" and takes lack of unanimity as a *prima facie* criterion for lack of truth and by implication for absence of progress. (cf. HR1, 3; AT10, 363). This does not necessarily imply the converse, that unanimity is a trustworthy indicator of truth and hence of progress. In speaking of Herbert of Cherbury's *De Veritate*, Descartes complains that "The author takes universal consent as the criterion of his truths; whereas I have no criterion for mine except the light of nature." What follows shows Descartes' absolutism nicely. He writes that "the two criteria agree in part": "for since all men have the same natural light, it seems that they should have the same notions; but there is also a great difference between them, because hardly anyone makes good use of that light of nature, so that many people— perhaps all those we know—may consent to the same error."[10]

For the relativist, especially the relativist for whom man is "in the making," it may be more difficult if not impossible to provide any criteria which would be of use to tell whether a present stage of

7. Additional aspects of these two factors come to the fore on p. 115f.

8. I use "public" here only in the sense of "anyone can do it for himself," and not in the sense of "it can be done in public so that all can see it, like an experiment in physics or chemistry."

9. Of course, for Descartes this phrase "reason used methodically" is a pleonasm.

10. Kenny, Descartes, *Philosophical Letters*, p. 66 (AT2, 597–98).

development is "better" than a previous stage. One criterion might be offered in terms of whether or not certain subjective likes can be satisfied, or certain subjective dislikes can be stilled more easily in the present than in a previous situation. Even if agreement on the degree of realization of these preferences were possible, that would still leave the question of whether these are the right preferences to be realized. Preferences whose realization would be an instance of progress for some might constitute retrogression for others. Moving from "unanimity" to "light of reason" and from there to "clarity and distinctness" allows Descartes to escape this type of problem.

Precisely how Descartes' absolutism and the use of the criterion of clarity and distinctness is to allow for a generally acceptable assessment that progress has been achieved, I will leave for a moment.

(ii) *The applicability of the criterion.* That question is related to the idea of infinity. It can be articulated as follows. If the infinite universe presents the scientist with an infinite number of problems, how can there be meaningful talk of progress in the first place?

One view of progress, a view which arose during the late Renaissance, remained current long after and is not infrequently met even in contemporary discussions, is that which sees progress in science as analogous to progress in the exploration of the earth's surface. Given the finitude of the earth, all its places could be "discovered" within a finite time span, so that eventually the work of the explorer would be complete. The analogue in science is that although man may be faced with a large number of problems, it is a finite number; and in view of the fact that science provides answers which are certain, the cumulation of these certain answers will eventually be complete and the scientists' work will be done.[11]

Descartes cannot accept this view of science and of progress. Given that man is a finite being in an infinite universe, his scientific task will never be complete. The "chains of reasoning" which constitute science will go on forever. As we read in the fourth Meditation, "although my knowledge grows more and more, nevertheless I do not for that reason believe that it can ever be actually infinite, since it can never reach a point so high that it will be unable to attain to any greater

---

11. See, for example, Radnitzky's "Justifying a Theory," an article in which he discusses this "finalization theory" of progress. He writes that "even today this conception has its advocates, and is popular among prominent scientists." See Radnitzky and Andersson, eds., *The Structure and Development of Science*, p. 217.

increase" (HR1, 167; AT7, 47). Hence progress can continue indefinitely. Man is perfectible but he will never become perfect. Can man
be said to be moving well along on the way of progress if he treads
an endless road? If he will never be able to say that he "has arrived."?[12]
Can there be legitimate talk of "progress" at all?

"Progress" may seem a legitimate concept if the balance between
the known and the unknown shifts continually in favour of the former.
But with the infinite set of problems posed by the infinite universe
there can never be a shift in balance in favour of the known; no matter
how much is known, the "problems solved" will always remain a finite
class and the class of "problems unsolved" will always remain infinite.
There can be no talk of progress where the ratio between what is
known and what remains unknown can never shift in favour of the
former.

Descartes does not have to worry about this problem because of,
first, his absolutism and, second, his concept of order in scientific
investigation. His absolutism allows him to say that once solved a
problem is solved forever. And his concept of order of investigation
allows for simultaneous solving of problems in the various sciences.

First, then, more about Descartes' absolutism. There may be an
infinite number of problems to be overcome, in mechanics, in medicine, and in morals. But each time a problem or part of a problem
is solved, it is solved once and for all. In the *Discourse* he writes that
"a child . . . who . . . has made an addition according to the rule prescribed . . . may be sure of having found as regards the sum of figures
given to him all that the human mind can know" (HR1, 94; AT6, 21).
That is because of the nature of the problem and because of the
nature of reason. As to the first, if the mind is trained in the use of
method (if it works "according to the rule prescribed") then it can

12. I am dealing with the general thrust of the Cartesian position. Not all of Descartes'
statements contribute to this thrust. Some perhaps oppose it. On the grounds of Descartes' belief—a belief which he articulated in various contexts—that man is a finite
being in an infinitely (or at least indefinitely) large universe, I concluded that, for the
Cartesian, man's scientific task will never be complete, that man is perfectible but will
never reach perfection. The concluding paragraph of the Introduction to the *Principles*
contains the words: "many centuries may pass until all the truths which may be deduced
from these principles are so deduced . . ." If "many" is to be taken as a finite number,
then Descartes here inconsistently seems to subscribe to a "finalization theory" of progress and perhaps, by implication, to the possibility of human perfection rather than
perfectibility.

deal with (though not always solve) whatever problems come before it. For the nature of these problems themselves is determined by the nature of the universe. But Descartes holds that the nature of the universe is such that when, in the various problems with which it confronts man, the universe becomes an object of knowledge, this object of knowledge is almost always susceptible to the use of resolution and compositon. He holds this belief because of his underlying position that the order which pertains in the universe is itself a rational order: both as to its elementary principles and its complex order, the universe's principles are reason's principles and its order is reason's order. Only problems which are not susceptible to reduction and composition are problems which the human mind cannot solve. But of such problems it can discern that they are either pseudo-problems, or that they are genuine but of the kind on which human progress does not depend. (Among the latter are those of the sixth Meditation, whether, for example, there actually exists heat in fire.) A genuine problem which is also important for human progress, can be solved once and for all because of the nature of the object: as to its principles and order, the rational universe remains eternally the same. But, in addition, the problem is solved once and for all because of the nature of reason.

For reason is complete in each human adult (even though it is often, or usually, obscured by prejudice). Each act or set of acts by which a problem is solved is a complete solving of that problem because it is a complete actualization of the potentiality of reason in that context. No subsequent developments in science will throw further light on that problem: having worked "according to the rule prescribed," "he may be sure of having found as regards" that problem "all that the human mind can know." Even the child's reason in the example is an instance of the fully actualized human reason. If, once an adult, the child has become a master-mathematician, he still will know no more about the problem he once solved. For the problem was solved completely; and his reason, being completely adequate to the task of solving it then, was then fully actualized.

Second, the other aspect of Descartes' position which allows him to speak of progress in spite of a never-ending task is his concept of order in scientific investigation. The mind is potentially capable of solving the problems that come before it as long as it deals with them in the "right order of philosophizing." That order is from "metaphysics" through "physics" to "all the other sciences," from the "simplest" or "most general" to the "most complex." But not all problems in metaphysics or physics need be dealt with before work in mechanics, medicine, and morals can be started. The "order of philosophizing" dictates only that the relevant foundations for that part of physics in which work is about to be done be established in metaphysics, and that the relevant foundations for such parts of mechanics, medicine and morals be established in physics. Establishing such foundations in, say, physics does not demand accomplishment of the impossible task that all problems of that science be settled. Cartesian methodology does not, therefore, dictate that there be a finite number of problems in any of the sciences. In spite of his acknowledgement of an infinite number of problems, Descartes can meaningfully speak of progress. He can do so in terms of the following considerations (and here I return to the first issue, that of a criterion which allows for the generally acceptable measurement of progress).

Some people never use their reason and remain forever ignorant of the method. Some people, through use of the method, come to shake off prejudice and succeed in gaining knowledge. All prejudice is characterized by obscurity, all knowledge by clarity and distinctness. To some minds nothing is clear and distinct, to some minds much. In the realm of science, progress can be measured quantitatively, in terms of the number of clear and distinct items. Even if the number of clear and distinct items potentially available is infinite, it is still the case for Descartes that someone who has even one clear and distinct idea is better off than he was before he had that one idea, or better off than someone who has none. For Descartes to be able to believe this he need not also believe that there is an end state for knowledge. All he needs is (i) knowledge characterized as absolutely certain or unchangeable, and (ii) a criterion which allows him to detect the presence of knowledge and to measure its extent. The first becomes possible because he adopts a non-relativistic position about the nature of both reason and the universe. The second he finds in the criterion of clarity and distinctness, a criterion which functions concomitantly with a reductionistic methodology and an atomistic epistemology. In the realm of knowledge, progress consists in moving from obscurity to clarity and distinctness. The nature of that move Descartes spells out for us in the argument which leads to the *cogito*. Subsequent to that move, the presence of continued progress can be discerned and measured because it consists in adding more certainties to those we already have, more clear and distinct items to those already systematized.

Descartes measures progress anthropocentrically. Thus the balance between knowledge and lack of knowledge can be known, because it is not the balance between what man already knows and what he does not yet know (between a finite and an infinite number of truths), but the balance between man's original state of ignorance and man's state of overcoming this ignorance. In the latter state the number of known truths may be any finite number, but as long as it is greater than zero, progress has been made.

(iii) *The framework.* These two problems, that concerning the existence of a criterion which allows for measurement of progress with a claim to objectivity and that concerning the meaningfulness of talk about progress to begin with, are problems Descartes would be capable of handling. The Cartesian solutions to these problems present important points of contact with many contemporary dogmas.[13] Nevertheless, many contemporary thinkers reject crucial details of the view of progress implicit in this position. They do so, first, because of apprehension about applied science: they do not accept that the application of scientific knowledge and the achievement of mastery necessarily go hand in hand. They deny that the application of science always leads to greater freedom and happiness for a person or mankind, and hence that it is necessarily good. Second, they do so because of misgivings about basic elements of the framework within which Descartes' view of progress is possible, a framework which to a large extent dictated how the questions concerning the criterion for and the possibility of measurement of progress were to be answered. Let us consider these two doubts.

(a) *Science and mastery.* Is Descartes committed to the view that any application of scientific knowledge is necessarily good? And if so, does that in turn commit him to say that the application of scientific knowledge is a necessary and sufficient condition for the achievement of mastery? When I raised that question near the beginning of this section, I said that the answer depends on how we take "scientific" in the phrase "the application of scientific knowledge." The answer calls

---

13. Of course, Descartes' absolutism makes his position on progress quite different from that of a number of recent thinkers. For Descartes, truth, method, reason, and nature are all essentially fixed. Truth itself does not develop. Neither does method itself ever change. Both pragmatists and existentialists would reject a position like Descartes'. Neither Dewey nor Sartre would hold that, once solved, a problem is solved forever. In this study I shall not deal with positions so far removed from Descartes'.

for implementation of the two different uses of "science." In a moment we shall be able to see why this is so.

Some contemporary thinkers believe that the application of scientific knowledge is evil; they often reach this belief through their fear of the potentiality for disaster which may attend this application. As we shall see, that is a belief which Descartes would have to reject. Others deem the application to be neither good nor evil but neutral, or value-free. They relate a person's talk of good or evil only to particular subjective values pertaining to particular uses he makes of science—to the decisions and the intentions of the user. That too is a position which Descartes would have to reject. This leaves the view that the application of science is objectively good. If we allow for one important qualification, we find here the view implicit in Descartes' position. This, however, would not commit him to the position that science cannot be misused.

For Descartes, science is of instrumental value; its end lies in its application. Hence the value of progress in science comes to the fore in the application of science. It is crucial to be clear on the qualification which allows Descartes to move from the goodness of science to the goodness of its application.

The goodness of science derives from its two roots. These are: the instrument through which knowledge is gained, and the object of knowledge. The instrument of knowledge is reason, and since for Descartes "methodic reasoning" is a pleonasm, I may also say that the instrument of knowledge is the method. From his earliest work Descartes considered reason or method to be good because it can only lead to truth and goodness and never to error or evil. Its utility derives from its necessary goodness. And so we read in the *Rules* that "the human mind has in it something that we may call divine, wherein are scattered the first germs of useful modes of thought" (HR1, 10; AT10, 373). In the *Rules* the human mind is said to "have in it" understanding or reason, imagination, memory, and sense. The latter three can lead man astray; they are never called "divine." The first, by its very nature, cannot lead astray; it, therefore, "we may call divine." That is the first root of science.

The second root, the object of knowledge, is man's total context, the universe. Because it is structured on rational principles also, the universe is good. Although evil may take place in it, it is itself neither evil nor can it lead to evil. Unlike man, the universe cannot behave in a way which violates its essential principles.

These roots together account for the goodness of science. Scientific activity results in reason's cognition of the rational principles which structure (parts of) the universe; and science as a body of knowledge is the articulate expression of that cognition. Neither scientific activity nor scientific knowledge can be anything but good.

Since the end of science lies in its application, it now becomes tempting to say without qualification that the application of science cannot fail to be good. However, all we can say so far is that this application is a necessary condition for the achievement of mastery. In the rational universe rational man has the opportunity to work at bringing himself to greater perfection. Through knowledge of the workings of his own reason—a knowledge he possesses once he is clear about the method— he can come to know the way in which the world around him works and, through this knowledge, he can come to control his world. The Cartesian ideal of mastery can find no realization apart from science.

But none of these points can settle the issue of whether scientific knowledge can be misapplied or used for wrong ends. Only when we introduce the crucial qualification does Descartes' position imply that the goodness of applied science cannot be called into question; that any development in the application of science is an instance of progress; that therefore whatever can be done through the application of science ought to be done. This qualification is that "scientific" in the phrase "applied scientific knowledge" be an instance of "universal Wisdom" rather than of isolated knowledge in, say, mechanics. Differently put, the qualification is that science be developed and implemented by the Cartesian wise person.

We can begin to get a picture of this wise person from what Descartes says in the first of the *Rules*. There we read that the sciences ought not "to be studied separately, each in isolation from the rest" for "the sciences taken all together are identical with human wisdom." This Rule's penultimate statement is:

If, therefore, anyone wishes to search out the truth of things in serious earnest, he ought not to select one special science; for all the sciences are conjoined with each other and interdependent: he ought rather to think how to increase the natural light of reason . . . in order that his understanding may light his will to its proper choice in all the contingencies of life.

These are words about both the unity and the utility of the sciences, as well as about the nature of human wisdom. They state that the wise person is the one who keeps the unity of the sciences firmly in mind and has a clear insight into all of them. When such a person applies the sciences, he harvests nothing but happiness.

This picture of the wise person fits the well known tree-simile from the Preface to the *Principles*: "just as it is not from the roots or the trunk of the trees that one culls the fruit, but only from the extremities of their branches, so the main use (*utilité*) of philosophy is dependent on those of its parts that we cannot learn till the end" (HR1, 211; AT9-2, 14-15). If we cannot learn something "till the end" that presupposes other things to be learned before it. The utility of philosophy (that is, of "science" in its broad sense) is therefore again taken to lie in the hands of the wise person, of the one who really knows mechanics, medicine, and morals because he also knows physics and metaphysics. Such a person knows when and how to apply mechanics, medicine, and morals and, when he does so, mastery is increased. Science cannot be misapplied by the wise man. For him, whatever can be done through the application of science, ought to be done. For him, power achieved through the application of science really is mastery; the results then achieved are all genuine instances of progress. The criterion for progress now becomes objective in the sense of "publicly verifiable": progress exists in the successes reached through this wise person's application of science.

When "science" in the phrase "the application of science" is science known and applied by the person who also knows the other sciences, then the application of science is not only a necessary but also a sufficient condition for the achievement of mastery. Regarding the contemporary situation, a situation in which the polymath is extinct, mastery can be achieved only by a community of competent scientists who, among them, adequately represent the various relevant disciplines, with much overlapping knowledge.

The application of science by the wise person, but only by the wise person, necessarily constitutes an instance of mastery. Scientific knowledge in the hands of the less-than-wise threatens mankind with its misuse; it may result in retrogression rather than in progress. Just as a person cannot start solving problems at random but, submitting to the discipline of the method, must move from the most simple and general to the most complex, from metaphysics through physics to mechanics or medicine or morals, so the sciences ought not to be applied "at random" either. Here I say "ought not" rather than "cannot," for clearly there are instances where someone partially ignorant possesses enough expertise in a delimited area to exert power. The intention behind that exercise of power may be praiseworthy or blameworthy. But, whichever it is, no power should have been exerted in that instance, just as no exercise of will in judgment should be permitted while that on which one is about to pronounce judgment is not clear and distinct.

The last part of the statement "the necessary and sufficient condition for the achievement of mastery is the application of science by the person who also knows the other sciences" requires explication. We still need to see more clearly what Descartes' text suggests about the extent of the phrase "the other sciences." The tree-simile from the Preface to the *Principles* is helpful on this point. It contains both "vertical" and "horizontal" imagery. I have made use of the vertical imagery so far, as for example in the preceding paragraph when I wrote that one must proceed from the roots by means of the trunk to the branches, "from metaphysics through physics to mechanics or medicine or morals." Only if we conjoin the vertical and horizontal imagery can we do justice to the text and at the same time give a full explication of the condition for achieving mastery.

It may well be Descartes' position that for the *development* of science only the implementation of the vertical imagery is required. But this awareness of the unity among only *some* of the sciences seems not to be what Descartes considers sufficient for *wisdom*. It is certainly a necessary and perhaps a sufficient condition that for the development of, say, medicine, one knows metaphysics and physics. But wisdom is the "universal Wisdom" which makes one the kind of person capable of *applying* the sciences in a way which equips one to deal rationally, effectively, with all of life's exigencies. To return once more to the penultimate sentence of Rule I: "If . . . anyone wishes to search out the truth of things in serious earnest . . . he ought . . . to think how to increase the natural light of reason . . . in order that his understanding may light his will to its proper choice in all the contingencies of life." For efficacious action *all* the sciences are to be involved, "for all the sciences are conjoined with each other and interdependent" (ibid.). The "good understanding, or universal Wisdom" of the first of the Rules is a wisdom which is universal in two respects: it allows for the "proper choice in *all* the contingencies of life," and it does so because it is rooted in knowledge of "*all* the sciences." For "utility," for wise practical action, the vertical needs to be complemented by the horizontal imagery. What is suggested by Rule I is confirmed by Descartes' formulation of the tree-simile:

Thus philosophy as a whole is like a tree whose roots are metaphysics, whose trunk is physics, and whose branches, which issue from this trunk, are all the other sciences. These reduce themselves to three principal ones, viz. medicine, mechanics and morals—I mean the highest and most perfect moral science which, presupposing a complete knowledge of all the other sciences, is the last degree of wisdom. (HR, 211; AT9–12, 14)

It seems to me that, to avoid ambiguities and to make explicit what is intended, the second of these two sentences should be rewritten. Earlier we saw that for Descartes "complete knowledge" of any *part* of a science is quite possible. On the other hand, given the belief that we live in an infinite universe which poses an infinite number of problems, no science will ever be "complete" and in that sense we can have no "complete knowledge of the sciences." Thus if "the highest and most perfect moral science" is to be a human possibility, the phrase "complete knowledge of" must be qualified by a phrase like "the relevant part of." When the vertical and horizontal imagery are conjoined, it is not just "morals" which "is the last degree of wisdom." Let me re-write the sentence so that it brings out clearly what I take to be Descartes' full meaning: "These reduce themselves to three principal ones, viz. medicine, mechanics and morals—I mean the highest and most perfect [medical, mechanical and] moral sciences[s] which, presupposing a complete knowledge of [the relevant parts] of the other sciences, [are] the last degree of wisdom."

On this reading we go from metaphysics through the relevant parts of physics, mechanics, and morals to medicine; from metaphysics through the relevant parts of physics, morals, and medicine to mechanics; and from metaphysics through the relevant parts of physics, medicine, and mechanics to morals. This reading has much to commend it when we focus on the *application* of the sciences. For the simile then allows the implication that, just as one would expect fruit on the same tree to ripen at about the same time, so that it would be unwise to pluck and dangerous to eat some of it before the rest, so it would be unwise, say, to implement certain types of medical knowledge before the requisite clarity has been reached in mechanics and morals. The wise man would then be the one who knows medicine because he knows physics and metaphysics, and who knows when to implement certain medical knowledge because he also knows the relevant mechanics and morals; he can bring "universal Wisdom" to bear on the particular situation because he possesses the requisite knowledge not just in the immediately relevant science but also in the "support" sciences. Because, for Descartes, science must order life if happiness is to be attained or increased, and because the wise person is the one who really knows when and how to apply what scientific knowledge to what specific area of life, therefore the wise person is the one who knows how to order life scientifically, how to attain or increase happiness.

For Descartes the necessary and sufficient condition of mastery is, then, the application of scientific knowledge by the wise person. This condition raises all sorts of questions with respect to the possibility of progress. Most people are not (or not yet) wise. What would prevent them for acquiring some applicable scientific expertise, say limited to medicine, exert the power which is then in their hands, and as a result at best halt progress? Or if they do not take this power in their own hands, what would persuade them to leave it in the hands of the wise scientists?

Even in the hands of the wise, progress is not absolutely guaranteed. For as we saw in the preceding chapter, no one needs to be compelled by reason, and that holds as much for those who have achieved a degree of wisdom as for those who have not. So even if all those who are now prejudiced and superstitious were to become enlightened and wise, progress is not guaranteed. For the sake of showing one's independence, even one's independence with respect to what one knows reason dictates and science promises, one could will to use reason for anti-rational and science for self-destructive purposes. If only because of the primacy it assigns to freedom, the Cartesian position cannot consistently present an argument for the inevitability of progress. Nevertheless, Descartes' writings exude confidence in the belief that progress will be achieved and that its advance will continue. This confidence is therefore based on faith rather than on reason. It is a faith in man to the effect that, although he need not, he will submit himself to the compulsion of reason. Descartes assumes that the wise man will steadfastly abide by his wisdom.

Many contemporary thinkers reject Descartes' faith in man's willingness to submit himself to reason's compulsion. With that faith removed, and with the assumption that science will continue to develop firmly established on empirical grounds, they fear the application of science. They see it as power in the hands of the less-than-wise. Thinkers like these may well be rationalists, even Cartesians—disillusioned Cartesians. All they deny is the inevitability that the wise will always rise above the unwise and will continue to act wisely, that power will never take the place of mastery. For the appearance of such thinkers we did not have to wait until the twentieth century; the eighteenth century already had its share of them.[14]

There are others who reject the view of progress implicit in the Cartesian position because of different kinds of misgivings: they have doubts about basic elements of the framework within which Descartes' view of progress is possible. This is the second point I wanted to discuss.

(b) *Is Descartes' criterion generally acceptable?* In Cartesian thought, the criterion used properly to judge an application of science to be an instance of mastery is a criterion intrinsic to science itself. If science is applied by the wise person then we have mastery. But the wise person is the well-rounded scientist. And therefore all criteria that determine mastery are strictly from the realm of science. Terms like compassion, need, love, respect, can play no role unless they do so through their incorporation in science. Suppose that today brings some development in mechanics or medicine. Is it good for man or all persons that it has occurred? Should it be applied in the lives of human beings? Such questions may have to be determined by further questions about a person's needs or by considerations of the respect due to people in general or to a particular person. But such questions and considerations can be brought to bear, if Descartes is right, only once concepts like these are incorporated in the science of morals. That science, as well as any other science, is one which Descartes has left highly coloured methodologically by reductionism, and epistemologically by atomism. Since the Cartesian wise man is the man of science, his wisdom is impossible apart from reductionism and atomism, and his mastery is as coloured by these factors as is any science or as are all of them taken together. The application of Cartesian science may therefore seem to be necessarily good only for the person

14. Some eighteenth-century thinkers who adhered to the doctrine of the primacy of free will were consistent and denied the inevitability of progress; if they also believed in human degeneracy, they would tend to deny the very possibility of progress. Rousseau's writings attest to the fact that not all were consistent. To quote Christopher Hill, "It is logically difficult to believe simultaneously in degeneration and progress, though Rousseau did his best." (*Puritanism and Revolution*, p. 115).

to whom fundamental tenets of this rationalist outlook, of its methodology and epistemology, are unobjectionable. For the non-Cartesian there need be nothing that is acceptable about a science founded on a rationalist epistemology and developed through a rationalist methodology; and the Cartesian person of wisdom need not be universally acknowledged as wise. For the non-rationalist there are solid grounds for witholding the epithet "good" from the application of rationalist science and I think this implies that also the label "neutral" should be withheld. To what is coloured by a particular epistemology and is developed through a particular methodology—where both the epistemology and methodology are directly linked to a particular set of metaphysical beliefs—the label of "neutral" or "value free" seems inappropriate.

Of course, if we were able to confront Descartes directly, he would reject any attempt to force him to answer the question "Are there any criteria in terms of which this claim about the goodness of an application of science by the wise person can be tested?" He would reject this attempt for the simple reason that allowing it would have been tantamount to questioning the autonomy of reason. Descartes holds that reason presents man with what is good and true, and that the significance of these products lies in their application. Behind the application of science there stands, for Descartes, the full authority of autonomous reason. Hence to question what he considers the laudable application of science by a wise person is tantamount to submitting reason to a norm. But for Descartes reason is itself the norm; reason is autonomous.

Such reflections push the problem back a few steps, to the question "How do you know that reason is autonomous?" The answer to that question Descartes had well prepared. He published it under the title *Meditations on the First Philosophy* . . .

Part of the basis of Descartes' position is the autonomy of reason. In the *Meditations* this autonomy becomes explicit in the attempt to show the absolute trustworthiness of reason through the use of reason. Many see this attempt as viciously circular. I disagree with this view. But for those who hold it, the position that the application of scientific knowledge by the Cartesian wise man is necessarily good will have to be rejected, unless a justification other than that provided by Descartes can be found for it.

I disagree with the view that there is circularity in Descartes' attempt to show the trustworthiness of reason by means of reason, because of the distinction which Descartes draws in knowledge between items known *per se* and items known *per aliud*. There is a corresponding distinction in the basic functions of reason: that between intuition (which is the ability to grasp items knowable *per se*) and deduction (the ability to develop knowledge in terms of such items). Under the attack during metaphysical doubt, intuition shows itself absolutely trustworthy. It is thanks to deliveries of this indubitably trustworthy intuition that the reliability of deduction is held by Descartes to be established. And so the autonomy of reason is maintained: reason validates itself.[15]

The doctrine of the possibility of knowledge *per se* crops up time and again at crucial points in Descartes' system. We have seen it function in his methodology and in his epistemology, in his metaphysics, in his very practice as a revolutionary, in science. And we now see it behind the view implicit in the Cartesian position, the view that the goodness of the application of science by the Cartesian wise person cannot be meaningfully questioned. Like those who impute circularity to the *Meditations*, so those who (like myself) find the doctrine of contextless knowledge untenable will have to look beyond rationalism for a justification of the view that the application of scientific knowledge (in whatever sense of 'scientific') is necessarily good. Of course, they will have to look elsewhere only if they want an argument to justify that view in the first place.[16]

15. For a detailed discussion of this facet of Descartes' position, see my *Imposition of Method*, chapters 2 through 5.

16. This discussion points us in a certain direction. When the question is asked whether the application of scientific knowledge is a good thing, or neutral, or evil, this should evoke another question, namely, the application of which sort of scientific knowledge? For it is clear that there can be various kinds, with those qualified as "reductionistic" and "holistic" as perhaps the major species. Which of these a person believes ought to be developed will depend on his view of man and of nature. This implies, I think, that no application of scientific knowledge can be "necessarily" good. Neither can there be an application which is neutral; since it incorporates a view of man and of nature, it is embedded in "metaphysical belief." Even the consequences of the application of science do not give us instances which can be generally accepted as either progressive or retrogressive. Neither an application of scientific knowledge, nor the criteria to evaluate the consequences of such an application, are free from "metaphysical belief."

VI

Progress and Enlightenment

WHEN, IN THE THIRD CHAPTER, I began to make explicit the relationship between Descartes and the *philosophes*, I emphasized some primary forms of resemblance. Although I shall continue to focus mainly on points of likeness in this sixth chapter, some points of difference will arise over the issue of the inevitability of progress. These, however, are differences not between Descartes and the *philosophes*, but between Descartes and some of the *philosophes*; others, in fact most of them, do not differ from him on this matter. In the third chapter, I limited myself primarily to issues in which the concept of freedom loomed large: for the issues in this chapter the notion of freedom is again important, but they also allow me to pay greater attention to the concept of progress.

The present treatment of Descartes' relationship to the Enlightenment now needs to cover the following topics. First, I shall make clear that for Descartes the connection between progress in science and the achievement of human happiness was as close a tie as it became for the *philosophes*. Second, I shall argue that the eighteenth-century debate about the inevitability of progress really creates no distance between the position implicit in Descartes' works and the position of many eighteenth-century thinkers. Third, I shall draw attention to the fact that the doctrine implicit in Descartes' position about the criterion to be met so that science can be shown to serve man's happiness is almost entirely ignored by the *philosophes*; in this respect Descartes' position is more advanced than that of these eighteenth-century thinkers. And, fourth, I shall point out that, as far as Descartes' stress on the utility of science and on the instrumentality of reason is concerned, he is at one with most eighteenth-century thinkers. For them these notions of utility and instrumentality had become commonplace.

(i) *Progress, science and happiness.* It is hardly controversial to say that for the *philosophes* happiness depends on progress in science. It is equally beyond debate that the modern idea of progress (modern because it directly links progress and science) occupies a major place in Descartes' thought. A thesis which may need further support is that for Descartes, too, progress in science is closely linked with human happiness. That is a tenet whose truth is still denied by some influential authors, often in a sweeping statement. It was John Plamenatz, for example, who wrote: "In the seventeenth century nobody was much concerned with . . . the belief . . . that progress in the arts and science makes for happiness" for the belief "was as yet seldom asserted."[1] It was, of course, something upon which Descartes did insist. It is not farfetched to say that Descartes is a major source of this modern belief too. There is clear evidence that he held the tenet and that it was no minor element in his thought. The *Principles of Philosophy* are his "principles" of all the sciences. And, as we saw in the preceding chapter, Descartes explicitly connects progress in science with happiness when he affirms of these principles: "the great array of truths which may be deduced from them" should lead people "to observe to what a degree of wisdom, to what perfection of life, to what happiness they may lead us."

Descartes held progress in science to be a necessary condition for increase in happiness. The happiness which attends freedom from toil in the gaining of one's daily bread depends on mechanics; that which comes from alleviating or ending of bodily suffering altogether derives from medicine. Of these I shall say little more beyond calling attention once again to Descartes' statement that we ought to "render ourselves the masters and possessors of nature," if only "because it brings about the preservation of health, which is without doubt the chief blessing in this life. For . . . we could be free of an infinitude of maladies . . . and even also of the infirmities of age, if we had sufficient knowledge of their causes . . ." (HR1, 119–20; AT6, 62). I call attention

---

1. Plamenatz, *Man and Society*, vol. 2, pp. 216–17. Earlier in the same chapter Plamenatz writes: "That knowledge is a means to the good was an opinion which nearly all moralists had shared since the time of Socrates: that the accumulation of knowledge increases the good was an opinion hardly worth denying before the eighteenth century, for almost no one held it." (p. 212)

to it because of the persistent echo of these words in eighteenth-century literature, either as an exact and acknowledged quotation as in the *Encyclopedia* entry "Cartesianism,"[2] or as in this passage from Condorcet:

The improvement of medical practice, which will become more efficacious with the progress of reason and of the social order, will mean the end of infectious and hereditary diseases and illnesses brought on by climate, food, or working conditions. It is reasonable to hope that all other diseases may likewise disappear as their distant causes are discovered. Would it be absurd then to suppose that this perfection of the human species might be capable of indefinite progress; that the day will come when death will be due only to extraordinary accidents or to the decay of the vital forces, and that ultimately the average span between birth and decay will have no assignable value?[3]

It would be wrong to think that in its last sentence Condorcet goes far beyond anything Descartes envisaged. In the year after publication of the *Discourse*, Descartes wrote to Huygens that through the results of medicine he expected man to live "much longer and happier"and that for himself he had "hopes" of living "more than a century" (25 January 1638; AT1, 507). A few years later these hopes had certainly not dwindled. Kenelm Digby requested that, in view of the brevity of life, Descartes should study the body in order to find the means to prolong life; Descartes replied that he was already engaged on this task and that although "he could not promise to make man immortal" he was "quite certain to be able to render one's life equal to that of the Patriarchs" (AT11, 670–71). For Descartes, the "average span between birth and decay" still had an "assignable value." But in less than 10 years his expectations had grown from the vague "more than a century" to a firm 175 years (if we take Abraham, the first of the Patriarchs, as the relevant example). Throughout the age, this sense of optimistic anticipation continued to spread and grow. Despite Descartes' death at the age of 54, and despite an average life span still well below that, it led Condorcet to "suppose" it not "absurd" to expect the duration of human life to become indefinite (though, modestly, still not infinite).

2. *Encyclopédia* 2 (1752), p. 719.
3. *Sketch*, pp. 199–200. In view of passages like these the *Sketch* has been aptly characterized as Condorcet's "dream of life unlimited in a world of peace." Cf. McManners, *Death and the Englightenment*, p. 118.

I will say no more about either mechanics or medicine and their promise of happiness. Instead, I shall offer some comments on what Descartes says about "morals" in *The Passions of the Soul*. That work—known better to the *philosophes* than to many a twentieth-century reader of Descartes—has a tone which is today usually associated with the eighteenth rather than the seventeenth century. In it, Descartes' optimism about human nature reveals itself again and again. It is an optimism both about man's capacities and about man's inclination to make good use of these capacities. It proclaims that if science is applied by the Cartesian wise person, happiness will increase also in the realm of morals. In this section I shall focus on just one set of statements, in which Descartes writes about the results achieved when scientific knowledge is applied to morals. In the following chapter (a chapter devoted entirely to a discussion of *The Passions*), I shall treat in detail the relationship which Descartes believes to pertain in the realm of morals between knowledge on the one hand and freedom on the other.

Eighteenth-century thinkers as diverse as, say, Voltaire and Condorcet, share with Descartes the view that scientific knowledge is the way to increase happiness in the realm of morals. They agree that it is science alone which dissipates ignorance and error and it is these, as the roots of vice, which ultimately make for unhappiness. Condorcet goes beyond Descartes, for he holds that science will necessarily weaken the passions and that, because science will progress indefinitely, it will lead ever closer to total eradication of vice. Because Condorcet holds that to know the good necessarily leads to doing the good, he is also convinced that the possession of a scientific psychology (the discipline which Descartes began to develop in *The Passions*) automatically brings with it the end of subjection to vicious passions. That position, as we have seen, is one which Descartes does not hold without qualification. Indeed, Descartes would agree that to know the good is to do the good. But we can decide not to have our will determined by the good, we can opt for vice rather than for virtue. Knowledge can be a means to virtue; in fact there is no path to virtue except that of knowledge. But for Descartes man possesses the freedom to turn his back on that path by distracting his attention from the good he knows. In this respect, Descartes' stress on freedom through his doctrine of the role of liberty of indifference seems to lead him to an accentuation of human autonomy beyond what we find in Condorcet. For Descartes, man is beyond Paradise but before the Fall. He is beyond Paradise because he is already in the position of "knowing good and evil"; and his situation is pre-Lapserian because, with respect to good and evil, the choice of which to take is still his own. In this respect, Descartes seems closer to Rousseau than to Condorcet. For all three of them it is knowledge alone which can lead to greater happiness. But neither for Rousseau nor for Descartes is it credible that increase in knowledge must necessarily be followed by greater human happiness. Rousseau's emphasis on this point has made some commentators wonder whether he should be counted as a member of the Enlightenment's prime movers at all. Rousseau's stress on the real possibility of retrogression, his so-called "pessimism," seems to some to preclude such membership.

Descartes allows no room for a "pessimism" like Rousseau's. As we have seen in the preceding chapter, at this point there is considerable tension in Descartes' position. On the one hand there is his insistence that man need not be compelled by reason unless he wants to be so compelled. On the other there is Descartes' strong belief in continuing progress, a belief which rests on the undefended assumption that man will always freely want to be compelled by reason. As I have shown, he cannot argue for that assumption without being trapped by overt contradiction. Descartes' optimistic belief in progress, and particularly the belief that progress in science and increase in happiness must go together, are subjects to which I should address just a few more words.

In *The Passions*, the notion of happiness comes to the fore stronger than in any of his other works; the degree of happiness attainable is linked directly with progress in science. The amplification of this theme, which we saw in both the *Discourse on Method* and the Preface to the *Principles of Philosophy*, unequivocally exhibits Descartes' optimistic Enlightenment spirit.

In article 154 of *The Passions*, he presents an optimistic picture of mankind in terms of "good-will." A person of "good-will" is one who possesses "a firm and constant resolution . . . never to fail of his own will to undertake and execute all the things which he judges to be best" (art.153). Article 154 states that human beings are creatures of "good-will." It is this optimism about "good-will" which helps to provide the foundation for his doctrine of progress in the realm of morals. Since we are all taken to possess "good-will," the only thing needed to end strife and create "generosity" among men and so augment the happiness of all, is an increase in knowledge. Again, man is seen as beyond Paradise and before the Fall, and doctrines about original sin are circumvented. For doing wrong does not come from an innate perverseness: in his ascription of "good-will" to man Descartes rules that no innate perverseness exists. Neither does it come from an inability to grasp the truth due to irreparable dimness of the understanding: Descartes holds that there is no dimness of the understanding which we ourselves cannot remove. Use of the method will overcome dullness of mind. And man can draw upon the innate quality of "good-will" to check the perversion embodied in the misuse of free will, which consists in the constant deliberate turning of one's back on the path of knowledge and virtue. Doing wrong comes from lack of knowledge, from making mistakes in judgment. To adopt a phrase from the next article: given "good-will" and increasing knowledge, we will no longer be entrapped by "the faults which we may formerly have committed." Article 155 begins to bring home the conclusion. It is that we have a remedy for the unregulated passions, a remedy which allows us freedom from vice and all unhappiness which attends it. This remedy consists in using our freewill to act only on the basis of that which we understand. If we apply this remedy, we are not dominated by our passions but are masters of them. As the next article (156) states explicitly, if we so wish we can be "entirely masters" of our passions, of "desires," "jealousy," "envy," "hatred," "fear," and "anger."

Thanks to knowledge coupled with "good-will," we need not stay beyond Paradise and before the Fall. We can attain the status of remaining beyond Paradise and not being threatened by the Fall. Traditionally, the Fall is said to be the result of pride. Descartes gives short shrift to that vice in article 155, where he states that pride is "unreasonable and . . . absurd." The proud have simply not thought about what they merit, and accept as due to them what is not their due; they are therefore of all men "the most ignorant and stupid." It follows that if, as is classically held, the Fall is due to pride, then it is due to ignorance and stupidity.[4] It is only for the proud that the Fall

---

4. For the man of "good-will" and knowledge there is no Fall because there is no sin. This person acts only when he sees clearly and distinctly whatever is relevant to his action (hence the person of "good-will" and of knowledge is Descartes' wise person). Only he who acts precipitously sees sin enter his life. The advent of sin is his own fault for he need not have acted precipitously; in the face of lack of clarity and distinctness he could have suspended judgment until clarity and distinctness had been achieved. As we read in Descartes' correspondence, "for if we saw clearly it would be impossible to sin, as long as we saw it in that fashion; that is why they say that whoever sins, does so in ignorance" (Kenny, *Descartes, Philosophical Letters*, p. 150; AT4, 110). The *philosophes*

exists; it exists for them because they are "slaves to their desires." For them, also hell exists, hell on earth. For being "slaves to their desires" they have "a soul incessantly agitated by hatred, envy, jealousy, or anger." Whosoever boasts, let him boast of "the will which we feel in ourselves always to make good use of our free-will"; let him boast of his "good-will" (article 157). Of those who make this good use of their free will, Descartes says that "although they often see that others commit faults which make their feebleness apparent, they are at the same time more inclined to excuse than to blame them, and to believe that it is rather by lack of knowledge than by lack of good-will that they commit them" (article 154).

This basic optimism about human nature, about man's capacities and here especially about the use he is inclined to make of them, is a note sounded not just in Descartes' last work. It is, rather, the persistence of a note which was sounded long before. It is the amplification of a theme present in the Preface to the *Principles* as well as in the *Discourse*. In that Preface we read of man's natural ability to become wise. And as we saw before, for Descartes' wise person all applications of science necessarily lead to an increase in happiness. Already in that Preface Descartes' note of optimism sounded clearly:

The brute beasts who have only their bodies to preserve, devote their constant attention to the search for the sources of their nourishment; but men, in whom the principal part is the mind, ought to make their principal care their search after wisdom. . . . There does not exist the soul so ignoble, so firmly attached to the objects of sense, that it does not sometimes turn away from these to aspire after some other greater good, even although it is frequently ignorant as to wherein that good consists. . . . And this sovereign good, considered by the natural reason without the light of faith, is none other than the knowledge of the truth through its first causes, i.e. the wisdom whose study is philosophy. (HR1, 205; AT9-2, 4)

In turn, that note was sounded a decade earlier, in the *Discourse*, whose original title, it will be recalled, began with the words "the project of

---

agree. "We sin only because the light of our reason is not as strong as our passions, and there is a certain truth in the theological maxim that all sinners are ignorant." Their wise person, the "philosopher," is the one who "when he does not have any proper basis, . . . knows how to suspend judgment"; this is his "most perfect trait." Hence the true "philosopher" cannot sin. (*Encyclopedia*, "Philosopher," in Hoyt and Cassirer, p. 288, 285).

a universal Science which can elevate our nature to its highest degree of perfection."

The idea of progress, central to Descartes' position, includes the idea of the steady advance of mankind towards ever greater happiness. The possibility of this steady advance he took to be provided by the existence of science itself; and its actualization depended only on action by the person of wisdom. Through science, developed and applied by the wise person, happiness will ever increase also in the area of morals.

(ii) *The "inevitability" of progress.* As we have seen. Descartes' position allows him to maintain that progress can continue indefinitely. Man is ever more perfectible because he can keep up his pace along the endless road of progress. His position does not allow him to maintain consistently that progress is necessary, or that man's perfectibility is inevitable. Apart from his arbitrary ascription of "good-will" to mankind, there is nothing in his position which makes it necessary for him to say that man cannot use his liberty of indifference to halt the development of science or to misuse its results. On the contrary, because it is ultimately nothing but his own free will which sets and keeps him on the path of progress, this free will can be exerted to keep him off that path or to abandon the path once he is on it. Persisting in such use of free will Descartes would not call a "good thing." Instead, persistent rejection of the promise of science he would consider a misuse of man's mind. His optimism amounts to a firm convinction that such misuse will not occur, or not prevail; it rests on the unargued thesis that "good-will" predominates in man. That optimism may seem strange in view of the fact that it is also his contention that all of history prior to his own day portrays the misuse of the human mind and hence the absence of "good-will." If it is objected that his contention and his optimism do not conflict at all because the optimism is really founded on the use of method—of a method which, although "necessary for finding out the truth" was not, or not sufficiently, known and hence not effectively used by his predecessors—then this simply takes us back to the first point, that progress is not inevitable. Progress is indeed contingent on the use of method; but whether or not the method, once it is fully known, is going to be used depends on man's will.

In the eighteenth century, there were those for whom progress was not inevitable. Rousseau, Voltaire, and d'Alembert are good examples. Their ground for this belief is the thesis that man is free. They are then not necessarily more consistent or more cogent than Descartes when, in relating human freedom and the possibility of progress, they present a pessimistic view of man's prospects for progress. Neither optimism nor pessimism necessarily follows from relating these two. They are, however, more consistent when they introduce an additional ground, for example, the thesis that a study of history shows that the past produced minds as methodic and as fertile as, say, that of Descartes; that, nevertheless, relapses into barbarism continually occurred. Such historical points offered some ground for d'Alembert to maintain consistently that periods in which reason rules alternate with those in which barbarism triumphs.[5]

But also many of those for whom progress looked inevitable (as it did for Condorcet and Kant) firmly believed in human freedom. They thus introduced an additional ground which made their optimism fit their position. For Condorcet this was the principle that progress is inherent in human nature. Just as it is the nature of the individual to progress from day to day as he grows to maturity, so the human race progresses as it grows older and each generation absorbs the experience of that which preceded it. This led him to the position "that nature has set no term to the perfection of human faculties; that the perfectibility of man is truly indefinite; and that the progress of this perfectibility . . . has no other limit than the duration of the globe upon which nature has cast us."[6] His program in the *Sketch* is therefore "to show why, in spite of the transitory success of prejudice . . . truth alone will obtain a lasting victory." To show that truth will be victorious is not enough, for truth must also be enacted in daily life. His program in the *Sketch* is therefore also to "demonstrate how nature has joined together indissolubly the progress of knowledge and that of liberty, virtue and respect for the natural rights of man."[7]

In this last statement Condorcet approaches the principle which allowed Kant his optimism about human progress, namely, that it is inherent in nature in general. Kant goes beyond Condorcet in providing a ground to support his principle: "if we turn away from that fundamental principle, we have then before us a nature moving without purpose, and no longer conformable to law; and the cheerless

5. As he does in the *Discours préliminaire*, I, p. xxxiii.
6. *Sketch*, p. 4.
7. *Sketch*, p. 10.

gloom of chance takes the place of the guiding light of reason."[8] This argument, though meant to give support to his principle, really does no more than make explicit the basis of Kant's faith in progress.

In the eighteenth century there was very wide disagreement about the inevitability of progress. In the debate one key term is "freedom." That debate did not really drive a wedge between the position implicit in Descartes' works and that of the eighteenth century. One might say instead that the debate is in terms of the unresolved tension within Descartes' position: that between the assertion of the primacy of freedom on the one hand, and the assertion of the triumph of reason or of the understanding on the other. Those, at least, are the poles between which d'Alembert moves before he opts for freedom rather than for the necessity of an enduring victory for the understanding. For a philosopher like Kant the issue becomes far more complex in its details. But perhaps it is not unfair to say that the tension submerged in the Cartesian system, that between the freedom of the will and the compulsion of the understanding, comes to explicit dominance in the Kantian position, and that, in spite of the many nuances which make them so very different, Kant and Descartes are really quite close in spirit in this crucial respect.[9]

(iii) *Progress and its criterion.* For Descartes, progress consisted in "raising our nature to its highest degree of perfection." The *philosophes* expressed the same ideal in the phrase "the perfectibility of man." Both took this ideal to involve mastery, and the positive expression of this ideal they took to consist in the freedom of self-realization. Assessment of the progress made with respect to the realization of this ideal they all assumed to be possible because they shared a set of absolutes. For in spite of the fact that some of the *philosophes* presented themselves as relativists, they nevertheless shared important Cartesian absolutes. All of them accepted the basic uniformity of nature in general[10] and particularly the basic uniformity of human nature and of human reason. Some commentators quite mistakenly present a position like that of Condorcet's as one which states that there is progress in human nature or in human reason in the sense that both

8. Quoted from Hastie, ed. *Principles of Politics*, p. 4.

9. In its various tables, Van Doren's *The Idea of Progress* contains much material which at a glance gives further information about the various positions of eighteenth-century thinkers on an issue like that of the necessity of progress.

10. See Gay, *The Enlightenment* vol. 2, *The Science of Freedom*, pp. 168–69 and pp. 380–85.

of these actually change in essence.[11] Progress was taken by the *philosophes* to be possible only in so far as human nature can come to self-expression or to the extent whereby reason can function without hindrance. The view that human nature and reason change in essence finds no support in Condorcet's writings. Furthermore, it conflicts with the position which, as we saw in the third chapter, the *philosophes* (including Condorcet) share with Descartes: that there is a single method which is universally applicable precisely because it is "derived entirely from those primary and evident truths which we can discover by observing the operations of the human mind." The universal applicability of the method demands the unchangeable nature of reason.

In addition, most of the *philosophes* believed in man's original freedom. In the *Encyclopedia* Diderot begins the article "Man" with a statement which includes the phrases, "A feeling, reflecting, thinking being, who freely walks the earth . . . who has given himself masters, who has made laws for himself."[12] This is a definitional statement which ascribes original freedom to man. At the same time it is a statement which confronts man with a task, a challenge, an ideal. Because man is a feeling, reflecting, thinking being, therefore he is capable of freely walking the earth; and he will freely walk the earth once he accepts no masters and obeys no laws but those which he gives to himself as a feeling, reflecting, thinking being. Progress consists in self-realization, in becoming in fact what one potentially is.

One difficulty with the *philosophes* is that they have little to say which is specific about how progress is achieved, let alone appropriately assessed. Of course, progress is said to consist in throwing off the yoke of all foreign authority, of superstition and of prejudice. Or if I may put things positively, of course progress is said to consist in freedom or mastery or self-realization. Nor are they silent about how

11. In *The Idea of Progress* Van Doren is one of those who ascribes such a view to Condorcet with respect to human nature (p. 15) and human reason (p. 51). So does Voegelin in *From Enlightenment To Revolution*. Van Doren does not support his contention. Voegelin attempts to offer support (cf. p. 133) but the passages he quotes from the *Sketch* fail to provide the support he needs. I find myself on the side of, for example, Miller, rather than on that of Voegelin, when Miller writes that for Enlightenment thinkers, there was no belief in change in human nature but, instead, the position that "human nature must be given the chance to show its essence anew." Miller aptly quotes Robespierre: conditions must be created which allow "what is written in the heart" to function publicly. Cf. *Rousseau, Dreamer of Democracy*, pp. 132–33.

12. From *Encyclopedia Selections*, Hoyt and Cassirer, p. 243.

the yoke is to be thrown off and about how to recognize whether or not it is thrown off. In these respects they implement the Cartesian methodology and apply the Cartesian criterion of clarity and distinctness (though often in Locke's language of "determinate ideas"). In this criterion they even believe that they have a device for discerning progress in the sciences. The problem is that although they hold any increase in happiness to depend on the application of science to everyday life, and although some are aware of the fact that scientific knowledge can be used to fetter and impede as well as to liberate, they remain largely silent about precisely how to judge which application of science would hinder progress and which would enhance it. Although they provide hints, they provide no more than hints and not enough of them. Hence an attempt to work towards articulation of a criterion on their behalf would be more speculative than in the case of Descartes.

The hints they do give, however, point in the direction of a further affinity with Descartes. One hint is that, even for those who do not believe in the inevitability of progress, the progress that does occur in the conditions of human life occurs because of the development of not just a single science but of the science in general. At this point we can discern the eighteenth-century's groping towards the equivalent of Descartes' notion of science as "universal Wisdom." A science cannot develop much in isolation to begin with, hence its salubrious potential effects on life cannot be appreciable. For Condorcet, "progress in politics and political economy was caused primarily by the progress in general philosophy" which allowed for the application of a common method in the various disciplines.[13] And of important questions in economics, he says that they "have been solved only by the aid of our knowledge of natural history, agriculture, the physical constitution of plants and the mechanical or chemical arts." He then generalizes that "Such, in a word, has been the general progress of the sciences that there is not really one of them whose principles and details can be fully developed without the help of all the others."[14] D'Alembert considered the *Encyclopedia* both as a manifestation of progress and as a tool for further advances. Its major aim should be to lay bare the order and the inter-connection of the various sciences.[15]

13. *Sketch*, p. 132.
14. *Sketch*, p. 162.
15. *Discours préliminaire*, I, p. i.

One hint they give, therefore, is that a condition for the achievement of progress in everyday life is the conjunctive development of various sciences.

Another hint is given in Antoine-Leonard Thomas's *Eloge de Descartes*, a hint made more conspicuous by Voltaire's praise of it. In the *Eloge*, Thomas presents what he takes to be the Cartesian ideal—that of achieving mastery—as a continuing task for the Enlightenment, as a task whose fulfilment demands communal scientific activity: "Let all scientists unite their forces. Let one group begin where another has left off. Thus, by joining together the lives of various persons and the labours of several centuries, a vast depot of knowledge will be formed, and nature will at last be subjected to man."[16] These two hints, one about the unity of science and one about the community of scientists, are the major indications they provide. Both trade on the distinction between "science" in the narrow and in the broad sense.

It is clearly their belief that science can and must serve progress. But even if we are generous about what their positions might imply, they have less to say about how science can serve progress than was implied in Descartes' position. For his system allowed us to draw the conclusion that it is the wise person's application of science which necessarily constitutes an instance of progress. And because quite a bit could be said about this wise person, this implied a good deal as well about the criteria to be met if science is in fact to serve the cause of improving man's condition. This wise person knows the sciences, their interrelation and their unity. For example, he really knows mechanics because he also knows physics and metaphysics. Moreover, this wise person knows mechanics in the context of his knowledge of both medicine and morals. He is therefore acquainted with what these sciences tell him to be man's legitimate needs and aspirations, and he possesses the wherewithal to begin to meet these needs and aspirations. Thus the Cartesian wise person not only knows the order among and unity of the sciences, but also the order among and unity of the various aspects of human life as they are to come to expression through the application of the "principal sciences" of mechanics, medicine and morals if happiness is to be gained or increased.

The *philosophes* said nothing explicitly analogous to this last aspect of the wise person, to his knowledge of the order among and unity of the various aspects of human life, and hence to his knowledge of when and how to apply the sciences so that their application leads to

16. Quoted in Vartanian, *Diderot and Descartes*, p. 16.

or increases happiness. Where one might have expected them at least to make explicit the implications of Descartes' position, they did not do so. Perhaps they had not travelled as far along this road as to reach the point which Descartes may have reached. For the analogue to that implication of Descartes' doctrine was not articulated in a clear manner and was not to exert its influence until the turn of their century when, in categories different from but not unrelated to those of Descartes, Saint-Simon made it explicit.

(iv) *The utility of science and the instrumentality of reason.* In the eighteenth century there was no longer any special stress on the doctrine that science is developed for the sake of its utility or that knowledge is of strictly instrumental value. This doctrine had become a commonplace. For Descartes it was not a commonplace but a revolutionary position, and therefore it was important to state it at several points during his career. Once one considers the passages in which he especially stressed this doctrine, it cannot but strike the reader how "eighteenth century" in tone and outlook these passages really are. Furthermore, the doctrine of the instrumentality of knowledge is accompanied by the contention that reason serves the passion for mastery. In Descartes' system the passion for mastery dominates, and so I called it the master passion. Apart from this master passion, reason is held to be of no use to man. Reason itself is instrumental in the satisfaction of the master passion. That alone is its value.

I shall not quote again well-known passage from the *Discourse* in which Descartes speaks of attaining "knowledge which is very useful in life," of "a practical philosophy" which allows us mastery over nature and freedom "even also possibly of the infirmities of age." Instead, let me draw attention once again to the Preface of the *Principles of Philosophy*. Its second and third paragraphs contain these statements:

I should . . . first of all . . . explain . . . what philosophy is, beginning with the more ordinary matters, such as that this word philosophy signifies the study of wisdom, and that by wisdom we . . . understand . . . perfect knowledge of all things that man can know, both for the conduct of his life and for the conservation of his health and the invention of all the arts; and that in order that this knowledge should subserve these ends, it is essential that it should be derived from first causes. . . .

I should in the next place have caused the utility of this philosophy to be considered, and shown that since it tends over the whole range of human knowledge, we are entitled to hold that it alone is what distinguishes us from savages and barbarians, and that the civilization and refinement of each nation is proportionate to the superiority of its philosophy. . . . living without philosophy is just having the eyes closed without trying to open them; and the pleasure of seeing everything that is revealed to our sight, is not comparable to the satisfaction which is given by the knowledge of those things which are opened to us by philosophy. And finally, this study is more necessary for the regulation of our manners and for our conduct in life, than is the use of our eyes in the guidance of our steps. . . . And [therefore the] sovereign good, considered by the natural reason without the light of faith, is none other than the knowledge of the truth through its first causes, i.e. the wisdom whose study is philosophy.[17]

In all of these statements there is not a sentiment expressed which the *philosophes* would not claim as their own.

For them, as for Descartes, the sovereign good is scientific knowledge, and the sovereign tool is reason. Both are placed so highly not for what they are in themselves, but because of what they allow man to achieve: the mastery of his enivronment to give him happiness. In the "Philosopher," the *Encyclopedia* entry which Hoyt and Cassirer so aptly characterise as "an idealized self-portrait" of the *philosophe*, the "philosopher" uses "the torch of his reason" to dispel "the night of unreflecting passion."[18] The "philosopher" knows that to escape corruption and misery he must use reason. He is therefore the one who "when he does not have any proper basis . . . knows how to suspend judgment" and who "is more pleased with himself when he is able to withhold conclusions than he would be if he had made up his mind before perceiving the proper grounds for coming to a decision."[19] The "philosopher" is the one who seeks to avoid whatever is "contrary to well-being and a reasonable life."

Perhaps the best known statement of this article is that "Reason is to a philosopher what grace is to a Christian. Grace impels the Christian to act, reason impels the philosopher."[20] Built into this comparison there is of course an implicit contrast: "grace" comes from without and, being irresistible, it masters man; "reason" comes from within

17. This stress on "utility" appears in many other places. In the *Conversation with Burman* it takes the form of de-emphasizing metaphysics and stressing the importance of the applied sciences ('it is just these physical studies that it is most desirable for men to pursue, since they would yield abundant benefits for life, p. 30).

18. These phrases are Hoyt's and Cassirer's, *Encyclopedia Selections* p. 283. The article itself speaks of the "philosopher" who "even in moments of passion, acts only after reflection; he walks through the night, but he is preceded by a torch," p. 285.

19. Ibid., p. 285.

20. Ibid., p. 284.

and, being resistible, only masters man if man wills it to master him. Through grace God employs man for His purposes; through free will, man uses reason for his ends. Grace robs man of independence; reason guarantees his autonomy. Descartes and the *philosophes* were on the side of reason. Through his emphasis on the instrumental role of reason and on the utility of science, Descartes was not far from being the *philosophes'* "philosopher."

It now remains to state a corollary. The proposition that man is an end in himself is one most often ascribed to Kant—and rightly so, for he articulated it most clearly. But the position it expresses is that of Descartes. When reason becomes characterized as instrumental because it allows for a science marked by its usefulness, then also nature, the object of science, becomes a means to an end. Through the application of the sciences of mechanics, medicine and morals nature is to serve human happiness. And so, by serving himself through his reason, his science and "his nature," man has become an end in himself.

VII

Self-Mastery

THE THESIS which I have developed throughout this study is that some often overlooked, but quite central tenets of Descartes' came to be shared by eighteenth-century Enlightenment philosophers. Descartes' concepts of freedom, mastery, and progress are concepts which belong to Enlightenment thought.

In rounding off my discussion of the two major parts of my thesis, this penultimate chapter deals again with freedom and mastery. It does so in a discussion which once more shows how fundamental these concepts are for Descartes. Here, I shall indicate their importance in *The Passions of the Soul*, the last work which Descartes wrote for publication. Then, with specific reference to eighteenth-century thinkers, in the final chapter I shall complete my discussion of why we should say that an Enlightenment spirit pervades Descartes' thought.

Before I enter upon my discussion of *The Passions* it will be helpful to recapitulate. A brief change in basic imagery may make the task easier and more effective. Rather than continue speaking of Descartes as a revolutionary, I shall simply view him for a few paragraphs as a thinker who is unwilling to accept anything on trust. Once I begin to deal with *The Passions*, I shall revert to the image of revolution.

Descartes' position is in great part a distrust of the past. What shall we say, he is asking, of acts in which people are content to order their lives in any way that just conforms to the past? He would have us call them acts in which one fails to realize one's autonomy and abrogates one's humanity to an intolerable extent. Since the past cannot be changed, its power to mould us must be rejected. The past comes to determine a person through his cultural milieu, not least by the forces of his education. Rejection of one's culture, especially through rejection of one's education, contributes much to man's fulfilment of a duty to himself—getting rid of the past as an enchaining tyrant. One might note that it is through such an attempt at freeing himself that a person is first revealed as a potential master: it is the first act of a series through which he intends to establish his autonomy more and more clearly. In the opening chapter we saw how Descartes saw the rejection of the past as dictated by the way in which he believes reason must first go about its business if truth is to be achieved. His attitude of distrust towards the past is therefore essential to his view of reasoning. And, since he takes reasoning to be a crucial expression of human nature, the attitude is at least implicit in his view of human nature itself.

Descartes also distrusts the present. He is wary of it to the extent that he experiences his inability to control this present. Regardless of what one senses or imagines to be true, no trust may be placed in sensation or imagination unless the beliefs arising from these sources are first reduced to their simplest elements, next reconstituted, and finally seen to fit in a rational scheme.

The arguments of the second and fourth chapters placed what I now discuss as a matter of trust or of distrust in terms of freedom, particularly in terms of liberty of opportunity and liberty of spontaneity. The fourth chapter established that the exercise of free will as liberty of opportunity must always precede the enjoyment of freedom as liberty of spontaneity. So it is always true that, in rational, autonomous thought, distrust necessarily precedes trust. As the second chapter made clear, no credence may be given even to the products of reason itself until reason has withstood the most severe test of doubt to which human freewill as liberty of opportunity could submit it. Both the second and the fourth chapters revealed Descartes' attitude of distrust: legitimate acceptance of what is presented by reason, by sense, or by imagination can occur only after reason has been shown to be trustworthy. Until this is done, we cannot legitimately accept reason's claim that it is qualified to analyse and reconstruct and fit into a rational scheme the beliefs of sense and imagination. Reason must first have been shown to be trustworthy. Only after the beliefs born of sense and imagination have *then* been fitted into a rational scheme, may these beliefs born of sense and imagination be accepted as true. The experience of liberty of spontaneity cannot come about beforehand. No recognition of truth can occur apart from acts of liberty of spontaneity. It follows that the experience of liberty of spontaneity, or of the legitimized trust of reason, sensation, and imagination, presuppose an autonomous will expressing itself in acts of liberty of opportunity.

These statements make it possible for me to articulate more correctly a point which I made earlier in this section. I said that the rejection of one's culture is really the first way in which a person reveals himself as a potential master, the first act through which he develops his intent to establish his autonomy. It now appears that a more correct formulation would run like this: such a rejection confirms what he has begun to believe is his proper state, the state of autonomy. Here his first and most fundamental assertion of mastery is found. For such a rejection implies the declaration that nothing shall be accepted unless the individual first vouches for the trustworthiness of that which requests or demands acceptance. It amounts to the proclamation that the criterion for acceptability resides in each individual. The criterion is to be applied by him—and by him alone.

Descartes is thus insisting that whatever custom, example, or education seem to combine, or whatever reason, sensation, or imagination appear to have joined together for eternity, can be broken. Indeed, each and every person can put them asunder. All the earlier chapters have given illustrations of such human powers. In discussing *The Passions of the Soul* I shall now provide one further illustration.

The concepts of freedom and of mastery play as important a role in *The Passions* as they do in, say, the *Discourse*. Even establishing that point alone would have much value, reinforcing my case for the pervasiveness of these concepts in Descartes' thought over many years of writing on many subjects. And that would further support the point that, in important respects, Descartes should be taken as the chief enlightener of later Enlightenment thinkers. There is, however, another reason why it is so profitable to scan *The Passions*. In my preceding chapters the concepts central to this study were discussed in an environment largely devoted to methodology and theory of knowledge. Now what if it is found that the same concepts belong in as central a place in a work of Descartes' where a human agent's "moral" conduct is the author's central concern, rather than issues of method or knowledge? That kind of discovery helps to provide more breadth and depth to the conclusion that a spirit, usually taken to originate with Locke or Newton and to be properly developed by the eighteenth-century Enlightenment, had saturated *all* of the works which Descartes had composed long before d'Alembert, or even Voltaire, was born.

In *The Passions* Descartes deals with mastery of the passions. This he calls self-mastery. It is not my intention to give a complete account of how Descartes believes self-mastery can be achieved. I shall limit myself to providing a proper basis for my argument that, in *The Passions*, concepts like freedom and mastery play as important a role as they do in the earlier works. I shall clarify the main thrust of *The Passions* and introduce those of the work's concepts and theories which are needed for background knowledge. This I shall do in the first of the following two parts. In the second, I shall deal with free will, as it comes to the fore both in acts of liberty of opportunity and in enjoyment of liberty of spontaneity, and with mastery, in relation to revolution as well as to autonomy.

I. THE THRUST OF THE PASSIONS

The thrust of Descartes' last work is that any person can attain full mastery over the passions. To grasp why Descartes is so confident of this position we are required to have (i) some understanding of what he means by "person." We also need (ii) to note that there are restrictions which surround the idea which Descartes called "mastery over the passions." We must further (iii) be somewhat acquainted with Descartes' ideas of physiology. Last we have (iv) to be clear about what he means by "virtue." Let me deal briefly with each of these in turn.

(i) *Person.* It is known that, according to Descartes, "my real nature" is in no way a part of physical nature because I am "a substance the whole essence . . . of which is to think" (HR1, 101; AT6, 33). The obvious conclusion he draws is equally well known: "so . . . this 'me,' that is to say, the soul by which I am what I am, is entirely distinct from body" (ibid.). His dualism nevertheless, should not detract from another set of tenets which are just as important to Descartes. These are that this "me" is joined to a body and that only as joined to a body can we conceive of it as a person. In addition, he holds that it is only as a person that I desire mastery over both nature and over the self, and that it is only as a person that I can attain such mastery.[1]

Without the existence of souls there is only nature. And nature, whether animate or inanimate, is nothing but a machine. With soul united to body there is the person—the being in this world for whom

---

1. The relationship between Descartes' dualism and his moral philosophy has been noted by many commentators. A helpful recent account is that in Blom's *Descartes. His Moral Philosophy and Psychology*, pp. 57–80.

it is beneficial that nature, as distinguished from soul, is nothing but a machine. It is only through this union that the soul can act on the body, that mind can influence matter. Because man is the only creature in whom there is the substantial union of thought and extension, man is the only creature capable of attaining mastery over nature. Hence man is also the only creature capable of the kind of self-mastery which involves mastery over a part of nature, namely, over that part of nature which a person calls "my body."

There is, of course, another side to this coin. For it is only because of this union that extension can influence thought, that nature can have power over a person. Whether a person is in bondage to tradition or enslaved by the passions, in either case such lack of freedom is, for Descartes, necessarily mediated by a particular body, which acts upon a particular soul through their union with each other. All human unhappiness and suffering and most human happiness[2] derive from this union: "there are . . . certain things which we experience in ourselves and which we should attribute neither to mind nor to body alone, but to the close and intimate union that exists between the body and the mind. . . . Such are the appetites of hunger, thirst, etc., and also the emotions or passions of the mind which do not subsist in mind or thought alone, as the emotions of anger, joy, sadness, love, etc.; and, finally all sensations such as pain . . ." (art. 48). The development of mechanics is to set us on the path of progress towards the kind of mastery which will abolish the pain which attends taking care of daily needs. The development of medicine is to guide us towards freedom from the miseries which result from bodily malfunctions. As we saw in a preceding chapter, in neither of these would Descartes hold mastery to be fully realizable. Of these two kinds of mastery *The Passions* has little or nothing to say and I shall largely overlook them in this chapter. Instead, my focus is on mastery over the passions. As distinct from what Descartes says about mechanics and medicine, it is the main thrust of *The Passions* that, in principle, self-mastery is fully within each person's reach.

(ii) *Restrictions.* We may begin to understand how Descartes can take such mastery to be within each person's grasp once we note the restrictions which surround his way of using "mastery over the passions." One of these restrictions concerns the extent to which *The Passions* is

2. Some happiness is intellectual only and exists regardless of the presence or absence of a body. Cf. *The Passions*, art. 91.

a treatise on ethics or "morals." Another concerns the denotation of "Passions" in the title of this work. And a third pertains to the question: what measure of trust should one accord to one's passions? All three of these sources of restrictions should be made clear at the outset and be kept in mind throughout the chapter.

First, we should keep in mind that *The Passions* is not meant to be a treatise on ethics or "morals" in general.[3] Rather, Descartes assumes that we already know good from evil and that we desire to pursue good and shun evil. Descartes then asks: how do we become successful in the pursuit of good and in keeping away from evil? How do we gain happiness and tranquillity? Even these questions may too easily suggest that Descartes' answers are broader than he intends. For in *The Passions* Descartes deals solely with that part of morals which he takes to admit of explanation only in terms which introduce nothing apart from the person. He there deals only with a person's passions. Suppose that I am quite in control of my passions. This does not tell me how I ought to behave when confronted by what I take to be injustice in my society. Nor do I then know which side to choose in a war and how to conduct myself as a member of that side. It may be objected that social injustice or war would not exist if we were all in control of our passions. This misses the mark. As long as there is no fully developed medical and mechanical science, there remain other moral questions. Two examples are: how should we deal with the handicapped? What is our duty to victims of natural disasters? Having the passions under one's control does not settle such moral issues. But within the area of morals there is one sector in which, Descartes holds, a person can in principle gain full control and achieve total mastery. That is the sector of what he calls the passions. In it total mastery is possible because we deal there with a finite, self-contained part of reality. It is true that objects or events external to the person arouse the passions. For we may be happy when we meet a long lost friend, or sad when we hear of a parent's death. But, replies Descartes, it is just as true that we need not suffer these passions simply because certain objects or events would tend to arouse them in us. That point is precisely the thrust of Descartes' discussions: regardless of what passions any objects or events would arouse in us,

3. In a letter he wrote three months prior to the publication of *The Passions*, Descartes states that he had not composed this work as a "moral philosopher, but only as a physicist." Cf. AT 11, 326.

we can gain complete control, we can determine for ourselves whether or not they will in fact affect us in certain ways. Of course this implies that Descartes does not use "passions" in what some commentators would call its *etymological sense*. This is the second point to be remembered from the outset.[4]

When he begins this treatise Descartes at first uses "passions" in its so-called etymological sense, so that seeing a tree is just as much a "passion" as is experiencing fear. But before we are very far into the treatise, the use of this word is restricted:

although all our perceptions, both those which we relate to objects which are outside us, and those which we relate to diverse affections of our body, are truly passions in respect of our soul, when we use this word in its most general significance, yet we are in the habit of restricting it to the signification of those alone which are related to the soul itself; and it is only these last which I have here undertaken to explain under the name of passions of the soul. (art. 25)

The rest of the treatise remains consistent with this restriction. In article 69, Descartes lists as the "six primitive passions" those of wonder, love, hatred, desire, joy, and sadness. What of other passions, such as anger, fear, hope, bravery, remorse, pity, pride? I mention some of those enumerated in articles 53 through 67. Descartes there says that they "are composed of some of these six, or are species of them." Both these "primitive passions" and their "compounds" or "species" are the kind of passions dealt with in this treatise. It is over passions like these that he claims a person can achieve full mastery.

The third restriction pertains to questions about when, and to what extent, one should trust one's passions. To grasp how the matter of trust is a relevant issue at this point, we should start with an aspect of Descartes' technical definition of "passions."

Descartes defines "passions" as "the perceptions, feelings, or emotions of the soul which we relate specially to it, and which are caused, maintained, and fortified by some movement of the [animal] spirits"

---

4 Neglect of this point mars the otherwise straightforward account in the twelfth chapter of Rée's *Descartes*. (See especially pp. 122–3). The editors of the Haldane and Ross edition of Descartes' works encourage such neglect. They annotate the word "Passions" in the title of this work with the following footnote: "The expression "Passions" is in this Treatise of course used in its etymological significance" (p. 331).

(art. 27). The important phrase is "caused . . . by some movement of the spirits." We need not know exactly what constitute "animal spirits" to be able to grasp that this definition does not tell the full story. For if the cause of the passions is to be found only in movement of the animal spirits, then they are to be explained entirely in terms of motion and extension. That is because "animal spirits" (as we shall see later) are wholly corporeal. In that case the whole story about the passions would be in mechanistic terms. Then the soul would merely suffer them and be entirely at their mercy. The notion of trust (or, for that matter, of distrust) would in that case be irrelevant. Accordingly, it would make as little sense to speak about acquiring "a very absolute dominion" over the passions (as Descartes does in article 50) as to prattle about acquiring such "dominion" over the perception of a tree.

It may at first sight appear as though Descartes thinks that being at the passions' mercy is not so bad. He writes that the passions' "natural use is to incite the soul to consent and contribute to the actions which may serve to maintain the body or to render it in some manner more perfect" (art. 137). This is only at first sight. A complication immediately arises because the passions do not always tell us what is really good or bad for us. Moreover, they sometimes lead us into excess in our pursuit of good or in our backing off from evil.

That complication Descartes takes to be a boon. If we could always rely on the passions, then our existence would in this respect tend to be sub-human. If we could always rely on the passions, we would be inclined to follow them from the beginning. In such a case it would be only the passions that would let us know what to do, leading us one way rather than another. But action so directed by the passions is not action purposefully directed by reason. Hence such action can never be autonomous action, even if it tends towards some degree of well-being.

So it is fortunate that the passions do not always tell us what is really good or bad, or always disclose what really leads to our well-being. It is even fortunate, according to Descartes, that they sometimes lead into excess. For that gives us the opportunity to discover that we cannot always trust our passions at our first experience of them. Initially we cannot know which to trust and which not to trust and, in each case, to what extent trust or distrust is in order. This brings us to the realization that before we can allow the passions to lead us at all, we must first lead them. Only when the passions are themselves directed by reason can we trust ourselves to be led by them. Once led by reason, we can trust the passions to lead us without endangering either our autonomy or our well-being.[5]

We cannot always rely on the passions' guidance at our first experience of them. This implies that we can never trust our passions to begin with. "That is why we should make use of experience and reason in order to distinguish good from evil [promptings of the passions], and to recognize their just value, so that we may not take the one for the other, or rush into anything too violently" (art. 138). If making use of the knowledge gained from "experience and reason" is going to be relevant at all, then the soul must be able to constrain and direct the passions. Descartes holds that such constraint and direction is possible. For the thrust of *The Passions* is that "there is no soul so feeble that it cannot, if well directed, acquire an absolute power over its passions" (art. 50).

The focus of the discussion in *The Passions* is therefore on the kind of mastery Descartes calls self-mastery. Once we are "masters of our passions" we can "so control and guide them that the evils which they cause are quite bearable, and that we even derive joy from them all" (art. 212). On such mastery, says Descartes, "all the good and evil of this life depend" (ibid.). For the person who has achieved such mastery, "the most violent efforts of the passions never have sufficient power to disturb the tranquillity of his soul" (art. 148). But we cannot become "masters of our passions" unless we know how the body functions. Such knowledge is indispensable if we are to mainpulate it to good purpose. Also it is necessary that we be "virtuous" if we are to manipulate the body consistently for our well-being.

Virtuous thoughts are necessary if mastery of the passions is to be achieved. Articles 49 and 170 alone would place this beyond doubt. But understanding of the body's physiology is equally necessary. We are, to begin with, prejudiced. Although we have all sorts of *beliefs* about what is and what is not virtuous, we do not *know* which of our thoughts are really virtuous. Our beliefs about virtue, which, as beliefs, are mere prejudices, are firmly established through the medium of

5. There is a clear parallel here between *The Passion* on the one hand the *Discourse* and *Meditations* on the other. In the latter works it is Descartes' position that it is fortunate that our senses sometimes deceive us and that our teachers are locked in controversy. For now each thinking person can come to the position that, whatever their source, only beliefs sanctioned by his own reason may be accepted without loss of autonomy and without danger of espousing prejudices.

habitual bodily behaviour. We cannot attain knowledge of virtue unless the mind is freed from the domineering influence of the body. A prerequisite for attaining this freedom is knowledge that the body exerts a domineering influence, and at least some understanding of how it does so. Only once we posses such an understanding are we able to neutralize the body's influence and to examine dispassionately our beliefs about virtue.

Even if it were possible to obtain knowledge of what is virtuous without understanding of physiology, it is still the case that possessing such knowledge does not automatically give dominion over the passions. Descartes denies that knowing the good automatically leads to doing the good. Virtuous thoughts may tend to move us one way, the force of habit another. The strife which results can enervate a person so that the outcome is inactivity rather than mastery. Here we find another reason (one which comes to the fore quite clearly in the *Passions*) why knowledge of physiology is necessary. It is needed in order to understand how the force of well-established habit may be broken so that knowledge of what is virtuous may come to triumph. Passages like those of articles 46, 50, 136, and 211 make it abundantly clear that knowledge of what is virtuous by itself is not enough to achieve full mastery, that understanding of how the body functions is equally necessary.

In the argument of this chapter's second part, I shall draw upon the passages I mentioned (and others like them), passages in which Descartes speaks about the role of virtue and of knowledge of physiology in the achievement of mastery of the passions. First in order, however, is the completion of the present section, which still demands a general sketch of Descartes' ideas about both physiology and virtue to the extent that such ideas are relevant as background for my argument in the second part.

(iii) *Physiology.* As Jonathan Rée has put it, "Descartes equated activity with freedom and passivity with bondage." He then adds that, for Descartes, "a person is active when his behaviour is an expression of his thought, and that otherwise he is passive." Such points imply that "human behaviour is not really free unless it expresses thought."[6] Rée here states a general case. It clearly fits Descartes' view as expressed, for example, in the statement to Regius which we noted earlier: "no actions can be reckoned human unless they depend on

6. Rée, *Descartes*, p. 120.

reason."[7] In the case of the passions we have a particular application of this general rule. To suffer the passions is to be passive, to be in bondage; to direct the passions through reason is to be active, to be free.

Mastery over the passions can be gained only indirectly, through control of the body based on knowledge of its physiology. Descartes' antiquated physiology itself is of no intrinsic interest. But there are bare minima needed for understanding his philosophical views. They call for only a few comments about the animal spirits and the pineal gland.

We meet the phrase "animal spirits" from the outset of *The Passions*. The "spirits" play a crucial role in Descartes' account of perception as well as in that of action. In spite of what the name might suggest, the animal spirits are entirely corporeal. As we read about them in article 10: "what I here name spirits are nothing but material bodies and their one pecularity is that they are bodies of extreme minuteness and that they move very quickly like the particles of the flame which issues from a torch." They serve to convey sensuous images from all parts of the body to the brain, and to transmit messages from the brain to all parts of the body. In these roles they are closely linked with the nervous system: "all . . . movements of the muscles, as also all the senses, depend on the nerves, which resemble small filaments, or little tubes, which all proceed from the brain, and thus contain like it a certain very subtle air or wind which is called the animal spirits" (art. 7).

These spirits play an equally crucial role in the account of the passions, so much so that they even appear in the definition of "passions." As we have seen, Descartes defines the passions as "the perceptions, feelings, or emotions of the soul which we relate specially to it, and which are caused, maintained, and fortified by some movement of the spirits" (art. 27). It is a certain movement of the animal spirits which places us at the mercy of our passions; similarly, it is a certain movement of the animal spirits which allows for mastery over our passions. In the first instance the body affects the soul, while in the second the soul affects the body. In the former, our "action" is mere reflex action, and we are caught up in the mechanism of nature. In the latter we can experience our freedom. If we ask Descartes how

7. Kenny, *Descartes, Philosophical Letters*, p. 102 (AT3, 371).

the body can affect the soul or how the soul can affect the body, his answer introduces the pineal gland.

This gland Descartes believes to be the point where the body chiefly affects the soul and where the soul particularly exerts its influence on the body. The soul, he says, "has its principal seat in the little gland which exists in the middle of the brain, from whence it radiates forth through all the remainder of the body by means of the animal spirits, nerves, and even the blood . . ." (art. 34). This gland is suspended in one of the brain's "cavities" in such a way that any motion of the animal spirits is communicated to it. But also any motion of the gland itself is communicated to the animal spirits. When the animal spirits move the pineal gland, this motion affects the soul as a passion. When the soul itself causes the motion in the pineal gland and so, indirectly, moves the animal spirits, Descartes speaks of action. (Cf. arts 29, 34, 35). Once the soul knows how to control all movements of the animal spirits, through its action on the pineal gland, then the person is in complete control of the passions. For in the words of article 37, all the passions "are caused by some particular movement of the animal spirits." One may speak of self-mastery in this instance because, whereas these passions are caused by movements of the animal spirits, such movements themselves are in turn caused by the soul's action on the pineal gland.

Later on I shall say more about the process through which this control is to be achieved. Nowhere does Descartes touch at all on the metaphysical question: How can the body affect the soul and how can the soul influence the body? He takes this interaction as a fact of experience. Personhood is to be accepted as a basic given. When friends pressed him to explain this interaction, no explanation was given.[8] This metaphysical question, however, is not relevant at this point. What is germane is to understand what Descartes says about self-mastery. Without knowledge of the mechanism of the body it is, for Descartes, impossible to rise above this mechanism and express ourselves as persons in "actions" which "depend on reason."

8. Descartes' response to Elizabeth's persistent challenge ("The senses teach me that the soul moves the body but neither they nor the intellect nor the imagination teaches me how") was one of evasion. Se his letters to Elizabeth of 21 May 1643 and 28 June 1643: Kenny, *Descartes, Philosophical Letters*, p. 137 (AT5, 663) and p. 140 (AT3, 690). In his earlier response to Arnauld, Descartes presented a more refined position, but not a more satisfactory answer. Cf. HR2, 102–03; AT7, 227f.

(iv) *Virtue*. We cannot become masters of our passions unless we know enough physiology to manipulate the body. Neither can we achieve self-mastery unless we know how to manipulate the body for our well-being. The latter requires what Descartes calls "virtue."

The second part of *The Passions* closes with these words:

> For whoever has lived in such a way that his conscience cannot reproach him for ever having failed to perform those things which he has judged to be the best (which is what I here call following after virtue) receives from this a satisfaction which is so powerful in rendering him happy that the most violent efforts of the passions never have sufficient power to disturb the tranquillity of his soul. (art. 148)

Absolute mastery over the passions is attainable only by the virtuous. "Virtue" consists in never failing "to perform those things" which one "has judged to be best." The meaning which Descartes gives to "virtue" differs from that of his predecessors. To Elizabeth he writes that "though I do not know that anyone has ever so described it," "virtue . . . consists precisely in firmness in this resolution": "to carry out whatever reason recommends without being diverted by passion or appetite."[9] Descartes wrote this letter a few months before he composed *The Passions*. However, this novel definition of virtue does not make its first appearance near the end of Descartes' career. It is already present in the first of his published works, in the *Discourse* (cf. HR1, 98; AT6, 28).

Virtue consists in acting only on the pronouncements of reason. Moreover, "no actions can be reckoned human unless they depend on reason."[10] If we place this statement to Regius next to the definition of virtue, it becomes clear that, for Descartes, the class of actions properly called "human actions" is the same as the class of virtuous actions. For Descartes, to be human is to be virtuous, to be virtuous is to be human. One cannot be virtuous, and one cannot be fully human, unless one's actions conform to reason. Actions which conform to reason are actions which depend on the co-operation of free will and reason. This is stating the general case. Insofar as we are dealing with *The Passions*, we should say that to be virtuous or human is to be master over the passions, and that such mastery can be achieved

9. Kenny, *Descartes, Philosophical Letters*; p. 102 (AT3, 371).
10. Ibid.

only once the passions are guided by reason. Also in his discussion of mastery over the passions, Descartes holds that to be human depends on the co-operation between the free will and reason—a point which (as we shall see) Descartes makes repeatedly in this work. A single example will suffice for now.

When in article 153 Descartes defines "generosity," he explicitly states that virtue depends on the co-operation of free will and reason:

> true generosity which causes a man to esteem himself as highly as he legiti-mately can, consists alone partly in the fact that he knows that there is nothing that truly pertains to him but this free disposition of his will . . . and partly in the fact that he is sensible in himself of a firm and constant resolution to use it well, that is to say, never to fail of his own will to undertake and execute all the things which he judges to be best—which is to follow perfectly after virtue.

Explication of this co-operative relationship between free will and reason re-introduces the notions of liberty of opportunity and liberty of spontaneity. That discussion belongs to the following part.

II. FREE WILL AND MASTERY

It now remains to show that the central concepts of my study, par-ticularly those of free will and of mastery, are as important to Des-cartes' final work as they were to all his earlier philosophical writings. First, then, let us deal with free will and its relation to reason. Next, let us see how Descartes employs "mastery" in relation to "revolution" and "autonomy."

(i) *Free will and reason.* The cause of the passions is not simply to be found in the animal spirits. If a person is to control and guide the passions, rather than to be merely subject to them, the mind must be able to affect the animal spirits. The animal spirits must be directed in a way which will result in mastery over the passions. Such mastery, and such direction of the animal spirits, requires knowledge. How-ever, knowing how to direct the animal spirits is only one of the conditions for the achievement of mastery. Because desire functions as intermediary between such knowledge and passion, another con-dition is related to desire. This condition is that also desire itself be "regulated" by knowledge.

Desire functions as intermediary between knowledge and passion.

Passion alone does not lead us to act: "the customary mode of action of all the passions is simply this, that they dispose the soul to desire those things which nature tells us are of use, and to persist in this desire" until the desired object is attained (art. 52). In article 144 Descartes succinctly connects passion, desire, knowledge, and action when he writes: "But because these passions can only bring us to any kind of action by the intervention of the desire which they excite, it is this desire particularly which we should be careful to regulate . . ." Desire must be regulated by knowledge. He adds: "desire is always good when it follows a true knowledge"; "it cannot fail to be bad when it is founded on some error."

Desire, the source of action, is to be regulated by knowledge of good and evil. Hence mastery of the passions requires knowledge on two counts: it demands knowledge of the workings of the body in order that the animal spirits may be directed, and knowledge of good and evil so that desires may be regulated. That self-mastery is impossible apart from reason is a tenet which, not surprisingly, underlies Descartes' entire argument. It is a tenet which he mades explicit at several points. In article 48, for example, we read:

those in whom by nature the will can most easily conquer the passions and arrest the movements of the body which accompany them, without doubt possess the strongest souls. But there are those people who cannot bring their strength to the test, because they never cause the will to do battle with its proper arms, but only with those with which certain passions furnish it in order to resist certain others. That which I call its proper arms consists of the firm and determinate judgments respecting the knowledge of good and evil, in pursuance of which it has resolved to conduct the actions of its life; and the most feeble souls of all are those whose will does not thus determine itself to follow certain judgments, but allows itself continually to be carried away by present passions, which, being frequently contrary to one another, draw the will first to one side, then to the other, and, by employing it in striving against itself, place the soul in the most deplorable possible condition. Thus when fear represents death as an extreme evil, and one which can only be avoided by flight, ambition on the other hand sets forth the infamy of this flight as an evil worse than death. These two passions agitate the will in diverse ways; and in first obeying one and then the other, it is in continual opposition to itself, and thus renders the soul enslaved and unhappy.

Self-mastery presupposes "firm and determinate judgments respecting the knowledge of good and evil." Knowledge never enslaves a person. It is the absence of knowledge which enslaves man, for then the "passions agitate the will in diverse ways" and the will is "in continual opposition to itself." In that situation the will is neither self-determined nor determined by reason; there is neither an exercise of liberty of opportunity nor an enjoyment of liberty of spontaneity. Absence of these kinds of determination or of these kinds of freedom destroys a person's efficacy. For Descartes, if one lacks these determinations or freedoms, one becomes part of the mechanism of nature. In that event, a person is ruled by necessity, in this case by the necessity involved in the agitation of the passions. If one is ruled by necessity one is merely a natural being. Without self-determination there is no self or person, no difference between man and beast. Hence also in *The Passions* Descartes holds that, in the end, it is only the self-determined action involving determination by reason which qualifies as human action. Descartes' statement to Regius remains of force: "no actions can be reckoned human unless they depend on reason." They alone result in true mastery.

These conclusions, that the absence of knowledge enslaves, and that self-mastery can result from actions which depend on reason, may appear to some to have been drawn too quickly. For in the article just quoted, Descartes only said that self-mastery presupposes "firm and determinate judgments respecting the knowledge of good and evil": he did not say that it presupposes firm and determinate judgments which are *true* respecting the knowledge of good and evil. To avoid confusion at this point it must be remembered that Descartes' use of "determinate" differs from that of some other seventeenth-century philosophers. For example, as is clear from the "Epistle to the Reader" which serves as Preface to the *Essay concerning Human Understanding*, Locke uses "determinate" interchangeably with "clear and distinct."[11] Descartes allows no such equivalence. Hence a "firm and determinate judgment" is, for him, not the same as a "firm and clear and distinct judgment." That may seem to imply the possibility of self-mastery on the basis of "firm and determinate judgments" which are false. Perhaps I should have said the absence of knowledge *can* enslave us, rather than the absence of knowledge enslaves.

The first of these two formulations may seem to be required by what Descartes writes in articles 49 and 170. In both, he allows for self-determination in spite of the absence of knowledge. He argues

11. Locke, *An Essay concerning Human Understanding*, ed. Nidditch, pp. 12–14.

that as long as one acts on one's own judgments, one remains self-determined and achieves a degree of self-mastery even if such judgments are false. As he says in the first of these articles, most people

have determinate judgments, in pursuance of which they regulate a part of their actions; and although often their judgments are false or even founded on certain passions by which the will formerly allowed itself to be vanquished or led astray, yet, because it continues to follow them when the passion which has caused them is absent, they may be considered as its proper arms, and . . . souls are stronger or weaker by reason of the fact that they are able to follow these judgments more or less closely, and resist the present passions which are contrary to them.

Similarly, in article 170 we read

the remedy against this excess [of irresolution] is to accustom oneself to form certain and determinate judgments concerning all things that present themselves, and to believe that we always do our duty when we do what we judge to be best, although we may possibly judge very badly.

To act on what may be quite possibly a false judgment is to exert the liberty of opportunity. Such an action prevents the agent at least in the first instance from being subject to a form of necessity. This is the necessity involved in agitation by the passions. Acting in this way involves self-determination. It allows for the achievement of a measure of self-mastery.

Nevertheless, in the end a form of bondage does result from actions like these. The passage cited from article 49 continues with the words:

Yet there is a great difference between the resolutions which proceed from a false opinion, and those which are founded only on the knowledge of the truth, inasmuch as if we follow the latter we are assured that we shall never regret nor repent it, whereas we do so always when we have followed the first-mentioned, and hence discovered our error in doing so.

The assertion of liberty of opportunity by itself ends in subjection to the passions of regret and repentance.[12] The presence of these two passions betrays a lack of self-mastery, and the definition of "repent-

12. Regret is "a species of sadness" which "proceeds" "from past good" (art. 68); and repentance is "excited" by "the evil" "which has been done by ourselves" (art. 63).

ance" indicates that those subject to this passion suffer because of their own deliberate fault. The "past good" of tranquillity need not have been lost if no actions had been based on ill-conceived judgments. Hence, for Descartes, complete self-mastery results only if one's actions "are founded on" "knowledge of the truth." In all other cases bondage of some kind is certain to follow. In the end, therefore, only the self-determined placement of oneself under the compulsion of reason results in action which qualifies as human action. The enjoyment of liberty of spontaneity is a necessary condition for self-mastery.

Passions lead to action only through desire, and desire is good only if it is founded on knowledge of good and evil. Hence the Second Part of *The Passions* closes with the statement that "whoever has lived in such a way that his conscience cannot reproach him for ever having failed to perform those things which he has judged to be the best (which is what I here call following after virtue) receives from this a satisfaction so powerful in rendering him happy that the most violent efforts of the passions never have sufficient power to disturb the tranquillity of his soul." Tranquillity, a state which is lasting only when all our actions are rational actions, is ours only when we perform those things which we "judge to be best." The judgment must then be a true judgment, so that the best is truly best.[13] The *Meditations* argue that we are entirely capable of making such judgments and of recognizing them as such when we make them. In addition, the *Meditations* make the point that we are quite capable of suspending action, including the action of making judgments, when that which is to be judged is seen by us not to meet the criteria of clarity and distinctness. If we then judge in any case, we judge precipitously; action based on such a judgment cannot be recognized as "the best." Since we are capable of suspending judgment, we can refrain from precipitous judgment and consequently keep ourselves from acting in foolish and dangerous ways. We are just as capable of exercising our liberty of

13. The point that lasting or "solid" tranquillity or contentment depends on following *true* judgments, on following what we discern to be the principle for action once we have "judged well," is a point which Descartes makes also to Elizabeth when he writes: "to have a contentment that is solid, it is necessary to follow virtue, that is to say, to have a firm will, and to perform constantly all the things we judge to be best, employing the entire force of our understanding to judge them well." This letter of 18 August 1645 (AT4, 271–78) is not included in Kenny's edition of Descartes' letters. It is printed by Blom in *Descartes, His Moral Philosophy and Psychology* (pp. 136–141); see p. 141; AT4, 277.

opportunity in keeping ourselves from judging precipitously and in determining ourselves to affirm as true only that which we have perceived as meeting the criteria of being clear and distinct. We are as capable of these careful exercises of liberty of opportunity as we are of abusing it, in affirming something that is not clear and distinct. We can, he concludes, determine ourselves to act only rationally. We have the power to act only as masters, and thus to "secure the tranquillity" of our souls. No one needs to err. Everyone can learn to handle the criteria of clarity and distinctness. Anyone can suspend judgment and can prevent precipitous action. Hence he writes, in the now well-known words of the heading of the fiftieth article: "there is no soul so feeble that it cannot, if well directed, acquire an absolute power over its passions." No one needs to be less than a master of himself, for no one needs to act in ignorance or embrace falsehood. No one, therefore, needs to be in bondage to the passions.

Each person possesses original freedom in the form of liberty of opportunity. And each can exercise this liberty to attain or to increase liberty of spontaneity. The parallel to Descartes' doctrine about the development of science is plain. Whether we look at the field of morals or that of physical science, we find that there can be no progress unless one exercises one's liberty of opportunity. In addition, there can be no progress unless one ceases exerting those forms of liberty of opportunity which do not lead to an increase in liberty of spontaneity. In both fields the prerequisite for progress is the co-presence of autonomy of the will and determination by reason.

The parallel in doctrine does not stop at this point. For the primacy of free will which, in the realm of thought, was to make possible the revolution demanded by Descartes' view of reason, that same primacy is to allow for a parallel development in the area covered by *The Passions*. In the realm of thought no beliefs were initially to be trusted; all one had learned from one's culture initially had to be rejected as false. The parallel to this in *The Passions* is that nothing which custom, or one's upbringing or education has joined together in this realm of practice should be accepted on trust. Each individual must start by separating what convention or tradition has made to seem inseparable. It is this aspect of Descartes' doctrine which I shall discuss next.

(ii) *Self-mastery, revolution, and autonomy.* Descartes holds that self-mastery cannot be attained unless one is willing and able to break asunder whatever custom or education have joined together: the notion of revolution reappears in the first step towards gaining self-mastery. That step consists in the practice of separating specific corporeal motions from specific thoughts. As we shall see, the notion of autonomy is already present in this practice. But it comes to the fore at least as much in the second step towards such mastery. That step is dictated by the "principle" which, according to Descartes, underlies the entire argument of *The Passions*. This is the principle that in order to gain self-mastery we must deliberately associate specific corporeal motions with specific thoughts, so joining together only that which each person's reason allows or demands to be joined. I shall deal first with separation and next with joining. Which is to say that I shall first pay attention to revolution and next to autonomy in Descartes' account of self-mastery.

(a) *Revolution*. Descartes' doctrine of self-mastery includes the advocacy of an activity which we may call revolutionary, because it is analogous to the revolutionary activity prescribed in the *Discourse*. In my discussion of methodology and epistemology, I called Descartes a revolutionary because his position demands total substitution. It demands, first, that one do away with the old and, second, that one replace it with what is new. Descartes' revolution requires that all one's opinions be completely swept away and that only such items as have been authorized by a person's own reason be accepted. We have seen before that, as a treatise on "morals", *The Passions* themselves are a revolutionary work in this sense.[14] For as Descartes writes in its opening paragraph, "that which the ancients have taught" regarding the passions is "so far from credible" that "I shall be . . . obliged to write just as though I were treating of a matter which no one had ever touched on before me." However, I am not concerned with how *The Passions* can come into existence as a treatise. Instead, I am interested in showing that Descartes' revolutionary stance appears as much in the instructions which he put down for the achievement of self-mastery as it did in his instructions for the learning and advancement of science. In both these areas, success is said to require that one first do away completely with the old.

In the realm of self-mastery, the old presents itself in what one "naturally" experiences. For example, when confronted with an act which threatens his life, a person may "naturally" experience fear. He experiences fear "automatically." In the same situation, another may "naturally" experience ambition. The former experiences fear

14. Cf. chapter 1, section 1.

because, when he was in a life-threatening situation for the first time, he judged death to be an extreme evil which one ought always to flee. The latter experiences ambition because when he first faced death he judged that to flee from such danger is infamous, and that the reputation of infamy is a fate worse than death.[15] Thus the first came to desire life above honour, the second honour above life. The judgments made during these first experiences were not, of course, necessarily true judgments. Education, example, or social pressure may have made one accept beliefs like these uncritically. However adopted, these beliefs and their concomitant desires and passions now arise "naturally." They now arise whenever a threatening object or event causes a certain kind of movement in the animal spirits which, in turn, causes movement of the pineal gland. Explication of this last sentence will allow us to see precisely how the first step towards self-mastery comes to possess its revolutionary character.

It is Descartes' belief that each movement of the animal spirits, and hence each movement of the pineal gland, has been "joined by nature to each one of our thoughts" (art. 50). Thus a particular movement of the animal spirits—a movement caused, say, by the apprehension of danger—in one person "naturally" arouses the thought and hence the desire to face it; it "naturally" causes the passion of ambition. All movements of the animal spirits are joined to particular thoughts. It often takes only one experience to forge this link between that particular movement and that particular thought. (Again, see art. 50). Which thought, and hence which passion, comes to be linked with a particular movement depends in the first place on contingent circumstances like education, example, or social pressure. This link becomes increasingly stronger if a particular movement recurs at various times, always joined to the same belief, the same desire, and hence the same passion. If, for example, in repeated danger there is always the belief that death is the ultimate evil, and always the experience of fear and the desire to flee this danger, then the particular motion of the animal spirits occasioned by the apprehension of danger becomes ever more strongly linked with the belief that death is the ultimate evil, with the passion of fear, and with the desire to flee. On the other hand, if in repeated danger there is always the belief that the infamy of flight is worse than death, and always the experience of ambition and the desire to face this danger, then the particular motion of the animal

---

15. Cf. article 48, of which these examples are adaptations.

spirits occasioned by the apprehension of danger becomes ever more strongly linked with the belief that infamy is worse than death, with the passion of ambition, and with the desire to face this danger. In each of these examples the person is subject to these passions. In each, self-mastery can be achieved only once the links in question have been broken.[16]

To achieve self-mastery these "natural" links must first of all be broken. This holds for all "natural" links. For one does not know, initially, whether at the moment a particular motion of the animal spirits and a particular thought were joined, the right thought—a thought authorized by reason—was joined to the right motion.[17] One does not know, initially, whether a particular case of life-threatening danger rationally calls for flight or for resistance. The links were established early in life—"from the beginning of our life," as article 50 has it—that is, during the time when we were particularly susceptible to the influence of others. We have no grounds to believe that any of the particular thoughts that accompany particular motions are anything except prejudices. What, therefore, "nature" or previous experience has joined together must be put asunder, if true and lasting self-mastery is to become possible. In his doctrine of the passions as in his methodology, Descartes' stance is that of the revolutionary: all links with the past must be broken, all "natural" givens must be rejected if mastery is to be achieved.

How, precisely, these links are to be broken is of no great interest at this point.[18] (Some of this part of Descartes' doctrine will become

16. Descartes usually speaks of particular thoughts joined to particular motions (e.g. art. 50), but sometimes of particular desires joined to particular motions (e.g. art. 44). Perhaps he uses these variations because, in the case of the passions, the thought in question always expresses a desire. When, in what follows, I use "thought" rather than "desire," "thought" stands for "thought expressing a desire."

17. Speaking this way presents an incomplete statement of Descartes' position, for it grants the "initiative" entirely to motion of the animal spirits. As we shall see, the initiative can also be on the side of will and reason.

18. Descartes presents this part of his doctrine succinctly in articles 45 through 48. In this part of his doctrine there is a further similarity with his methodology. Methodological doubt becomes successful in clearing the mind from prejudice through the technique of "balance": beliefs accepted in the past and retaining the force of conviction in the present are neutralized by "of set purpose" opposing to them "contrary" beliefs. (See Meditation I, paragraph 11; and chapter 3, subsection 3). In *The Passions*, one purposefully opposes to the belief which "naturally" arises in a certain situation and which always accompanies a particular passion, a contrary belief which arouses a con-

explicit in the next section, with the introduction of the notion of "strife.") That in all instances they can be broken is a conviction which Descartes states with great assurance: "there is no soul so feeble that it cannot . . . acquire an absolute power over its passions" (art. 50). Each human being is capable of attaining absolute self-mastery because we can all acquire "the forethought and diligence whereby we can correct our natural faults in exercising ourselves in separating within us the movements of the blood and spirits from the thoughts to which they are usually united" (art. 211).

(b) *Autonomy.* In *The Passions* we find a stress on autonomy, especially in the account of two major steps towards self-mastery. It is clearly present in what I just described as the first step, in the persistent attempt to separate all specific corporeal motions from all specific thought as long as these motions and thoughts were joined "naturally" in the course of life, under the pressures of custom, education, and example. All links forged in one's past have to be broken because, for all one knows, none of them were established through a person's own self-determined rational activity. They have to be broken because it is only self-determined rational action—which, for Descartes, is autonomous action—that qualifies as human action and that therefore allows self-mastery.

Autonomy is present also in what I call the second step towards self-mastery: the conscious joining of specific thoughts to specific corporeal motions. Since only rational action allows for mastery, new links must be wrought self-consciously by each person's reason rather than through some haphazard interaction between his physical and his cultural environment. I shall bring this chapter to a close by considering this second step.[19]

As we have seen, when he defines "passions" Descartes says that they are "caused, maintained, and fortified by some movement of the [animal] spirits." This movement can, in turn, be caused by the pineal

---

trary passion. If this move is successful, the latter will at least neutralize the former and the person is "cleared" from being subject to that passion.

19. The idea of autonomy also presents itself in Descartes' position concerning the kind of desires which allow for self-mastery. This position involves the doctrine that the desires of which reason approves are strictly of the kind whose realization demands no action but that of the individual whose desires they are. For this part of Descartes' view see, for example, article 144. Although it plays an important role in *The Passions*, and is one ground for my conclusion in the closing paragraphs of this chapter, I shall not discuss this part of Descartes' doctrine.

gland. This gland Descartes takes to be in place at which the soul chiefly influences the body: the gland can be set in motion by the soul willing it to be moved. Because the soul can set the pineal gland in motion, it can produce motion in the animal spirits and thus, indirectly, control the passions. Particular passions accompany particular thoughts. The soul can take the initiative and can will that a certain passion accompany a particular thought. Mastery calls for the separation of habitually associated thoughts and motions which one finds to be "naturally" joined. Then there must be a joining of thoughts and motions which reason wants to be joined. Descartes writes of both this separation and this joining in article 50:

And it is useful here to know that . . . although each movement of the gland seems to have been joined by nature to each one of our thoughts from the beginning of our life, we may at the same time join them to others by means of custom. . . . It is also useful to know that although the movement both of the [pineal] gland and of the [animal] spirits of the brain, which represent certain objects to the soul, are naturally joined to those which excite in it certain passions, they can at the same time be separated from these . . . and also that this . . . can be acquired by a solitary action, and does not require long usage.

He then illustrates this point in terms of animal behaviour, and draws the conclusion which leads us to see the presence of autonomy:

So when a dog sees a partridge he is naturally disposed to run towards it, and when he hears a gun fired, this sound naturally incites him to flight. But nevertheless setters are usually so trained that the sight of a partridge causes them to stop, and the sound which they afterwards hear when a shot is fired over them, causes them to run up to us. And these things are useful in inciting each one of us to study to regard our passions; for since we can with a little industry change the movements of the brain in animals deprived of reason, it is evident that we can do so yet more in the case of men, and that even those who have the feeblest souls can acquire a very absolute dominion over all their passions if sufficient industry is applied in training and guiding them. (ibid.)

The picture is clear: not only can a person put asunder what "nature" has joined but, through "training and guiding" of the passions, he can bring together what reason demands him to join. That the "training and guiding" in question is to be training and guiding by reason is apparent from the facts that animals cannot train or guide themselves and that the only thing which makes them incapable of it is said to be their lack of reason. Moreover, it is plain that self-mastery is not reserved for those of extraordinarily strong character or unusually skilful mind: even the "feeblest souls" can attain "a very absolute dominion over all their passions" by breaking asunder what was originally joined by "nature" and by coupling only that which reason authorizes to be joined.

Two things are crucial in the attaining of self-mastery. One of these we already considered; that the will be guided by reason. The other concerns what may be called "the principle of association." If the will is guided by reason, then the passions which result from the will's indirect manipulation of the animal spirits are such that we can trust ourselves to them without abrogation of our autonomy or without danger to our well-being. In that situation, autonomy is left intact since one allows oneself to be guided by one's passions only because one has oneself caused these passions. To say that no such situation can come about unless the will is guided by reason would not be telling the full story. Introduction of "the principle of association" completes the discussion of how one comes to occupy the position in which the passions can legitimately be followed.

Of the importance of that principle Descartes speaks most clearly in articles 107 and 136. In the latter he states that what he has written about "the divers effects or the divers causes of the passions" all rests on a single principle. It rests on the principle that "there is a connection between our soul and our body of such a nature that when we have once connected some corporeal action with some thought, the one of the two does not present itself to us afterwards without the other presenting itself also."[20] The "corporeal action" in question consists in movement of the animal spirits and of the pineal gland. The principle of association states that there is a constant conjunction between an event in the realm of extension (the "corporeal action") and an event in the realm of thought.

The mind knows that the body is a machine or automaton. If it

20. In neither article 107 nor 136 does Descartes argue for the correctness of this principle. Instead, he presents it as one particular aspect of the interaction of soul and body. This aspect, like all other aspects of this interaction, one "experiences" or "knows" through a "primitive notion." A "primitive notion" cannot be explicated. The principle of association is, therefore, presented as a basic fact of which anyone can be directly aware in his own experience.

knows the particular ways in which this automaton functions then the mind can, as it were, program the automaton so that it need fear no loss of either autonomy or well-being in following the body-based (but now reason-directed) passions. This possibility of programming assumes the programme (knowledge of good and evil); it also assumes ability to handle the automaton (which rests on knowledge of the body as a machine). In *The Passions* Descartes does not develop the former, but he says a good deal about the latter. He speaks as a "physicist" rather than as a "moral philosopher."

These two realms of knowledge, "morality" and "mechanics," interact in the programming which follows the de-programming of the atuomaton. That is, they intersect in the making of new connections between particular thoughts and motions once the old connections are broken. Both the de-programming and the programming introduce personal autonomy; and taken together they present autonomy in a bold relief. For what is really to take place if one could follow Descartes' directives is what might be called a "reconstituting of the person."[21] In the realm of the passions the person is reconstituted because, through the breaking of all the old connections, all passions or emotions are suspended. The person is then reconstituted when, in the subsequent programming of the automaton, he comes to be characterized only by passions or emotions of which his own reason has already approved.

All the passions are "caused by some particular movement of the spirits." A person is subject to a passion when these animal spirits move the pineal gland, which then affects the soul and arouses a particular desire in it. On the other hand, through desire the soul can move this gland and so cause motion in the animal spirits. The soul has complete control over the passions once it knows how to control all movements of the animal spirits through its action on the pineal gland. Since, as an expression of free will, desire can be under a person's direct control, he can indirectly gain control over his passions through the effect which a particular desire has on the pineal gland. As we read in article 41: "And the whole action of the soul consists

21. I adapt this phrase from Blom, *Descartes, His Moral Philosophy and Psychology*, who comes to a similar conclusion when, in the chapter entitled "Passions, or emotions, reconsidered" he writes: "the point of emphasizing the mechanistic character of the body is to remind us that we might have fallen into untoward dispositions for no good or worthy reason; he then prods us to rational consideration of genuine values and to efforts toward reforming or reconstituting the self." p. 96.

in this, that solely because it desires something, it causes the little gland to which it is closely united to move in the way requisite to produce the effect which relates to this desire."

The possibility of the soul's indirect influence on the animal spirits allows for self-mastery. There is, of course, another form of indirect influence. An object or event can indirectly cause a desire in the soul. In that case the soul suffers a passion, and there is no self-control. But in that case self-control can nevertheless still be achieved. As article 44 puts it, the soul can indirectly alter the movements of the animal spirits which produced this passion, because although "each desire is naturally united to some movement of the [pineal] gland," such movement may come to be connected to a different desire "by intentional effort." How this is to be accomplished, Descartes states in article 45. Our passions can be "indirectly" "excited or removed by the action of our will" when, through enlisting the senses, imagination or memory, the will presents to the mind things "which are usually united to the passions which we desire to have, and which are contrary to those which we desire to set aside." For example, when afraid, we cannot simply through an act of will or through desire cease to be afraid. But we can "consider the reasons, the objects or examples which persuade us" that there is little danger, that defence is a better policy than flight, that vanquishing whatever makes us fearful gives us glory and joy, while if we submit through fear we will have nothing but shame and regret. In this way courage and ambition can come to replace fear and, in words from article 44, the soul "gets the better of" its passions rather than being subject to them.

The soul's "getting the better of" a passion is often a process which involves a considerable time; it is often an experience of strife. Strife is caused by competing desires, the one induced by the animal spirits which affect the pineal gland, the other by the will's action on this gland. Strife, in other words, is between passions and acts of will. Yet there need not be strife between these two. As the penultimate article of this work puts it, the passions "are all good in their nature" and "we have nothing to avoid but their evil uses or their excesses." There is nothing wrong with desire either, as long as it is approved by reason. An enlightened will, which is a will guided by reason, pursues right desires and is capable of checking those desires which it deems wrong (that is, those which could result in evil use or excess of passion) by halting or changing the corporeal motion of the animal spirits which caused them.

In the realm of the passions, therefore, attainment of true good lies entirely within a person's power. In spite of custom, example, and education, no one needs to have his passions or emotions forced upon him through his physical or cultural surroundings. Also in the realm of the passions, a person can achieve autonomy. Hence, also in this last work, the comparison of man and God comes to the fore:

I only remarked in us one thing which might give us good reason to esteem ourselves, to wit, the use of our free will, and the empire which we possess over our wishes. Because it is for those actions alone which depend on this free will that we may with reason be praised or blamed; and this in a certain measure renders us like God in making us masters of ourselves . . ." (art. 152)

Descartes' correspondence with Queen Christine of Sweden unmistakably shows that he was in earnest both about the possibility of complete mastery over the passions through the proper use of free will, as well as about the comparison of man to God. He reaffirms both of these points in a letter he wrote after *The Passions* was completed.[22] In it the notion of autonomy comes to the fore in a formulation more striking than any of those he used in his published works. He writes that since "the goods of the body and of fortune do not depend absolutely on us . . . there remains only our will of which we can dispose outright." He thus again locates the realm in which we can gain total mastery and enjoy full autonomy. Attainment of such mastery and autonomy he calls a person's sovereign good:

I do not see that it is possible to dispose it [the will] better than by a regular and constant resolution to carry out to the letter whatever one judges best, and to employ all the powers of one's mind in informing this judgement. This by itself constitutes all the virtues; this alone really deserves praise and glory; this alone, finally, produces the greatest and most solid contentment of life. So I conclude that it is this which constitutes the supreme good.[23]

He then draws the comparison between God and man and he stresses the theme of human autonomy when he declares that, through the right use of free will, man can withdraw himself from subjection to God. This declaration clearly supports the conclusion I drew in earlier

22. Kenny, *Descartes, Philosophical Letters*, pp. 225–28 (AT5, 81–86).
23. Ibid., pp. 226–27 (AT5, 83).

chapters, namely, that Descartes' thought tends towards making God irrelevant for a person's theory and practice. He writes:

Now freewill is in itself the noblest thing we can have because it makes us in a certain manner equal to God and exempts us from being his subjects; and so its rightful use is the greatest of all the goods we possess, and further there is nothing that is more our own or that matters more to us. From all this it follows that nothing but freewill can produce our greatest contentments. Thus we see that the repose of mind and interior satisfaction felt by those who know they never fail to do their best is a pleasure incomparably sweeter, more lasting and more solid than all those which come from elsewhere.[24]

Strictly speaking Kenny's translation ("freewill . . . exempts us from being his subjects") presents a doctrine which is stronger than Descartes' language warrants ("*le libre arbitre . . . semble nous exemter de luy estre suiets*"). On the other hand, it perfectly captures the drive and direction of Descartes' thought. That drive is towards mastery in all areas of life, to freedom from drudgery (through mastery over nature by means of mechanics), freedom from pain and decay (through power over the body by means of medicine), and freedom from perturbation (through control of the passions by an enlightened will). In the first of these two realms, complete mastery and total freedom remains an ideal. Although Descartes believes in the possibility of constant progress towards realization of this ideal, its full actualization presents man with an infinite (or, at least, an indefinite) task. He declares that only in the realm of the passions can this task be fully accomplished.

It is in this respect of complete fulfilment alone that Descartes' final work differs from all his earlier writings. It is the only work in which he deals with an area of life in which he believes each individual can walk the road of progress to the end. Once that journey has been completed, the highest level of autonomy which is possible in that area of life has been reached: man then has exempted himself from being subject to God and has achieved complete mastery in that area of life. In this declaration of independence, *The Passions of the Soul* present what is perhaps Descartes' clearest articulation of the spirit which pervades the Enlightenment.

24. Ibid., p. 228 (AT5, 85).

VIII

Mastery, Method, and Enlightenment

TWO MAJOR POINTS remain to be made, completing some lines of thought from preceding chapters.

First, many of those who discuss the influence of the seventeenth on the eighteenth century stress the importance of thinkers like Bacon, Locke and Newton. That thinkers like these are very important to the eighteenth century I would be the last to deny. What I hope to have counteracted in this study is the belief that whereas the relationship between, say, the *philosophes* and Locke was one of deep affinity, that between the *philosophes* and Descartes was one of profound and total antagonism. I now want to stress that if—as Peter Gay will have it— Locke belongs to the Enlightenment's trinity of greatest men in history, so does Descartes. If we want to retain the notion of a "trinity," Descartes' name should replace Bacon's. This substitution will not often find support in what commentators have written; but it does justice to those about whom they wrote. Whereas the *philosophes* exalted Descartes' method, they soundly condemned Bacon's "methods for discovering truth": these methods "in no way influenced the course of science."[1]

Second, many of those who perpetuate the myth of antagonism between eighteenth-century thought and that of Descartes draw an opposition between the two in terms of methodology. They write that while Descartes proceeded on "the mathematical model," eighteenth-century thinkers in contrast adopted "the mechanical method." This juxtaposition violates the facts.

1. Condorcet, *Sketch*, p. 121.

I. THE ENLIGHTENMENT'S TRINITY

Many of those who today relate eighteenth-century thought to that of Descartes speak of antagonism or, at the least, of full-scale opposition between the two. This view of antagonism or of such opposition may without exaggeration be called that of the majority. It has been stated by influential writers such as Isaiah Berlin and Crane Brinton. This view tends to be accompanied by the judgment that Descartes has not really had a profound, enduring influence on Western thought. Although he is recognized as the father of modern dualism, most thinkers now take such dualism to belong to the past. Often, the contemporary image of Descartes is that of a philosopher whose influence today is negligible outside elementary classes in philosophy.

This majority view is opposed by a position which itself has roots in the eighteenth century. The position is the one I have propounded: that Descartes is the most important formative influence on eighteenth-century French thought. It tends to be accompanied with the judgment that Descartes did not only influence the *philosophes*, but that his thought is foremost among that which shaped the modern mind. Jonathan Rée (who belongs to those holding the minority view) concludes the argument of his *Descartes* with the words:

This modern image of Descartes [the majority view] has almost completely obliterated the old view that he was the founder of the "new philosophy", whose work was carried on by Newton and later scientists; but it is the old view which is closest to the truth. The principles of the "new philosophy", and the theory of knowledge and the theory of human nature which go with it; the concepts of an idea, of mathematical laws of nature . . . are so fundamental to modern consciousness that it is hard not to regard them as part of the natural property of the human mind. But, in fact, they are a product of the seventeenth century, and above all of the work of Descartes.[2]

Before I turn to "the old view" again, let me make a few comments

---

2. Rée, *Descartes*, p. 157. On pp. 30–31 of his *Descartes and Hume*, Ezra Talmor presents a nearly identical passage: "Descartes' theory of knowledge and his theory of human nature which goes with it, his concepts of an idea and of mathematical laws of nature are so rooted in our modern consciousness that it is difficult not to see them as the natural property of the human mind when actually they were created mainly by Descartes." Neither Rée nor Talmor introduce these statements as a quotation, although Talmor does provide a reference, namely: Étienne Gilson, *Discours de la Méthode: Texte et Commentaire*, cinquième édition, Paris, J. Vrin, 1976, p. 322.

about "the modern image of Descartes." Part of that image is that Descartes is not one of the great progenitors of the Enlightenment, let alone one of the Enlightenment's members.

In *Philosophers of the Enlightenment*, S. C. Brown answers his question "Who belongs to the Enlightenment and who does not?" with "Everyone would include Diderot, d'Alembert and Voltaire. Everyone will allow honorary and retrospective membership to Locke . . . and Newton."[3] If this statement does not precisely pinpoint Locke's position, it at least claims for it a close affinity with Enlightenment thought— and that is far more than many have been willing to say about Descartes'. Like many others, Brown introduces a representative from the eighteenth century to condemn Descartes: "D'Alembert attacks . . . Descartes . . . not for giving *too much* weight to Reason but for not giving *enough*." Many Enlightenment figures agreed with d'Alembert that, in spite of Descartes' protestations to the contrary, he often paid greater attention to the imagination than to reason. Items frequently cited as proof are his preoccupation with the building of systems and his dualism, with its accompanying doctrine of psycho-physical parallelism. It is undeniable that the *philosophes* rejected Descartes' metaphysics as the product of an "impatient imagination," as dogmatic and irrational. I, too, drew attention to this rejection at the beginning of my study.[4] To take their antagonism to his metaphysics as the one true indicator of how the *philosophes* saw their relationship to Descartes, however, inevitably results in a wrong depiction of this relationship. Those who over-emphasize their rejection of Cartesian metaphysics conclude that Descartes completely debarred himself from serving as a model for the Enlightenment, for the true age of reason. And so, continues Brown, "The age of reason," as understood by D'Alembert, was not inaugurated by those now commonly called 'rationalists' but by Locke and Newton. In championing Reason D'Alembert was championing *their* cause."[5]

It is fair to say that if d'Alembert championed Locke's cause, then he also embraced Descartes.[6] Even if none of the *philosophes* would have recognized themselves for the spiritual heirs of Descartes which

3. Brown, *Philosophers of the Enlightenment*, p. vii.
4. This point occupied a central place in the Introduction. See also the Introduction's footnotes, especially notes 8, 10, 11.
5. Brown, *Philosophers of the Enlightenment*, p. xv.
6. I have provided extensive grounds for this judgment in *The Imposition of Method*, chapter 6.

they were—and very few if any of them were altogether unaware of Descartes' influence—their acceptance of Locke would have made them Descartes' heirs. Most *philosophes* recognized their kinship with Descartes. *They rejected his metaphysics, but accepted his goals of freedom, mastery and progress.* They adopted his *method* as the only way to the realization of these goals. They shared his *view of man* as the being who possesses the wherewithal to shake off the shackles of the past and to forge for himself a life sanctioned by each person's own reason. They shared Descartes' *spirit.* They bewailed as tragic the fact that Descartes himself was, after all, incapable of fully acting in accordance with his own spirit: Descartes became dogmatic as a metaphysician. That was Descartes' failure. Their very recognition of an intimate spiritual kinship made them often vehement and always intolerant with respect to Descartes' failure. They wanted no one to identify them with Descartes the dogmatic metaphysician. Especially because some of the anti-Enlightenment movements of the day attempted to support their claim to authority with an appeal to Descartes' metaphysics, the *philosophes* presented themselves as radically averse to this metaphysics.[7] But in their adoption of his goals, of his method, and of his view of man, they championed Descartes' cause. They also championed the cause of Locke and Newton. In the works of Locke and of Newton they recognized important steps towards the realization of what they took to be each person's proper end, the end first articulated by Descartes, that of radical human autonomy. They understood that these steps had become possible through an application of the method which Descartes had made available.

Commentators who overstress (and consequently misjudge the significance of) the rejection of Descartes' metaphysics, without fail misconstrue the relationship between Descartes and the Enlightenment. Sometimes their misconstrual is abetted by the fact that they seem to have a limited acquaintance with Descartes' position, and take the metaphysical reflections as its most important part. These commentators do not give proper weight to Descartes' own statements in which he de-emphasized metaphysics and stressed the importance of reason's employment in the area of applied science: "you should not devote so much effort to the *Meditations* and to metaphysical questions . . . they draw the mind too far away from physical and observable things, and make it unfit to study them. Yet it is just these physical

7. See Vartanian, *Diderot and Descartes*, pp. 308–09.

studies that it is most desirable for men to pursue, since they would yield abundant benefits for life."[8]

One result of an exaggerated emphasis on the *philosophes'* rejection of Descartes' metaphysics is the elevation of thinkers like Locke and Newton to a position of greater originality—and hence of a more decisive influence—then their accomplishments warrant. Brown's attitude is shared by many, three of the more prominent commentators being Richard I. Aaron, Crane Brinton, and Peter Gay.

Aaron holds that it is "Locke . . . and not Descartes" who "is the supreme formative influence on the France of the eighteenth century . . ."[9] Brinton asserts that "the importance of Locke for the world view of the Enlightenment can hardly be exaggerated."[10] Rather than refer to Descartes, Brinton adds that it is "Bacon, Locke, Newton" who "have some claim to being the originators, the adventurers in ideas which the French did no more than develop and spread."[11] Brinton's three thinkers are introduced by others as the Enlightenment's "new trinity." Peter Gay, for example, writes that "the philosophes" celebrations of Newton all bear a certain family resemblance: . . . d'Alembert and Jefferson displayed his portrait in their studies; all of them, following Voltaire, included him in their trinity of the greatest men in history, placing him beside Bacon and Locke or (if they were Germans) Locke and Leibniz."[12]

Descartes' name is conspicuously absent from this trinity. It is absent, in part, because of an unsupportable wholesale opposition drawn between Descartes and eighteenth-century thinkers. This mistaken opposition is behind Gay's statement that "Of all the labels imposed on the Enlightenment, the label "Age of Reason" has been the most persistent, and the most damaging." He adds that this label "is accurate only if 'reason' is read to mean 'criticism' and counterposed to 'credulity' and 'superstition'."[13] But as we have seen, this counterposition of reason to credulity, and this identification of reason (at least in its analytic function) with criticism is precisely the counterposition and identification made by Descartes. The *philosophes* inherited it from

8. Cottingham, *Descartes' Conversation with Burman*, p. 30. See also Descartes to Elizabeth, 28 June 1643 (Kenny, *Descartes, Philosophical Letters*, pp. 141, 143; AT3, 694, 695).
9. Richard I. Aaron, *John Locke* (third edition), p. 334.
10. *Encyclopedia of Philosophy*, vol. 2, p. 519.
11. Ibid., p. 523.
12. *The Enlightenment, 2: The Science of Freedom*, pp. 129–30.
13. Ibid., p. 625.

Descartes, either directly or by way of Locke. The opposition of Descartes to the *philosophes* is as unwarranted as is the drawing of a special relationship between the *philosophes* and Locke if that relationship excludes Descartes. Both these points may be illustrated from Gay's account.

About Locke's *Some Thoughts concerning Education*, Gay writes that "it was a pioneering essay of vital interest to [eighteenth-century] reformers partly because it advocated far-reaching reforms, but mainly because it was an evident offspring of Locke's major work, the *Essay concerning Human Understanding*."[14] This filial relationship Gay explicates by saying that *Some Thoughts concerning Education* was the *Essay*'s "new philosophy in action," that it was "Locke's philosophy in education."[15] Gay is correct: Locke's works on education resulted from an application of the *Essay*'s central doctrines to educational practice. Consequently, Gay is also correct when he adds that when the Enlightenment appropriated Locke's theory of education, it accepted the central doctrines of Locke's *Essay*. This correctness, however, points up the superficiality of the views of those (including Gay) who deny the status of "Enlightenment thinker"—even if only "honorary" or "retrospective"—to Descartes but accord it to Locke.[16] It is correct to say that the central doctrines of Locke's *Essay* determine Locke's thoughts on education. It is equally correct to say that Locke shared these doctrines with Descartes, and that Descartes had published them more than a decade before Locke became an undergraduate at Christ Church, Oxford. In Descartes' works these doctrines play as crucial a role as they do in Locke's. The doctrines in question are those about man as a rational being and about method or the nature of reasoning, about man as a free being questing for mastery, about man as an autonomous

14. Ibid., p. 502.
15. Ibid.
16. The same holds for those who accord the status of "Enlightenment thinker" to Newton but deny it to Descartes. As Voltaire said, it was after all Descartes who discovered "new territories," while Newton was one of those "who came after him" and could only "make these lands fertile" because of Descartes' pioneering work. If we compare the work of Descartes and of Newton, then it is true that "the first is a sketch, the second is a masterpiece." But it is also correct to say that "the man who set us on the road to the truth is perhaps as noteworthy as the one who since then has been to the end of the road." These are quotations from Voltaire's essay "On Descartes and Newton," in his *Letters on England*, translated by Leonard Tancock, pp. 71–72.

being whose destiny lies in his own hands and who is capable of progressing on the way of the realization of his destiny. To posit a conflict between these central doctrines of Descartes' thought and those of the *philosophes* is doing as great an injustice to the facts as would be committed if such a conflict were said to exist between Locke's thought and French Enlightenment thought. One never comes across statements which assert the latter. Statements asserting a profound and full-scale conflict between Descartes and the *philosophes* are commonplace. In view of so many acknowledgements of indebtedness to Descartes by the *philosophes* themselves, the persistent recurrence of assertions that there is such a conflict is surprising.

Their persistent recurrence continues to feed the myth of wholesale antagonism between Descartes and the Enlightenment. This myth shows its blinding effect on the authors of much outstanding writing about the eighteenth century. Isaiah Berlin, for example, writes about that century's "noble faith" and "central dream." This "faith" and this "dream" he sees expressed in the belief that "all evils could be cured by appropriate technological steps."[17] These words could fairly be used to describe also Descartes' "faith" and "dream." In Berlin's work, Locke appears as one of the philosophers of the Enlightenment. It allows no such place for Descartes. Instead, although Descartes' pioneering work receives a commendation or two on the opening pages of *The Age of Enlightenment*, he is soon misinterpreted as one who eschews empirical observation. On this matter of empirical commitment, he is construed as much inferior to Locke.[18] For Berlin, this contrast is one factor which precludes the possibility that Descartes might be a member of the Enlightenment's trinity.

Those who have a clear sense of Descartes' importance for eighteenth-century thought correctly see this importance as deriving particularly from the Cartesian method. In his *French Enlightenment*, J. H. Brumfitt concludes that "Cartesianism had been absorbed rather than rejected" by the Enlightenment. He comes to this conclusion because he recognizes that Locke and Newton, the two Englishmen who so profoundly influenced the French, "were Cartesians with a difference rather than something totally new."[19] He recognizes that

17. Isaiah Berlin, *The Age of Enlightenment*, pp. 28–29.
18. Ibid., p. 31.
19. Brumfitt, *The French Enlightenment*, p. 43.

"Cartesianism remained a living force . . . because its spirit of me-thodical inquiry" was taken over by Locke and by Newton, and came to be applied by the French in fields like history, ethics, and religion.[20]

Writers who perpetuate the myth of thoroughgoing antagonism fasten on statements by the *philosophes* in which Descartes' failure is pointed out. They neglect to give proper weight to a different group of statements, to acknowledgments which are so much more important because they reveal the deep continuity between them. Let it first be recognized that Descartes and the *philosophes* shared a common method, a method from which both expected liberation and mastery. Then it can also be recognized that the *philosophes*' awareness of mistakes which their predecessor had made need not create much distance, let alone antagonism, between predecessor and progeny. Ira Wade has put this well: "Under these circumstances it does not really matter whether his [Descartes'] scientific world view is correct or not. What is really important is whether Cartesianism was capable of releasing within man his inner powers and whether this knowledge of himself could reestablish his true relationship with God and nature."[21] Because the *philosophes* adopted Descartes' method as the means to release what they took to be man's essential powers, their work can be seen as an attempt to carry out Descartes' "messianic" program of becoming fully autonomous through achieving mastery over self and nature.[22]

Let me conclude this section with a story about Locke and William Molyneux. During the closing decade of the seventeenth century, a friendship developed between Locke and Molyneux. This friendship grew by way of correspondence, Locke writing from Oates and from London, Molyneux from Dublin. Both eagerly sought ways to come to a personal meeting but no such meeting took place until the summer of 1698, barely two months before Molyneux's death. In 1696, after hopes of meeting had been frustrated more than once, Molyneux requested Locke to sit for a portrait. Locke granted this request and wrote to Molyneux:

The honour you do me, in thus giving me a place in your house, I look upon as the effect of having a place already in your esteem and affection; and that

20. Ibid., p. 33.
21. Wade, *The Intellectual Origins of the French Enlightenment*, p. 243.
22. See Vartanian's *Diderot and Descartes*, pp. 15–16 for this characterisation of the work of both Descartes and the *philosophes* as "messianic."

made me more easily submit to what methought looked too much like vanity in me. Painting was designed to represent the gods, or the great men that stood next to them. But friendship, I see, takes no measure of anything, but by itself; and where it is great and high, will make its object so, and raise it above its level. This is that which has deceived you into my picture, and made you put so great a compliment upon me; and I do not know what you will find to justify yourself to those who shall see it in your possession.[23]

Molyneux was at no loss for a reply: "Painting, it is true, was designed to represent the gods, and the great men that stand next them; and therefore it was, that I desired your picture."[24]

If during Locke's lifetime some, though very few, would want a justification for having Locke's portrait in the house of a man of science, no such justification was called for in the age that was about to dawn. Molyneux leaves it nicely ambiguous whether he desired the picture because it was an instance of representing a god or one of representing a great man next to the gods. Little of this ambiguity remained for the eighteenth-century Enlightenment. The idea of an absolute difference between gods and men came to be abandoned by many of its leaders. New gods were adopted, gods who were men. But if, with Peter Gay, we want to speak of the Enlightenment's trinity, this trinity cannot rightfully be that of Bacon, Locke, and Newton. Neither can it be that of Leibniz, Locke, and Newton. Descartes must be one of the three. His articulation of the precepts of method—which, it must be remembered, he himself and the *philosophes* believed to be the unveiling of reason's self-portrait—would make many *philosophes* demand such a place for him. And his use of the method, at least in the essays appended to the *Discourse* and in *The Passions of the Soul*, would guarantee him such a place. After all, as Turgot said, "What mortal dared to reject the insights of all past ages, and even the ideas he believed most certain? . . . Great Descartes, if it was not always given to you to find the truth, you did at least destroy tyranny and error."[25] And what mortal *could* destroy all links with the past except one who adhered strictly to the precepts of the method? Even then, what *mortal* could accomplish such a task? In the words of the Abbé Terrassen, "The new method of philosophy was first introduced into the world by the famous Descartes. . . . 'Twas then indeed, it might

23. Locke, *Works*, ed. 1823, vol. 9, p. 386. The letter is dated 12 September 1696.
24. Ibid., p. 391. This letter is dated 26 September, 1696.
25. Turgot, *Œuvres*, vol. 2, p. 89.

be justly said, that . . . a God had come down to clear this chaos, dissipate the darkness, and create light."[26]

Descartes must be a member of the Enlightenment's trinity. Without him it lacks its father-figure. Molyneux had a portrait of Locke. Newton's portrait graced the wall of Jefferson's study. Descartes' portrait occupied a place of honour in d'Alembert's room.[27]

II. MASTERY AND METHOD

In each of the preceding chapters, I have stressed the role which Descartes' method was expected to play in man's liberation from prejudice and in his achievement of mastery. My first chapter emphasized the revolutionary nature of Descartes' method, and the third stressed the point that the *philosophes* adopted this method and celebrated its revolutionary nature. The continuity between the seventeenth and eighteenth centuries is very much related to the methodology so clearly articulated in Descartes' *Discourse*.

Those who today oppose eighteenth-century thinkers to Descartes often do so with respect to method. Precisely where they should see a major dimension of continuity, they assume the existence of conflict. Of such writers, Berlin is again a good example. "If the model that dominated the seventeenth century was mathematical, it is the mechanical model . . . that is everywhere imitated in the century that followed."[28] Berlin argues that thinkers like Locke, Voltaire, Hume, Condillac, de la Mettrie, all implement "the mechanical model"; "it is this that forms a common characteristic" of all these "very different philosophers."[29] It is this which, primarily, is supposed to make these various philosophers so different from Descartes. It is true that "There are 'organic'—anti-atomic—notions in the writing of Diderot as well as those of Maupertuis or Bordeu . . . but the dominant trend is in favour of analyzing everything into ultimate, irreducible atomic constituents, whether physical or psychological."[30] What Berlin fails to recognize is that Descartes' method is not a "mathematical method,"

---

26. Quoted by Frankel in his *The Faith of Reason*, p. 13.
27. As Grimsley reports, next to that of Voltaire, Henry IV and Frederick II. *Jean D'Alembert*, p. 272.
28. *The Age of Enlightenment*, p. 14.
29. Ibid.
30. Ibid., p. 20.

but is the analytical method. The rational enquirer applies this method to any kind of subject-matter, analysing it into ultimate, irreducible, atomic constitutents. When Descartes applied it in arithmetic, the method would give him ultimate, atomic (that is, "indivisible" or "indefinable") concepts like "unity" and "equality." When he applied it in metaphysics and epistemology, it gave him ultimate, "atomic," indefinable, and underivable concepts like "thought" and "existence," as well as ultimate, underivable principles like the causal principle. When he applied it in physics it gave him irreducible "points of force." When Locke applied this method in his *Essay*, he too came to propound a doctrine of epistemic atomism; and when he applied it in the field of politics, he came to rest his political theory on the irreducible concept of "the individual."[31] When Newton applied it in physics it gave him his physical atoms and it allowed him to construct his mechanical universe. But Newton's universe was not any more (or less) mechanical than was Descartes'. Whether at the basis of it there were atoms or "vortices" made little difference. To speak of Descartes' method or model as "mathematical" and by contrast of Newton's or of Condillac's as "mechanical" is simply an incorrect portrayal of the situation. They all shared the analytical method. When any one of them—whether Descartes, or Newton, or de la Mettrie—applied this method in his account of the physical universe, the picture that resulted was that of a mechanical universe. As far as accounts of the universe were concerned, the mechanical model dominated the eighteenth, but also the seventeenth century—at least since the time of Descartes. Vartanian hits the nail on the head when he labels Diderot and his *confrères* as "Cartesians" *because of* their mechanism.[32]

Of all of Descartes' works it is, therefore, the *Discourse on Method* (whose original title, it should be remembered, contained the words *Le project d'une Science universelle qui puisse élever notre nature a son plus haut degré de perfection*) which is most important in determining whether—and, if so, to what extent—there is a spiritual kinship between Descartes and the *philosophes*. My study has aimed to show that this kinship is very deep: the Enlightenment, I have argued, is properly to be seen in important aspects as Cartesian in origin. In Vrooman's words, the

31. For a detailed justification of these last two statements, see *The Imposition of Method*, chapters 6 and 7.

32. *Diderot and Descartes*, p. 10.

Discourse is "the manifesto of the Cartesian revolution. It heralds . . . a heroic ideal."[33] Vrooman adds that the *Discourse* is in a sense Descartes' autobiography, but that it also transcends such personal limits. For although "René Descartes is the hero of his own autobiography . . . as the central figure of the *Discourse*, he is also a symbol of humanity." When, therefore, Descartes' "words narrate his own career" they at the same time "reflect the search for truth, particularly in the sciences." Vrooman correctly labels the *Discourse* as "the story of a quest not only for certainty but also for utility."[34] It is the story of Descartes', but also of the Enlightenment's quest for certainty and (through utility) for mastery.

Descartes' method dominated the world of the *philosophes* because they took this method to be reason's self-portrait, and because they expected mankind to be able to attain high achievements if only it determined itself to be led by reason. To proceed methodically is to proceed in a way the agent is compelled by reason to follow. Only when compelled to follow a path by reason, they held, can man be master of his fate.[35] It is no belittling of Descartes to say that "The only really lasting influence of the Cartesian system lay in its method . . . which was everywhere adopted by educated men in Western Europe."[36]

III. CONCLUDING COMMENTS

The task I have set myself in this study is to show that there is a far greater affinity between Descartes and the *philosophes* than many have allowed to exist. I have used the *philosophes* as a group of thinkers representative of the Enlightenment's stance. By this means I intended to reveal that one and the same spirit drove both Descartes and eighteenth century Enlightenment thinkers. Both wanted autonomy with respect to their inherited cultural conditions, and both wanted to conquer as much as possible the physical limitations which attend human life. Central to the thought of both therefore, are, concepts like those of freedom, mastery, and progress.

That such concepts play a crucial role in Enlightenment thinking is known well enough. That they are of vital importance also to Des-

---

33. Vrooman, *René Descartes, A Biography*, p. 111.
34. Ibid., p. 112.
35. For an excellent, detailed account of the predominance of Descartes' method in the world of the *philosophes*, see chapter 3 of Vartanian's *Diderot and Descartes*.
36. These words are from von Leyden's *Seventeenth Century Metaphysics*, p. 19.

cartes is less often recognized. Hence, fulfilment of my task demanded a careful re-evaluation of Descartes' writings. The interpretation which I have presented reveals the close affinity between the positions of Descartes and of thinkers who dominated the Western world's intellectual scene during the century and a half which followed Descartes' death.

One important root—quite possibly the main root—of Enlightenment thought is to be found in Descartes. That this root exists there, and that it is of prime importance, are facts often glossed over or denied. In this respect my study is meant to increase our understanding of the Enlightenment. The process of tracing this root also shed greater light on the nature of Descartes' position.

Descartes and the leading thinkers of the eighteenth century shared a particular goal. Depending on one's emphasis, this goal may be discussed in the terms of either freedom, or mastery, or progress. I have not made it a part of my task to criticize what one might call the sense and reference of the terms for this goal, even though I find many aspects of man's aspiring to express and attain this goal quite unattractive. Nor have I evaluated the means by which this goal was thought to be properly achievable. But, I should add, it is not only the most admirable figures and projects which we must study in order to understand the present and learn from the past.

The ideal of autonomy, expressed through what Descartes called freedom or mastery, belongs to humans almost obsessed with a belief in a fundamental conflict between each individual and the cultural as well as physical conditions in which he finds himself. The means to freedom or mastery is a method properly pleasing to those who confuse analysis with reduction. This method belongs with an epistemology which is atomistic. It calls for man's perception of what is ultimately and perfectly simple. This notion of simplicity betrays epistemic and semantic confusion. Both the Enlightenment's thinking on its ideal, and the means by which it expected to realize this ideal, can be rationally criticized in terms of what is intelligible and what is patently right and wrong. The fact that the means carries the label method or scientific method or rational procedure ought in no way to place it beyond rational criticism. I trust that one fringe benefit of this study is that it provides a solid foundation for the deepening of criticism regarding both Descartes and the Enlightenment thinkers, who drew far more from his writings than most of their commentators have been willing to admit.

Bibliography

Aaron, Richard I. *John Locke* (third edition). Oxford, 1971.

Adam, C. and Tannery, P. *Œuvres de Descartes*. Paris, 1965–75.

Anscombe, Elizabeth and Geach, Peter Thomas. *Descartes, Philosophical Writings*. London, 1954.

Arblaster, Anthony. *The Rise and Decline of Western Liberalism*. Oxford, 1984.

Arendt, Hannah. *On Revolution*. New York, 1963.

Berlin, Isaiah. *The Age of Enlightenment, The Eighteenth Century Philosophers*. Oxford, 1956.

Blom, John J. *Descartes, His Moral Philosophy and Psychology*. Hassocks, Sussex, 1978.

Brinton, Crane. "Enlightenment," in *The Encyclopedia of Philosophy*. ed. Paul Edwards. New York and London, 1967. Vol. 2, pp. 519–25.

— *Anatomy of Revolution*. Revised edition. London, 1953.

— *The Shaping of Modern Thought*. Englewood Cliffs, 1950, 1963.

Broadie, Frederick. *An Approach to Descartes' Meditations*. London, 1970.

Brown, S. C., ed. *Philosophers of the Enlightenment*. Hassocks, Sussex, 1979.

Brumfitt, J. H. *The French Enlightenment*. London, 1972.

Butler, R. J., ed. *Cartesian Studies*. Oxford, 1972.

Caton, Hiram. *The Origin of Subjectivity, An Essay on Descartes*. New Haven and London, 1973.

—"Will and Reason in Descartes' Theory of Error." *The Journal of Philosophy* 72 no. 4 (1975): 87–104.

Condillac, Etienne Bonnot de. *An Essay on the Origin of Human Knowledge*. Translated by Thomas Nugent. New York, 1974.

Condorcet. *Sketch for a Historical Picture of the Progress of the Human Mind*. Translated by June Barraclough. London, 1955.

Cottingham, John, ed. *Descartes' Conversation with Burman*. Oxford, 1976.

Doren, Charles Van. *The Idea of Progress*. New York, Washington, London, 1967.

Elliott, J. H. "Revolution and Continuity in Early Modern Europe." *Past and Present* 42 (1969): 35–56.

Finlayson, Michael G. *Historians, Puritanism, and the English Revolution.* Toronto, 1983.

Frankel, Charles. *The Faith of Reason, The Idea of Progress in the French Enlightenment.* New York, 1948.

Friedrich, Carl J. *Revolution.* New York, 1966.

Gabaude, Jean-Marc. *Liberté et Raison, La liberté cartésienne et sa refraction chez Spinoza et chez Leinbiz.* 3 vols. Toulouse, 1970.

Gay, Peter. *The Enlightement, An Interpretation. Vol. 1: The Rise of Modern Paganism.* London, 1966.

— *The Enlightement, An Interpretation. Vol. 2: The Science of Freedom.* London, 1970.

Gilson, Etienne. *Discours de la Methode.* Paris, 1925.

Gouhier, Henri. *Essais sur Descartes.* Paris, 1949.

— *La Pensee Métaphysique de Descartes.* Paris, 1969.

Grimsley, Ronald. *Jean D'Alembert.* Oxford, 1963.

— *Jean-Jacques Rousseau.* Sussex and New Jersey, 1983.

Haldane, E. S. and Ross, G. R. T. *The Philosophical Works of Descartes.* Vols. 1 and 2. Cambridge, 1911.

Hampshire, Stuart. "Introduction" to *Sketch for a Historical Picture of the Progress of the Human Mind.* Edited by June Barraclough. London, 1955.

Hardesty, Kathleen. *The Supplément to the Encyclopédie.* The Hague, 1977.

Hastie, W., ed. *Kant's Principles of Politics.* Edinburgh, 1891.

Hill, Christopher. *Puritanism and Revolution, Studies in Interpretation of the English Revolution of the 17th Century.* London, 1958.

Hoyt, Nelly S. and Cassirer, Thomas. *Encyclopedia Selections.* Indianapolis, 1965.

Hume, David. *A Treatise of Human Nature.* Edited by P. H. Nidditch. Oxford, 1978.

Kenny, Anthony. "Descartes on the Will." In *Cartesian Studies,* edited by J. Butler. Oxford, 1972.

— *Descartes, Philosophical Letters.* Oxford, 1970.

— *Will, Freedom and Power.* Oxford, 1975.

Koyré, Alexandre. "Condorcet." *Journal of the History of Ideas* 9, no. 2 (1948): 131–52.

— "Introduction" to *Descartes, Philosophical Writings.* Edited by E. Anscombe and P. T. Geach. London, 1954.

Krüger, Gerhard. "Die Herkunft des philosophischen Selbstbewusstseins." *Logos* 22 (1933): 225–72.

Lefèvre, Roger. *La Métaphysique de Descartes.* Paris, 1966.

— *La Pensée Existentielle de Descartes.* Bordas, 1965.

— *L'Humanisme de Descartes.* Paris, 1957.

Leyden, W. von. *Seventeenth Century Metaphysics*. London, 1968.

Locke, John. *An Essay concerning Human Understanding*. Edited by P. H. Nidditch. Oxford, 1975.

— *Works*. 1823 edition. Scientia Verlag Aalen, 1963 reprint.

Lough, John. *The Encyclopédie*. London, 1971.

Maritain, Jacques. *Le Songe de Descartes*. Paris, 1932. Translated by Mabelle L. Andison as *The Dream of Descartes*. New York, 1944.

McManners, John. *Death and the Enlightenment*. Oxford, 1981.

Meek, Ronald L., ed. and translator. *Turgot on Progress, Sociology and Economics*. Cambridge, 1973.

Mettrie, Julien Offray de la. *Man a Machine*. Translated by Gertrude Carman Bussey. La Salle, 1912.

Miller, James. *Rousseau, Dreamer of Democracy*. New Haven and London, 1984.

Pascal, Blaise. *Pensées*. Edited by H. S. Thayer. New York, 1965.

Plamenatz, John. *Man and Society*. Vol. 2. London, 1963.

Porter, Roy and Teich, Mikuláš. *The Enlightenment in National Context*. Cambridge, 1982.

Prior, O. H. "Introduction" to *Esquisse d'un Tableau Historique des Progrès de l'Esprit Humain*, edited by O. .H. Prior. Paris, 1933.

Radnitzky, G. and Andersson, G., eds. *The Structure and Development of Science*. Dordrecht, Boston, London, 1979.

Reé, Jonathan. *Descartes*. London, 1974.

Robinson, Daniel N., ed. *Significant Contributions to the History of Psychology, 1750–1920*. Washington, 1977.

Rousseau, Jean-Jacques. *Emile*. Translated by Barbara Foxley. Everyman Edition: London and New York, 1911, 1976.

Schouls, Peter A. "Peirce and Descartes: Doubt and the Logic of Discovery." In *Pragmatism and Purpose: Essays Presented to T. A. Goudge*. Edited by L. W. Sumner, John G. Slater, Fred Wilson. Toronto, 1981.

— *The Imposition of Method, A Study of Descartes and Locke*. Oxford, 1980.

Stewart, M. A. "Peter A. Schouls, *The Imposition of Method: A Study of Descartes and Locke*". Review in *Canadian Philosophical Reviews*, 1, no. 2/3 (1981): 119–23.

Talmor, Ezra. *Descartes and Hume*. Oxford, 1980.

Turgot, A. R. J. *Œuvres*. Vol. 2. Paris, 1808–11.

Vartanian, Aram. *Diderot and Descartes, A Study of Scientific Naturalism in the Enlightenment*. Princeton, 1953.

— *La Mettrie's L'HOMME MACHINE, A Study in the Origin of an Idea*. Princeton, 1960.

Voegelin, Eric. *From Enlightenment to Revolution*. Durham, 1975.

Voltaire. *Letters on England*. Translated by Leonard Tancock. New York, 1980.

Vrooman, Jack R. *René Descartes, A Biography*. New York, 1970.
Wade, Ira O. *The Intellectual Origins of the French Enlightenment*. Princeton, 1971.
Wittgenstein, L. *Philosophical Investigations*. Oxford, 1953.

Index

Aaron, R., 177
action, 154–55, autonomous, 166; and
bondage, 160-61; and clarity and
distinctness, 161-62; and desire, 158;
and free will, 156-57; and judgment,
161–62; and reason, 155, 161-62, 166;
and self-determination, 159-60; and
will, 169-70
animal spirits, and the passions, 153–55,
157, 164-70
Archimedean point, 48–62; and the
cogito, 50–51, 58–60; and self-
consciousness, 56
Aristotle, 28, 36, 70
attention, 90–91, 96; and clarity and
distinctness, 95; and freedom, 131–32;
and liberty of indifference, 90, 94; and
liberty of spontaneity, 89-90, 92; and
truth, 100; and will, 95.
autonomy, 3, 57, 94, 131-32; and action,
166; and agency, 99; and determination, 79-85, 95; and doubt, 36, 95; and
essence, 107-08; and freedom, 185;
and free will, 42-43; as free will,
108–09; and man and God, 171–72;
and mastery, 101, 107–08, 110, 143–47,
162–63, 165–68, 171–72, 180, 185;
and method, 176; and the passions,
168–69, 171; and reason, 57, 60, 75,
109, 126–27, 143; and revolution,
162–63; and self-determination, 104–5;
and spontaneity, 77–98; and will, 46,
74–75, 77–79

Bacon, F., 74, 173, 177, 181
being, and thinking, 57

Berlin, I., 4, 67, 174, 179
body, 47
Brinton, C., 4, 7, 62, 174, 177

Caton, H., 60
clarity and distinctness, 19, 91, 112–13;
and attention, 95; criteria for, 20-22;
and error, 34; and judgment, 121-22,
161–62; and progress, 112–14; and
reduction, 106; and truth, 37, 46,
112–13; and understanding, 87, 89;
and will, 45
cogito, 40, 51, 56, 92, 94; and
Archimedean point, 50–51, 58–61; and
epistemic priority, 50; and freedom,
40, 44–46; and free will, 40, 50–51,
58–60; and knowledge, 45–46, 57; and
primacy of free will, 49; and reason,
45; as source of knowledge, 57; and
will, 50
composition, 113
Condillac, E., 6, 7, 64, 71, 182, 183
Condorcet, 6, 7, 64, 67, 68, 70, 71, 73,
74, 106, 130, 131, 136, 137, 138

D'Alembert, 6, 7, 66, 71, 135, 136–37,
139, 175, 177
deduction, 19, 57–58, 127
desire, and knowledge and passion,
157–58
Diderot, 66, 69, 138, 175
doubt, 32, and autonomy, 36, 95; as a
defect, 35–36; and freedom, 35, 37,
40, 44, 49, 52–53; and free will, 35, 56,
57, 59–60, 89; and knowledge, 56; and
liberation of reason, 28, 35–36; and

McGill-Queen's Studies in the History of Ideas

5